FAITHLINES
Muslim Conceptions of Islam and Society

FAITHLINES

Muslim Conceptions of Islam and Society

RIAZ HASSAN

OXFORD

UNIVERSITY PRESS

OXFORD
UNIVERSITY PRESS

Great Clarendon Street, Oxford OX2 6DP

Oxford University Press is a department of the University of Oxford.
It furthers the University's objective of excellence in research, scholarship,
and education by publishing worldwide in

Oxford New York

Auckland Bangkok Buenos Aires Cape Town Chennai
Dar es Salaam Delhi Hong Kong Istanbul Karachi Kolkata
Kuala Lumpur Madrid Melbourne Mexico City Mumbai Nairobi
São Paulo Shanghai Taipei Tokyo Toronto

Oxford is a registered trade mark of Oxford University Press
in the UK and in certain other countries

ISBN 0 19 579930 5

This edition in Oxford Pakistan Paperbacks 2003

Typeset in Times
Printed in Pakistan by
Mas Printers, Karachi.
Published by
Ameena Saiyid, Oxford University Press
5-Bangalore Town, Sharae Faisal
PO Box 13033, Karachi-75350, Pakistan.

For
Selva, Haroon and Tirana

The views of the Qur'an will ... remain at the level of pure abstraction unless a thorough *factual* survey is made of the relevant social data. It is of the greatest importance to determine exactly where society is at present before deciding where it can go. To talk about reforming society without scientifically determining where the society is, is... like a doctor treating a patient without taking his case history or examining him. In fact, there is a sense in which even a meaningful formulation of Qur'anic thought would be dependent upon such a factual study and a proper method for interpreting facts; the converse...is also true. In other words, as with other fields...the study of the social sciences is a process, not something that is established once and for all. In fact, it is more so than any other field, for its subject matter—social behavior—is constantly in the process of creation.

– Fazlur Rahman, *Islam and Modernity*

By various obvious criteria—universalism, scripturalism, spiritual egalitarianism, the extension of full participation in the sacred community not to one, or some, but to *all*, and the rational systematisation of social life—Islam is, of the three great Western monotheisms, the one closest to modernity.

– Ernest Gellner, *Muslim Society*

CONTENTS

LIST OF TABLES

Chapter 3

Chapter 4

Chapter 5

PREFACE

I first became interested in the sociology of Muslim society in the 1960s after reading Ibn Khaldun's magisterial work *The Muqaddimah*, which, among other subjects, included an insightful analysis of medieval Muslim social formations. This interest was further stimulated by the works of Ernest Gellner and Fazlur Rahman in the 1970s and 1980s. Gellner's work on Muslim society has played a critical role in shaping my own understanding of some of the issues which have been explored in this book.

The conceptual and empirical explorations of the study began in 1994 when Professor Ivan Szelenyi invited me to teach a course on the Sociology of Islam in the Department of Sociology at the University of California, Los Angeles. I accepted the invitation with some trepidation, as I had never taught such a course before. The opportunity to teach a course on the Sociology of Islam, however, was intellectually challenging. It also made me aware that, notwithstanding an increasing global fascination with Islam, there were very few, if any, comparative sociological studies of contemporary Muslim societies. This is not to deny the contributions made by the studies of Muslim societies and sociology of Islam by social scientists like Ernest Gellner, Clifford Geertz, Fazlur Rahman, William Montgomery Watt, Ruben Levy, Ali Sharaiti, Fatima Mernissi, Mohammad Arkoun, John Esposito and Nikki Keddie.

The course gave me a valuable opportunity to identify a number of issues which merited comparative analysis in order to explain the differences in political, social, and religious trajectories of Muslim societies from Morocco and Nigeria to Indonesia. My association with the Department of Sociology at the University of California, Los Angeles, also allowed me to become more familiar with the approaches to comparative studies conducted by Ivan Szelenyi and other members of the department. On my return to Flinders University I began to work on a research proposal for a comparative sociological study of Muslim societies. I was fortunate to receive funding from the Australian Research Council for such a study, the results of which are the basis of this book.

The experience of carrying out the study in four Muslim countries proved to be a logistically complex and an intellectually challenging exercise. It presented many obstacles that needed to be overcome before the study could be carried out. The most notable of these was the deep suspicion I encountered not only from official bureaucracy but also from some academic circles in these countries for the motive for undertaking my study. I learned a great deal about the deep suspicion of alleged Western 'conspiracies' against Islam held by many highly educated people in the Muslim countries.

Some of the suspicions seemed to me to be far-fetched. There were international events which evoked great concerns among many people from all walks of life in these countries, and these undoubtedly influenced their perceptions of the Western countries. Among the events mentioned frequently were the indifference, and even reluctance, of major Western countries to intervene to stop the human tragedy and bloodshed which took place in Bosnia-Herzegovina, the American support of the Israelis against the Palestinians, destruction of Chechnya by the Russian Army and the Western-inspired economic and political sanctions against Iraq which were contributing to the suffering of the Iraqi people.

I also learned that a large majority of the people whose cooperation was necessary to carry out the study successfully were willing and able to rationally evaluate my requests for their participation in the study and extended their cooperation. The fact that the research team was able to survey over 4000 respondents from diverse backgrounds in the four countries is an eloquent testimony of their support. I am indebted to the members of Islamic organizations such as Muhammadiyah, Nahdatul Ulama, Jama'at-i-Islami, Tablighi Jamaat and

Jam'iyyat al-Ikwan al-Muslimin as well as to the many professional and civic organizations in Indonesia, Pakistan, Egypt and Kazakhstan for their participation in the study. I do not want to repeat here the information about the fieldwork, which is included in the appendix except to reiterate that, contrary to what I myself believed and was also told by many colleagues, it is possible to conduct research on 'sensitive' issues, including Muslim religiosity in Muslim countries. I hope that the presence of this study will act as a catalyst for similar studies in the future.

The social pervasiveness of Islam in the modern world and the social, political and religious trajectories of Muslim societies raise important issues for social scientists. Empirical studies of Muslim societies can be a rich source for evaluating and testing the validity of some of the major propositions of social theory that have been formulated in the context of increasingly secular social settings of modern Europe and North American countries. Through systematic and comparative studies of Muslim societies, modern sociological scholarship can lay the foundations for a more informed understanding of the social reality of the Muslim world.

It would not have been possible to carry out the study without the help of many people. I would like to express my indebtedness, in particular, to Dr Agus Dwiyanto, Drs Sukmadi, Professor Mohammad Anwar, Dr Muneer Ahmad, Mrs Razia Rafiq, Mr Shaukat Abbas, the late Dr Oumerseric Kasenov, Dr Sabit Jousupov, Dr Hassan Essia and Professor Saad Eddin Ibrahim for their invaluable contribution in managing the survey fieldwork. The study would not have been possible without a research grant from the Australia Research Council for which I am grateful. I would like to thank Noel Biggins for his valuable assistance throughout the research project and to Julie Henderson and Lynne Giles for their work in data analyses and to Nena Bierbaum for the editorial assistance.

I am also indebted to Professors Ivan Szelenyi, Georges Sabagh, Joseph Tamney, Irene Beirman, Afaf Marsot and Drs M. Amien Rais and Zafar Ishaq Ansari for their support and encouragement. My thanks to the Department of Sociology, Flinders University, the Department of Sociology and the Centre for Near Eastern Studies, University of California, Los Angeles, for their support at various stages of the study. I would like to thank Ms Uzma Gilani and Mrs Daleara Hirjikaka of the Oxford University Press, Pakistan for their support and assistance at various stages of the publication of this book and Ms Aquila Ismail for the editorial assistance and advice. It is impossible to imagine how the research, which is the basis of this book, could have been conducted without the willing and generous participation of my respondents in the four countries, and they deserve my greatest debt.

At the personal level, my wife Selva helped me in more ways than I can say. This study owes much to her and to our children Haroon and Tirana. Their affection and support was a source of constant encouragement and gave me perspective. All the people mentioned here are, of course, not responsible for any shortcomings, which may be identified in this book. I accept full and sole responsibility for that.

Riaz Hassan
Flinders University
Adelaide, Australia
April 2001

1

INTRODUCTION

Social Reality of the Islamic World

In the annals of human history, Islam occupies an illustrious position. Besides being one of the great religions, it gave rise to some of the greatest civilizations the world has known. The successor states of these civilizations are not as vibrant today as they once were but echoes of their past achievements still reverberate in their social, cultural and physical landscapes. Islam is the second largest world religion. An estimated 1.2 billion followers constituted about 20 per cent of the world population in 1998. Of these, approximately 800 million live in the forty-five Muslim-majority countries—the remaining 400 million live as Muslim minorities in 149 countries. In terms of size alone, the Islamic world constitutes a significant part of humanity and, therefore, warrants a sociologically informed understanding and analysis of religious, social and political trends which characterize it.

Most serious observers of contemporary Muslim societies will recognize their economic, social, educational and scientific backwardness. According to the World Development Reports published by the World Bank, most of the Muslim-majority countries are classified as low to medium income countries. About 66 per cent of Muslims live in low-income countries and about 32 per cent live in the medium income countries. Only 2 per cent of Muslims live in the high-income countries. All high income and a majority of the middle income Muslim countries are petroleum exporting countries.[1]

The general socioeconomic and demographic characteristics of Muslim countries confirm the causes and effects of low income. Most of them are largely rural, have relatively high inflation, low economic growth, low life expectancy and a high illiteracy rate. The quality of human capital is adversely affected by low educational attainment, poor nutrition and gender bias. The broad conclusion which can be drawn from the above is that the quality of human capital in Muslim countries is at severe risk, and, because of the widespread prevalence of the above-mentioned conditions, it is likely to get worse in the foreseeable future. In the third industrial revolution with its 'knowledge economy' in which the creation of wealth will depend primarily on skills, these conditions would have serious repercussions for the economic and social position of the Muslim world.[2]

These conditions are being addressed by the governments of Muslim countries with varying degrees of success. Perhaps the most notable among the Muslim countries for making great strides in educating its people has been Indonesia, the largest Muslim country in the world. In thirty years, Indonesia has been transformed from a semiliterate to a highly literate country.[3] In addition, it was able to achieve a very substantial rate of sustained economic growth until 1997. In neighbouring Malaysia the rapid economic growth of the past three decades has also brought about a radical social and economic transformation of its people. These successes, however, have not altered the fact that most of the Muslim world remains relatively poor, underdeveloped and technologically backward. These conditions have made Islam and Muslim countries a subject of numerous debates in the modern world.[4]

Debates about Islam and Muslim Societies

Reformulation of Islam

The key debates are centred on the political and economic crises, Islamic activism, backwardness in science and technology, position and status of women, and international relations. This list is not meant to be exhaustive but refers to subjects which are the focus of this study. There are numerous works dealing with the causes and consequences of political and economic crises in the Muslim world. It will be an impossible task to try to cover all of them. I will focus on a few selected works which are indicative of the analysis relevant to this study.

In his book *Crisis in the Muslim Mind,* the Saudi Arabian political scientist and educationist Abu Sulayman argues that a 'flawed sense' of *ummah* (community of believers) is responsible for the political, social and economic decline of the Muslim world over the past three centuries. He contends that coercion and authoritarianism of the political elite and emotional and psychological oppression of the masses by the intellectual (religious) elite have adversely affected the creativity of the Muslim mind. The results of these policies have created inhibitions which caused the mentality of the ummah and its character to develop in such a way that it lacks initiative and the ability to innovate and think for itself.[5]

He outlines a framework which is predicated on the integration of political and religious leadership in order to revive the past glory and the 'true' spirit of the Islamic ummah. Unfortunately his analysis, wittingly or unwittingly, conceptualizes the ummah as a kind of static social organization unaffected by major historical developments such as modernization and globalization. There is also no critical assessment of the bifurcation of leadership and how it is to be integrated in modernizing and globalizing contemporary Muslim societies.

Another Arab Muslim political sociologist, Bassam Tibi, in his provocative book *The Crisis of Modern Islam* (1988) provides a more historically grounded and theoretically informed analysis of the political, economic and scientific underdevelopment of the Muslim world, especially of the Islamic Middle East. His conclusions can be summarized as follows. The modern era rests on a technological-scientific culture based on rationality. The historical experience of the Protestant

Reformation was instrumental in separating the sacred from the political, which laid the grounds for the enlightenment with its emphasis on reason to control nature and reform society. Having undergone these processes the Europeans have developed, whereas Muslims are backward because they have not yet appropriated the technological-scientific culture.

He agrees with Islamic modernist thinkers like Muhammad Abduh and Jamaluddin Afghani that it is the structural conditions which have caused the backwardness of the Muslim world. Following the Qur'anic injunction that 'God does not change a people's lot unless they change what is in their hearts' (13:11), Muslims need a (new) normative orientation. This could be achieved by treading the path of *ijtihad* (considered judgement) rather than of *taqlid* (thoughtless imitation). He also argues that the modern crisis in the contemporary Islamic world is the product of economic poverty of Muslims and the identity crisis brought on by westernization. Despaired by the crisis, Tibi argues that Muslims are turning to Islam as the promise for a better future and as the basis for a cultural identity. The product of this development is a repoliticization of Islam which can be observed throughout the Islamic Middle East. This cultural retrospection, which is a dominant feature of Islamic repoliticization, can produce certain sociopsychological effects, but it certainly cannot contribute to the conquest of underdeveloped structures and the concomitant global inequalities.[6]

The Algerian philosopher and historian Mohammed Arkoun, using the methodology of modern social sciences, explores the identity crisis that has left many Muslims alienated from both a modernity imposed upon them and Islamic tradition subverted by the nationalists and Islamists for their own narrow ideological purposes. A key concern of Arkoun is the tyranny of reason, western and Islamic, and its impact on the image Muslims hold of themselves. He is critical of the West for projecting the total superiority of its secular, rational and universalist ideals and of the Muslims who, by virtue of superior knowledge, claim to distinguish the 'true Islam' from the 'false Islam' and 'true

Muslim' from 'false Muslim'. He is critical of contemporary Islamist movements which seek to subordinate reason to faith but subsequently embrace it as a tool for the confirmation, clarification, and administration of faith.

According to Arkoun, Islam has meant many things to many people in different epochs resulting in various expressions of Islam. He rejects the idea of one 'true Islam'. Instead, he suggests that the one and possibly the only way to establish an understanding of historically authentic Islam is to know and understand all that Islam has been, all that has been thought about it, and all that has remained unthinkable or unthought. In the totality of this understanding lies an important set of truths about Islam that can serve as a marker of identity for Muslims and also a bridge to other societies.

Through the methodology of human sciences, Arkoun wants to integrate the fragmented Islamic tradition and incorporate it into the world (human) history of which it has always been a part. For him the history of Islamic society is inextricably linked with that of the West. There is no dichotomy between the western reason and Islamic reason. Both must be viewed in the context of a single history, that of the peoples of the Book, which regenerates universality while destroying particularity. He is very critical of Islamists who, like the 'orientalists' have been seeking to marginalize the Islamic world. For Arkoun the only path for Islam and for humanity is to be a part of the world without margins.[7]

A prominent Muslim intellectual and the Prime Minister of Malaysia, Mahathir Muhammad, is a vocal critic of the social and economic conditions of the Muslim ummah. For him the decline of the Muslim ummah has been accelerated by the inability of Muslims and their leaders to:

> …understand Islam within the context of the contemporary world, with the changed conditions of life. We cannot recreate the world of the early years of Islam. The changes that have occurred in recent years are fundamentally the biggest changes human society has ever experienced, but in practical and intellectual terms, we

Muslims have not been able even to conceive of how to reorganise our political, social and economic lives to take in changes that have taken place.[8]

He criticizes Muslims for accepting, in their ignorance, the current conditions with pride. He argues that the Muslim world is in acute social, economic and political agony, although many Muslims have adopted a false sense of security by resorting to traditional Muslim piety. For Mahathir Muhammad the Muslim world is heading towards an 'aimless future' which would not only aggravate their present conditions but, worse, it will separate them from their faith. He sees the viable Muslim future only in a rationally planned, efficient economy based on modern industrial technology and which is grounded in interpretations of Islamic injunctions with reference to contemporary reality. In short, his prescription is the interpretations of sacred texts in the context of a modern world and a rationally planned industrial economy. The absence of such a world is owing to Muslim complacency based on an emphasis on the practice of traditional Muslim piety. These views have generated considerable controversy within and outside Malaysia, but, at the same time, he is given grudging credit for transforming Malaysia's economy along his vision of the Islamic future.

Ernest Gellner, in his seminal analysis of Muslim society, explores the reasons for the resistance to industrialism in the Islamic world. He argues that it was the distinctive pattern of distribution of scripturalist Puritanism and hierarchical ecstatic medianist styles in Islam which may explain both why industrial society failed to be born within it, and why Islam in the end may be more adaptable to industrial society than Christianity which provided the historical matrix for its development. For Gellner, the Islamic norms and values of universalism, scripturalism, spiritual egalitarianism, the extension of full participation in the sacred community not to one, or some, but to *all*, and the rational systemization of social life make Islam, compared with Christianity and Judaism, closest to modernity.[9]

According to Gellner the egalitarian scripturalism of Islam is more suited to a mobile, technical society than the ascriptive, medianist, manipulative spiritual brokerage of Christianity:

> To *engender* industrialisation, it is presumably best if the scripturalism is insulated and protected in a more or less peripheral part of the older society within which a New World can emerge in a relatively undisturbed way. But to *survive* in conditions of emulative industrialisation, it may be better if the scripturalism is at the very centre rather than at the periphery, and can slough off the peripheral styles as superstitions and unworthy accretions— thereby simultaneously affirming its own continuity and local roots *and* explaining away its political and economic retardation. It can then simultaneously affirm an ancient identity *and* justify a strenuous leap forward.[10]

Gellner's key argument that the core values of puritanical scripturalist Islam are compatible with industrial society is also echoed by Islamic modernists like the Algerian Muhammad Arkoun, who, while seeing the need for adaptation of Islam to the scientific age, sees no contradiction between Islam and science.

One of the most important Islamic scholars of this century was Fazlur Rahman—a Pakistani. He has provided the most systematic analysis of Islamic intellectual tradition as well as of the current crisis in the Muslim world. Rahman claims that a central aim of the Qur'an was/is to establish a viably just and ethically based social order on earth.[11] This aim was declared against the background of an Arabian society characterized by polytheism, exploitation of the poor, general neglect of social responsibility, moral degradation, injustice towards women and the less powerful, and tribalism.

The Qur'an and the genesis of the Muslim community occurred in the light of history and against a social historical background. The Qur'anic response to specific conditions is the product of a 'coherent philosophy' and 'attitude towards life' which Rahman calls the 'intellectual tradition' of Islam. This intellectual tradition was subverted and undermined by emphasis

on 'literalist' interpretations of the Qur'an by the ulama—
Islamic scholars. The Islamic scholarship moulded by the ulama
came to emphasize 'minimal Islam', focusing on 'five pillars'
and negative and punitive Islam. Islamic scholarship thus
became rigid, fossilized and largely removed from the
intellectual traditions of the Qur'an. Rahman argues that the
intellectual tradition of the Qur'an requires that Islamic thought
be dependent on a factual and proper study of social conditions
in order to develop appropriate Islamic social norms for
reforming society.[12]

Rahman sees intellectual and social reform as an important
part of the development of contemporary Muslim social
formations. These reforms require objective social scientific
studies of modern societies and a deeper understanding of what
he calls 'social thought in the Qur'an', which deals with the rise
and fall of societies and civilizations, moral decrepitude of
nations, function of leadership, conditions conducive to creating
peace and prosperity and 'the inheritance of the earth'. This
body of social thought should be organized next to the pure
moral thought of the Qur'an and the lessons from history upon
which the Qur'an is insistent. He argues that unless the material
of the Qur'an is well systemized it can be dangerously
misleading to apply individual and isolated verses to situations,
as Muslim preachers and many intellectuals tend to do.[13]

Rahman further elaborates his methodology and approach to
social engineering. The views of the Qur'an will:

> ...remain at the level of pure abstraction unless a thorough *factual*
> survey is made of the relevant social data. It is of the greatest
> importance to determine exactly where society is at present before
> deciding where it can go. To talk about reforming society without
> scientifically determining where the society is, is certainly like a
> doctor treating a patient without taking his case history or examining
> him. In fact, there is a sense in which even a most meaningful
> formulation of Qur'anic thought would be dependent upon such a
> factual study and a proper method for interpreting facts; the
> converse...is also true...the study of the social sciences is a process,
> not something that is established once and for all. In fact, it is more

so than any other field, for its subject matter—social behaviour—is constantly in the process of creation.[14]

There is also a large body of literature, which emanates from what Tibi and Rahman call Islamic apologists, which argues that backwardness of the Islamic world is a consequence of Muslims not acting according to the commands of the Qur'an and not carrying out the *jihad* (holy war/struggle). Most of them are transfixed by the assumption that any diminution of traditional religious piety will lead to secularization, which will be a harbinger of moral degeneracy. They see the present conditions in the Muslim world as evidence of the decline of tradition-grounded religious piety among Muslims. Their solution is the Islamic revival, which will lead to the re-establishment of the pristine Islamic era.

A typical example of the Islamic apologia is the writing of the Pakistani intellectual Hamid Gul, a retired Pakistani army general. Without any evidence and only a very superficial analysis of the relations between the West and Islam in this century, Gul argues that:

> The natural movement of history itself is paving the way for the acceptance of the eternal values embedded in Islamic teachings. Humanity is adopting these values and principles, and since Islam is a universal ideology it travels like the wind and is spreading like sweet fragrance. The wind and the sweet fragrance cannot be encountered by the sword.[15]

Gul sees the division between the Muslim ummah as being perpetrated by a Western, and in particular American, conspiracy designed with the specific agenda to keep the world devoid of the benefits and virtues of Islam. The Qur'an and Sunnah are the basis of Muslim solidarity and the West is conspiring to keep Muslims aloof from this foundation. The objective is to fan the flames of sectarianism among Muslims and to promote secularism. He urges Muslims to confront the West with a feeling of unity whose spirit is manifested in the Afghan *jihad*.

He sees only Islam as being capable of alleviating human sufferings which have been inflicted by the Western capitalism and communism under the former USSR.[16] This kind of reasoning is fairly typical of the Islamic apologists and they make no attempt to give any objective analysis for their assertions except rhetoric.

The revivalist movements led by Islamicists have performed the desired function by reorienting the modern, educated, lay Muslims emotionally toward Islam. But these movements also tend to perform a serious disservice to Islam by inhibiting the positive and critical Islamic thinking and scholarship among its ranks. According to Rahman,[17] while traditionalist ulama have built up an imposing edifice of learning that invests their personalities with certain depth, the revivalists have no serious intellectual depth or breadth. They have produced no Islamic educational system worthy of the name primarily because, having become dissatisfied with much of the traditional learning of the ulama, the revivalists themselves have been by and large unable to devise any methodology, any structural strategy, for understanding Islam or for interpreting the Qur'an.[18]

The biggest challenge facing Muslims at the present juncture is the task of rethinking and reformulating Islam. Muslims must decide what exactly is to be conserved, what is essential and relevant for the establishment of an Islamic future, what is fundamentally Islamic and what is purely historical. In other words, they must develop an enlightened conservatism. The conservative ulama and intellectuals strenuously resist this process, and this resistance lies at the heart of many fundamentalist movements. To secure a relevant future for Islam the Islamic world must undertake the process of reformulation of Islam.

Religious Fundamentalism

As implied in the discussion above, religious fundamentalism is a major arena of debate inside and outside the Islamic world.

Fundamentalism is not unique to Islam. It has emerged in all major world religions over the past thirty years and has gained prominence and influence in the 1990s.[19] It is defined as a:

> ...distinctive tendency—a habit of mind and a pattern of behaviour—found within modern religious communities and embodied in certain representative individuals and movements. Fundamentalism is, in other words, a religious way of being that manifests itself as a strategy by which beleaguered believers attempt to preserve their distinctive identity as people or group.[20]

Feeling this identity to be at risk, fundamentalism seeks to fortify it by a selective retrieval of doctrines, beliefs and practices from a sacred past as well as modern times. This renewed religious identity becomes the exclusive and absolute basis for a recreated political and social order. While there are differences between various fundamentalist movements in general, their endeavour to establish the new political and social order relies on charismatic and authoritarian leadership. These movements also feature a disciplined inner core of elites and organizations, as well as a large population of sympathizers who may be called up in times of need. Fundamentalists often follow a rigorous sociomoral code and have clear strategies to achieve their goals.

Religious fundamentalism is a growing and important part of social change in Muslim countries. Its main goal is to establish the *shariah* (the Islamic law) as the explicit, comprehensive and exclusive legal base of society.[21] Hardly a day passes without a reference to Islamic fundamentalism in the international media. All Muslim societies are affected by it, although, in its presence and power, there are large differences among them.[22] Is Islamic fundamentalism an inevitable destiny of all Muslim countries or is it only a part of a larger process of social change? Are there certain social, economic, historical and other preconditions which predispose some Muslim countries to Islamic fundamentalism more than others? Are there different types of Islamic fundamentalisms? These and related questions have been posed and explored by several contributors to the Fundamentalism Project of the American Academy of Arts and Science.[23]

There appear to be at least three competing theories of Islamic fundamentalism. These are Watt's[24] 'crisis of self image', Gellner's[25] 'pattern of distribution of dominant religious traditions' and the 'modernization and religious purification' theory advanced by a number of social scientists.[26] The following provides a brief account of the three theories.

Crisis of Self-Image

Distilling insights from his works on the history and sociology of Islam, Watt[27] has proposed that the principal root of Islamic fundamentalism is the domination of the traditional 'Islamic world view' and the corresponding 'self-image of Islam' in the thinking of Islamic intellectuals and of great masses of ordinary Muslims. According to Watt:

> ...the important distinction is between those Muslims who fully accept the traditional world view and want to maintain it intact and those who see that it needs to be corrected in some respects. The former group are fundamentalists...while the latter group will be referred to as Liberals.[28]

Among both groups many different political movements and attitudes are to be found. The ulama, who are the primary bearers and transmitters of the traditional world view, are mostly reactionary in the sense that they tend to oppose reforms. However, other Islamic intellectuals subscribe to a variety of reformist elements and they are sometimes very critical of the ulama. The reforms they are interested in, however, are mostly social and political and leave the traditional worldview of Islam unchanged.

Watt then identifies important aspects of the traditional worldview. These are:

- The unchanging static world which is predicated on the complete absence of the idea of development;
- The finality of Islam;
- The self-sufficiency of Islam (Watt sees this reflected in the Muslim's conception of knowledge. When a Muslim thinks of knowledge it is primarily 'knowledge for living' whereas when a Westerner thinks of knowledge it is mainly 'knowledge for power');
- Islam in history. (This idea refers to the widespread belief that Islam will ultimately be triumphant in changing the whole world into *dar-al-Islam* (the sphere of Islam);
- The idealization of Prophet Muhammad (PBUH) and of early Islam.

This renders critical and historically objective scholarship highly problematic in Muslim consciousness and deviation from the idealized and romanticized notions as heretic and 'unthinkable'. For Watt, these features of Islamic worldview and the corresponding self-image are the basis of Islamic fundamentalism. The support for fundamentalism is embedded in the consciousness, which fully accepts the traditional worldview and wants to keep it intact.

Patterns of Distribution of Dominant Religious Orientation

Building on the previous sociological and historical analyses of Muslim society by Ibn Khaldun,[29] Weber,[30] Hume,[31] Hodgson[32] and others, Gellner has advanced a theory of Muslim social formation based on his conceptualization of 'two strands of Islam'. One strand is characterized by 'scripturalist puritanism' and represented by the ulama. This is the Islam of the 'fundamentalists'. The other strand is characterized by 'hierarchical ecstatic mediationist style and is represented by the saints'. These two strands have evolved historically as representing two major social structural features of Muslim society, namely the city and the countryside. He then combines these strands of Islam with political orientation of the elites and proposes a model of Muslim social formations. If we contrast 'fundamentalism' with 'laxity' along one dimension and 'social radicalism' with 'traditionalism' along another, according to Gellner we get four types of Muslim societies or social formations.

The old style Puritanism prevails where a traditional elite survives, but is still fairly close to its own origin in one of those Ibn Khaldunian swings of dynastic change which had brought it to power in a fusion of religious enthusiasm and tribal aggression. The new style Puritanism, with its elective affinity for social radicalism, prevails where colonialism had destroyed old elites and where a new one had come from below rather than from the outer wilderness.[33]

Modernization and Religious Purification

This theory holds that religious fundamentalism is one of the consequences of the modernization process. Building on the studies by Mol[34] and Folliet,[35] Tamney[36] proposed that one way modern people are different from traditional people is that they practice 'purer' religious styles. The relation between modernization and religious purity can take two forms. In its general sense, purification is simply the opposite of syncretism. Purification means the differentiation of religious traditions at the personality level so that the individual's religious lifestyle reflects just one of the traditions. If being modern means people are more conscious about the history and internal structures of various religions, modern people could realize the inconsistencies in a syncretic lifestyle, feel uneasy or even insincere, and seek to purify their lives by deliberately eliminating elements from religious tradition other than their own. Using this conceptualization, Tamney hypothesizes that modernization will be associated with religious purification. His empirical examination of this hypothesis in Indonesia tended to support his theory. Other studies by Hassan[37] and Irfani[38] provide some support for Tamney's theory.

This study does not claim to test these theories using the logic and framework of the classical experimental design, but it will attempt to examine some of the theoretical insights of these theories in order to assess their analytical usefulness in the study of contemporary Muslim societies. In particular, the empirical evidence from this study will be used to examine Watt's theory of self-image of Islam. The study will also examine the perception of religious institutions under different institutional configurations and whether religious fundamentalism produces anti-Western attitudes.

Islamic State

The relationship between politics and religion in Muslim societies has been a focus of debate among scholars of Islam for most of this century. A commonly stated view of many Western and Muslim scholars of Islam is that Islam is not only a religion but also a blue-print for social order and, therefore, encompasses all domains of life, including law and the state.[39] This view is reinforced by the fact that Islam does not have a 'church' separate from the state, although it does have the institutions of *ulama* (religious scholars), who act as the guardians of the interpretations of the sacred tests, and *imams* of *masjid* (leaders of the mosques), who lead the mandatory daily prayers in the Muslim mosques. It is further argued that this characterization sets Islamic societies apart from Western societies that are built on the separation of state and religious institutions.

After reviewing the evidence about the separation of state and religion in Islamic history, Lapidus[40] concludes that the history of the Muslim world reveals two main institutional configurations. The undifferentiated state-religious configuration characterized a small number of Middle Eastern societies. This configuration was characteristic of lineage or tribal societies. The historic norm for agro-urban Islamic societies was an institutional configuration that recognized the division between the state and religious spheres:

> Despite the common statement (and the Muslim ideal) that the institutions of state and religion are unified, and that Islam is a total way of life which defines political as well as social and family matters, most Muslim societies did not conform to this ideal, but were built around separate institutions of state and religion.[41]

Keddie[42] has described the supposed near-identity of religion and the state in Islam more as a 'pious myth than reality for most of Islamic history'. While it is true that Muslims widely subscribe to a basic Islamic belief that *Islam din wa dawla* (Islam is religion and state), the fact that this precept contains two distinct elements in its predicate signifies that those two elements are in reality separate, and the ultimate relation between the two can take many forms.[43] Similar views of Islamic history have also been advanced by others.[44]

The weight of historical scholarship indicates that the institutional configurations of Islamic societies can be classified into two types: 'differentiated social formations' (i.e., societies in which religion and state occupy different space); and 'undifferentiated social formations' (i.e., societies in which religion and state are integrated). While a majority of Islamic societies have been and are 'differentiated social formations', a small but significant number have been and are societies which can be classified as 'undifferentiated social formations'. A common label used in contemporary discourse for undifferentiated Muslim social formations is 'Islamic State'. The contemporary Muslim world contains examples of both types of social formations.

While the majority of Muslim countries are differentiated social formations, an important group of countries also claim to be undifferentiated social formations. These include Saudi Arabia, the Islamic Republic of Iran, the Islamic Republic of Pakistan, and, more recently, the Sudan and Afghanistan have also joined this group. We know very little about how religious institutions relate to state power in the two types of institutional configurations; in particular, how these institutional arrangements influence the attitudes of Muslims towards religious and other institutions of the state and civil society. This is a significant issue since the legitimacy and stability of political structures ultimately depends on the perceptions and attitudes they evoke and instill in the citizens. One aim of this study is to explore this important but neglected area of social reality. This study will examine the level of trust and legitimacy accorded to religious institutions compared with the other institutions of the state in order to assess the public influence of religion under different institutional configurations.

Gender Issues in Muslim Societies

Attitudes towards Gender Roles

For many Islamic and Western scholars of Islam the status, role and position of women are important distinguishing features of Muslim societies which set them apart from their Western counterparts. Many people in the West regard the status of women in Muslim society as symptomatic of their oppression in Islam.[45] It is further argued that gender relations in Islam have been primarily shaped by its Arabian origins. While it is true that throughout its history Islam has borne the marks of its Arabian origin, in regard to the position held by women in his community, Prophet Muhammad (PBUH) was able to introduce profound changes.[46]

Islam was instrumental in introducing wide-ranging legal-religious enactments to improve the status and position of women in Arabian society and to protect them from male excesses. There are numerous Qur'anic injunctions to give effect to these changes.[47] These Qur'anic injunctions brought about significant improvements in the status of women in a wide range of public and private spheres, but most importantly these injunctions gave women a full-fledged personality.[48]

However, selective literal, non-contextual and ahistorical interpretations of sacred texts by Islamic scholars over time have shaped the average Muslim's conservative views and attitudes towards women. One of the major dilemmas faced by the nationalist leaders who spearheaded the independence movement from Indonesia to Pakistan and Egypt was the 'woman issues'. Their problem was how to respond to the questions raised regarding women about their role, status and function in the new independent states. This generated highly emotive and divisive debates between the Islamic scholars and the nationalist leaders which centred around the issues of marriage and family law, and the role and status of women in a modern independent Muslim state.[49]

Notwithstanding strong resistance from Islamists in several countries, the new nationalist leaders were able to overcome centuries of resistance and introduce modest changes to family and marriage laws. These changes were introduced within an Islamic framework that did not expressly violate the appropriate Qur'anic injunctions and Sunnah.[50] These reforms have continually been criticized and opposed by a majority of Islamic ulama and their followers who regard them as violations of Islamic law and commandments as codified in classical Islamic legal texts, as well as thinly veiled attempts to find an Islamic justification for an essentially western approach to the issues of interpersonal relations.[51] This debate between nationalists and Islamists continues and, according to some evidence, is becoming an important part of the political agenda of Islamic fundamentalists.[52]

Attitudes towards Veiling and Patriarchy

Veiling and seclusion of women and patriarchy have been important features of Islamic societies. In recent years they have attracted much criticism from Muslim and Western feminist scholars. The tradition and custom of veiling in Islam can be attributed to Islamic history, Islamic texts and the privileged position of males and their control and dominance over positions of power and authority in Muslim society. Veiling and seclusion of women and their role and function in society are also intertwined with the management of sexuality in Islam.[53]

Islam recognizes sexual desire as a natural endowment of the human body and enjoins its followers to satisfy and even enjoy fulfillment of this desire, and provides a framework enunciated in the sacred texts to do so. Unlike Christianity, it does not sanction or idealize celibacy. Over the centuries the interpretations of sacred texts by the ulama have led to the development of an institutional framework for the management and satisfaction of human sexuality by the imposition of control over women. As women are seen not only as sexual beings but also as the embodiment of sex itself, the social framework that has evolved has, consequently, sought to view the woman's body as pudendal. This conceptualization has led to the development and observance of strict dress codes for women, including veiling and seclusion, in order to prevent them from displaying their bodily charm and beauty.[54]

Other features of the institutional framework arose out of women being made the principal actors responsible for preserving the sanctity of the family and social reproduction. This led to strict injunctions on the types of roles they could play in the public sphere. Strong social and cultural traditions evolved which placed serious obstacles in the way of women seeking to succeed in public roles. Men, on the other hand, were assigned all public roles as providers, protectors and arbiters, and this reinforced their power in the domestic domain as well. Patriarchal family structures thus became more functionally suitable to ensure the perpetuation of the institutional framework for the satisfaction and management of the family.

Such an institutional framework and its accompanying normative requirement as they apply to gender roles, dress codes, veiling and seclusion, and patriarchy is by and large universally accepted in Muslim societies, although their observances vary according to economic conditions. For most ordinary Muslims this practice is in keeping with the supremacy of the male over the female as postulated by the Qur'an. However, the vagueness of these edicts has given ulama greater authority to interpret them as the local custom demanded. Some ulama even appear to have invented 'tradition' in order to bolster their interpretations which may in fact be in conflict with the Qur'anic statements.[55]

Owing to internal and external pressures, governments of most Islamic countries have initiated reforms to improve the quality of citizenship accorded to Muslim women. These reforms have sought to remove some of the obstacles that have prevented gender equality. While they vary in their scope and intensity from country to country, such reforms have been initiated in most Muslim countries. Some of these reforms have been successful, and in some instances, like Iran and Pakistan, the pendulum has swung to more traditionalist views which have gained favour with the current ruling elites. In general, the reforms are having a positive effect, although the obstacles still exist. These obstacles will continue until such time as the rigid attitudes of the ulama change or lose significance for the general body of Muslims owing to the decline of their religious authority.

While these issues occupy an important part of discourse on Islamic society, there is little attention paid to comparative studies of Muslim attitudes towards gender issues and how these are shaped and articulated under different social and political settings. Like all human attitudes in general, attitudes towards gender issues are formed and shaped by the prevailing social, economic and legal conditions, and by the nature of interactions between them and religious institutions. The Muslim attitude towards gender relations and issues require explanations which are empirically grounded in the concrete social realities of Muslim societies, and not simply by the fact of their religiosity. Any observer familiar with the social conditions in contemporary Muslim countries such as Saudi Arabia, Pakistan, Indonesia, Afghanistan, Egypt, Turkey and Kazakhstan would know how differently gender relations are structured in these countries.

The differences and similarities between them on gender relations cannot be simply attributed to Islam. Any meaningful explanation would require an examination of the social, economic and political conditions and how they mediate between traditional Islamic norms and their expressions in the local milieu. One of the aims of this research was to focus on these issues.

The Aims of This Study

There is now a considerable body of literature which purports to describe and analyse the kind of issues which have been identified in the discussion above. Some of it is informed and the rest highly biased and subjective. Studies which purport to be comparative are often based on the comparisons of single country studies. One aim of the research to be reported in the following chapters was to undertake a systematic comparative investigation of everyday beliefs of Muslims, with special reference to the middle classes in a number of national settings. The focus on everyday beliefs was based on the assumption that moral consciousness is closely related to political and social conditions. The compatibility between the two is an important condition for the formation and maintenance of individual and collective identities. The selection of the middle class was guided by the well-known sociological insight that the middle class plays an important role in shaping the social, economic and political conditions in modern societies. The countries selected for the research were chosen for the geographical, historical, cultural and political characteristics which have influenced their religious milieu.

The research sought to investigate Muslim perceptions of religion and society. It was assumed that religious perceptions would influence the perceptions of society. It was designed as an empirical study and this meant that its focus and scope had to be confined to selected aspects of religious and social phenomena which could be investigated within the constraints

of available resources. The other factors which influenced the
focus and scope of the study were their relevance to some of the
debates which have been mentioned here.

The focus on religion was confined to Muslim piety, Muslim
ummah and 'images of Islam'. Similarly, the focus on society
was confined to the relationship between politics and religion,
gender issues and the image of the 'other'. The notion of Muslim
piety refers to the degree and nature of an individual's religious
commitment. The investigation of the Muslim ummah focused
on the one widely held belief that all Muslims belong to a
'community', loyalty to which transcends other forms of
primordial loyalties. The 'images of Islam' focus sought to
explore the propositions advanced by Watt, Gellner and others
about Muslim ideals of Islam, and their relationship, if any, to
Muslim piety and to modernization. These dimensions can be
considered as three key dimensions of Muslim religious
consciousness.

The three aspects of Muslim perceptions of society related to
the debate among Muslim intellectuals and Islamic activists
about the relationship between religion and politics in Islam.
There is now considerable literature that examines this
relationship in historical as well as contemporary Muslim
societies. The focus in this study was not on examining the
competing theories of this relationship but the consequences of
different institutional configurations on the public influence of
religious institutions.

The gender issues are an important part of modern Islamic
discourse. The research focused on two aspects of this discourse,
namely Muslim perceptions of gender roles in modern society,
and their attitudes towards veiling and patriarchy. Finally, the
focus on the perception of the 'other' was aimed at exploring
Muslim perceptions of Christianity and Judaism, as well as of
the West. As mentioned earlier, it was assumed that there is a
relationship between the moral consciousness and social and
political conditions. This relationship will also be examined in
the light of the empirical evidence gathered on this relationship.

Countries Studied

The research was carried out in four Muslim countries, namely Indonesia, Pakistan, Egypt and Kazakhstan. These countries were chosen for their distinctive geographic, historical, cultural and political conditions. The religious developments in them are strongly influenced by these differences. In this respect it was expected that they would provide contrasting environments for sociological explorations of the research. These four countries have a combined population of about 400 million, which is about half of the population of Muslim-majority countries and one-third of the total Muslim population in the world.

Indonesia

Indonesia is the largest Muslim country, with an estimated population in 1998 of about 200 million of which 88 per cent are Muslims. Like most other Muslim countries it is a developing country with a per capita gross national product (GNP) in 1997 of US$1110.[56] Until recently it was one of the most rapidly developing economies in the developing world. Unlike many other Islamic countries, Indonesia has also been very successful in making great strides in providing universal education to all its citizens. The success of the Indonesian government's education policies over the last thirty years has transformed the country's educational profile.[57] After two years of economic crisis its economy appears to be recovering and it is likely to resume its growth trajectory.

Almost all Indonesians are Sunni Muslims and followers of the Shafii school of Islamic law. Islam was introduced by South Asian and Arab traders and Sufi scholars in the thirteenth century. Its rapid expansion occurred in the fifteenth and sixteenth centuries, and by the eighteenth century the majority of the population in Java and Sumatra had become Muslim. Because of the Sufi influence, Sufi mysticism became an important feature of Indonesian Islam.[58] This religious orientation allowed it to assimilate the images and metaphors of the local cultures. Consequently, Indonesian Islam has been remarkably malleable, syncretistic, multi-vocal and multi-layered.[59] Its expressions are closely intertwined with the social structure of Indonesia's dominant island of Java. The ruling classes and peasantry assimilated and absorbed Islamic concepts and practices into their Indic pantheism and animism. The trading classes, which also made up the middle classes, were more exposed to the Islamic world of the Middle East and South Asia as a result of their trading activities and consequently acquired doctrinal and puritanical Islam.[60]

As a result of these influences, contemporary Indonesian Islam has two well-established traditions. These are represented by two mass organizations. The Sufi, or popular, Islam which dominates the rural areas and *pesantren* (religious schools) is represented by Nahdatul Ulama, and the modernist-scripturalist Islam which dominates the urban areas is represented by Muhammadiyah. The Islamic teachers, known locally as *kiyais,* are the symbols of Sufi or popular Islam, and the Islamic intellectuals dominate the activities of Muhammadiyah.[61]

The constitutional framework of the secular Indonesian state is based on strict separation of religion and the state. In this respect the Indonesian governments have continued the policies of Indonesia's former Dutch colonists. The state ideology is known as *Pancasila* (five principles) and is strictly enforced. Since its formation in 1949, the Indonesian state has been governed by authoritarian, military-dominated governments. As a result, the evolution of civil society has been thwarted and many institutions of civil society are dominated by the state functionaries. Although the state ideology has encountered resistance, which at times has been militant, Indonesian governments have been largely able to enforce strict adherence to *Pancasila,* a result of which has been that Indonesian society has evolved as a secular, modernizing capitalist society.

Pakistan

Pakistan, with its estimated population of 142 million in 1998, is the second-largest Muslim country in the world. It came into existence in 1947, after the independence of the Indian subcontinent from Britain which lead to its partition into India and Pakistan. It was founded to provide a separate homeland for the Indian Muslims and consisted of the Muslim-majority areas in the northern and eastern parts of the Indian subcontinent. In 1972, the eastern part of the country, known as East Pakistan, seceded to form the new country of Bangladesh. Pakistan now consists of the provinces of the Punjab, Sindh, Balochistan and the North West Frontier Province.

It is a developing country and its per capita GNP of US$490 in 1997 makes it one of the world's poorer countries. Unlike Indonesia, it has a very patchy development record. It has a very high illiteracy rate, and the government's efforts to provide mass education have not been very successful owing to social, cultural and economic obstacles. Over 95 per cent of Pakistan's population is Muslim. About 85 per cent of Pakistanis are Sunni and largely subscribe to the Hanafi school of Islamic law. About 15 per cent of Pakistanis are Shia Muslims. Since independence it has gradually developed as an Islamic Republic.

While Pakistan is not theocratic, its constitutional framework stipulates that Pakistan would be a democratic state based on Islamic principles. Article 198 of the constitution stipulates that all laws shall be in accordance with the injunctions of Islam as laid down in the Qur'an and Sunnah. Since 1971, Islamization has been adopted as a state policy.

Paradoxically, the adoption of the Islamization policy has proved to be socially and politically divisive. For much of Pakistan's political history it has been governed by an authoritarian, bureaucratic, military oligarchy. But with urbanization and industrialization, the pressure for democratization of the political processes has been gaining momentum.[62]

At the sociocultural level, Islam plays an important role in the lives of Pakistanis. But, like many other Muslim countries, religious sectarianism is a fact of life in Pakistan and a source of political and social instability and increasing violence. There are considerable variations in the way people articulate, interpret and practise their faith and work out its implications in their individual and collective lives. For analytical purposes, one can describe the religio-intellectual situation of Islam in Pakistan with reference to at least four distinct categories, namely legalistic, Sufi/popular, reformist/liberal, and revivalist/ fundamentalist Islam. The ulama play a prominent role in orthodox Islam, the Sufi saints and Pirs dominate the Sufi/ popular Islam, Islamic intellectuals are active in the reformist/ liberal Islam and the religious political party Jamaat-i-Islami together with Jamiat-e-Ulema Pakistan and Jamiat-i-Ulema-i-Islam plays an important role in the revivalist/fundamentalist Islam. In recent years a number of splinter fundamentalist groups have also emerged but it is difficult to determine their impact as yet.[63]

Kazakhstan

Kazakhstan is a Central Asian country of about eighteen million people. The indigenous Kazakhs, who are Muslim, constitute over half of its population. According to 1998 estimates, little over 30 per cent of the population was made up of ethnic Russians and about 15 per cent belonged to other European (mostly Germans and Ukrainians) and Central Asian ethnic groups. Kazakhs are Sunni Muslim and follow the Hanafi school of Islamic law. Kazakhstan had been under Russian control for several centuries. This control was exercised most ruthlessly under communist rule. In 1991, after the collapse of the Soviet Union, Kazakhstan became an independent country. It is a resource-rich country with a relatively literate population and a per capita GNP of $1340 in 1997.[64]

The spread of Islam in Kazakhstan began in 714 AD with the opening of Transoxiana by the Qutayba Muslims. However, because of their nomadic lifestyle Islam made little impression on the Kazakhs until the late eighteenth century, when Catherine the Great used the Tartar missionaries to spread Islam in Kazakhstan in order to 'civilize' and pacify the pastoral Kazakh nomads with whom her expanding empire was coming into increasing conflict. The nomadic lifestyle of the Kazakhs made proper religious training difficult. Consequently, the Islam of the Kazakhs was syncretic and not dogmatic. By the middle of the eighteenth century, however, a scripturalist tradition of Islam had taken root in Kazakhstan with the establishment of Qur'anic schools in several Kazakh cities and towns. By the end of the nineteenth century, Islam was firmly established among the Kazakhs and had become part of their identity.[65]

Under the Soviet rule, anti-religious pressure all but eliminated doctrinal Islam. The independent religious organizations were practically eliminated. The *Waqfs* (religious trusts) were taken under state control, mosques and Muslim courts and schools were closed. Kazakhstan was placed under the jurisdiction of the Spiritual Board for Muslims of Central Asia and Kazakhstan (DUMSAK), which supervised the functioning of the few remaining religious institutions. By 1989, when under *glasnost* the Soviet authorities relaxed their opposition to religion, all Kazakhs identified as Muslims as part of their ethnic and linguistic heritage. Their 'Muslimness' was more cultural than religious. Kazakhs are very particular in differentiating themselves from the neighbouring Uzbeks, whom they view as very religious. According to Kazakh ethnologist Raushan Mustafina, many Kazakhs observe Muslim ceremonies but they regard these ceremonies as part of their national rather than religious heritage.[66]

Since independence, the role of Islam at the individual and national levels is becoming more visible. At the national level, a new Board for the Muslims of Kazakhstan (DUMK), separate from the original Central Asian spiritual board which had regulated Kazakh religious affairs for about half a century, has been established by the Kazakhstan government. This development may be viewed as a response to greater religious adherence among the local Muslim population. There is increasing evidence that ethnic Kazakhs are now displaying a greater interest in Islam. The state, however, remains committed to secularism. The Muslim religious festivals are not public holidays and the government has refused to allow the most Islamic of the Kazakh nationalist parties, Azat, to be legally registered.[67] In 1997 and 1998, when the survey fieldwork was done, Kazakhstan was going through a very difficult economic period and there was widespread disillusionment among the people about their economic and political future.

Egypt

Egypt, with its population of sixty million, is the largest Arab Muslim country. It is also one of the most influential countries not only in the Middle East but also in the Muslim world. Approximately 90 per cent of Egyptians are Sunni Muslim. The majority of the remaining Egyptians are Coptic Christians. Egypt is a developing and economically poor country, with a per capita GNP of $1180 in 1997.[68] It has been a Muslim country since the seventh century when (in 642 AD) the Muslim troops from Arabia conquered it and made it a province of the Arab empire. It remained a province of the Arab empire for 200 years, and during that period its population was gradually converted to Islam and also became Arabic speaking. From 800 AD onwards, Egypt was ruled by different Muslim dynasties from Baghdad, Tunisia, Cairo and Istanbul. In 1882, Britain occupied Egypt, and after the First World War—with the defeat of the Ottoman Empire—Egypt became a British protectorate. In 1922, Egypt gained independence from Britain and became a kingdom. In 1952, an Egyptian Army coup abolished the monarchy, and in 1954 Colonel Gamal Abdel Nassar came to power and laid the foundation of the Arab Republic of Egypt.

Islam plays an important role in the public and private lives of Egyptian Muslims.[69] As the site of Al-Azhar, the oldest Islamic University, Egypt has played an important role in the development of Islamic learning in the Muslim world. Egyptian Muslim intellectuals like Muhammad Abduh, Muhammad Rasid Rida, Syed Mohammad Qutb and Hassan al-Banna are some of the most influential Muslim thinkers and scholars of modern times. They have inspired several influential Islamic activist movements inside and outside Egypt. These movements have been influenced by their ideas about the legitimacy of political authority and the nature of Muslim society. These movements included the Salafiyya, Jihad Organization, Jama'at al-Muslimin and the Muslim Brotherhood *(Jam'iyyat al-Ikhwan al-Muslimin)*.[70]

The Muslim Brotherhood has been probably the most important and influential Muslim organization in Egypt, as well as in the Arab world. From a reformist Muslim organization, it was transformed into a radical Muslim organization committed to the establishment of an Islamic state through armed resistance. Nassar banned it, but after his death the state control on it was relaxed. It is no longer a radical militant organization, but still remains enormously influential in Egypt as well as in the Sudan and Jordan. As a result of the realities of Egyptian politics, the Muslim Brotherhood now emphasizes the creation of an Islamically oriented society through sociomoral reform rather than political reform. Its present leadership is focusing on building its base of support through educational and socioeconomic programmes.

Islam has played an important role in Egyptian political processes and in the civil society. It continues to play a vital but constantly changing role in the development of Egyptian public life. Prominent Islamist intellectuals and the organizations which were formed by them[71] have shaped its role and influence. These intellectuals and organizations have articulated unique and diverse responses to modernism and the influence of the West.[72] These responses have ranged from violence directed against the political leaders, which included the assassination of the

Egyptian President Anwar Sadat, and periodic attacks on Western tourists to movements seeking to make Muslims Islamically observant in order to rebuild the ummah to redress the balance of power between Islam and the West.[73] The Egyptian state remains a secular state founded on a constitution which stipulates separation of the state and religion. It is ruled by an authoritarian government whose power base is in the armed forces and the bureaucracy.

The most important feature of Islamic revivalism in Egypt in the 1990s is that it has become part of the mainstream Egyptian life and society, rather than a marginal phenomenon confined to the margins of society. This development is credited to the institutionalization of a more open political system under President Hosni Mubarak. Emphasis on Muslim piety is now found across all social classes, educated and uneducated, peasants and professionals, young and old, women and men. The Qur'an study groups are becoming a popular form of social organization. Islamic identity is expressed not only in formal religious practices but also in the social services offered by professional and social welfare organizations. The ulama and the mosques have also taken on a more prominent role.

Like the Jamaat-i-Islami of Pakistan, the Muslim Brotherhood denounces the evils of imperialism and the cultural hegemony of the West. But both have realized that the Muslim predicament was first and foremost a Muslim problem, caused by Muslims who had failed to be sufficiently Islamically observant. They both re-emphasize the necessity of Muslims to cultivate Islamic piety, which will then pave the way for the establishment of a true Islamic society.[74]

Methodology: How the Study was Done

The following is a brief overview of the methodology. A fuller account is provided in Appendix A. The data was collected through a structured survey questionnaire, which consisted of ten parts. These were: sociodemographic, educational and occupational background of the respondents; social and political attitudes; religious socialization, belief and practice; images of Islam; social class, lifestyle and housing; self-esteem; media exposure; attitudes towards the 'other' and household composition. The details of how the survey questionnaire was developed are provided in the above-mentioned appendix. The questionnaire was professionally translated into the languages of the countries surveyed, namely Indonesian, Urdu, Arabic, Russian and Kazakh languages.

The rationale behind the inclusion of the countries mentioned was guided by pragmatic and theoretical considerations. Indonesia was chosen because it represented South-East Asian Islam. Pakistan represents South Asian and non-Arabic Middle Eastern Islamic traditions. Egypt was selected because of its position in the Middle East. It represents the Arabic Middle Eastern Islam. Kazakhstan represents the West Asian Islamic traditions which have been influenced by communism.

The fieldwork was carried out by well-established social science research centres in each country. In Indonesia, the survey was carried by the Population Studies Centre of Gadjah Mada University in Yogyakarta, Java and was coordinated by the Director and Deputy Director of the Centre, Dr Agus Dwiyanto and Drs Sukmadi. In Pakistan, the fieldwork was carried out by the Social Science Research Centre of the University of Punjab, Lahore, under the direction of its Director, Professor Muhammad Anwar. In Kazakhstan, the research was carried out by the Kazakhstan Institute for Strategic Studies in Almaty, and was coordinated by the late Dr Oumirseric Kasenov and Dr Sabit Jousupov, Director and Deputy Director of the Institute. In Egypt, the survey was conducted by the Ibn Khaldoun Centre for Social Development in Cairo, under the direction of its Director, Professor Saad Eddin Ibrahim and coordinated by Professor Hassan Eissa.

The study focused on individuals and groups who influenced governance of the society. The initial plan was to focus on a randomly selected sample of the elite as well as the general public in each country. This plan could not be realized because of funding and logistical constraints. Perhaps the biggest constraint was imposed by the suspicion about the study. Unfortunately, one lesson learnt while carrying out the study was that in the late twentieth century the Muslim mind is very susceptible to conspiracy theories which invariably involve some vision of a western villain trying to undermine the Islamic world and, in particular, Islamic resurgence in order to keep Muslim countries weak and dependent on the West. Some permutation of this theory was pervasive in all social classes. Under such conditions the resources required to carry out a survey of randomly selected individuals would have made the exercise highly resource intensive. Given the resource and time constraints (the funding agencies require the research to be completed within the stipulated time frame) a modification of the sampling frame was required.

After consultations with the country coordinators it was decided to administer the questionnaire to a purposively selected sample in each country. The composition of the sample, however, was maintained. The elite focus was modified to a focus on highly educated professional individuals and groups. Wherever possible the individuals interviewed were those who held a formal management position in an organization. In each country the sample consisted of three groups; these were Muslim professionals, religious activists (the middle-class-educated respondents) and the general public.

The Muslim professionals were individuals mostly with a university education and who were employed in professional occupations or were active in the management boards of professional organizations. They included university teachers, teachers, business people, medical professionals, engineers, bureaucrats, army officers, journalists, trade unionists and managers. The religious activists were also selected from among people who were active in legal religious organizations either as members of management boards or as religious functionaries such as *imams* of *masjids* and ulama. In most cases they had a university education or were trained as religious functionaries. The general public respondents were drawn from the working class areas. The proportion of each group was approximately one-third in the sample. These sub-samples were also stratified by gender to ensure that in each country at least one-quarter of the respondents were females. All respondents in the study were Muslims and so were the interviewers.

The focus of the study was on the individuals and groups who influence the governance of society, as mentioned previously. Insights of sociological theory indicate that the middle classes play a key role in determining the state and success of public institutions as well as the health of the civil society. The educational, employment and housing quality profiles of the country samples given in Table 1.1 indicate that the majority of the respondents had middle- or upper-middle class origins. It can be argued that in some of the countries studied it is not the middle classes but a coalition of feudal, bureaucratic and military elites who dominate the public institutions. However, it was assumed that the middle classes are a significant part of the ruling classes through their linkages by kinship, professional and civil ties. Whether or not these assumptions are valid perhaps can be indirectly tested by the findings of this study.

The sample in each country was drawn by the country coordinators who used their networks of contacts to identify key individuals among Muslim professionals and religious activists. These individuals were then used to identify other suitable respondents. In other words, a snowball-sampling technique was employed. The general public samples were also purposive types of samples and were drawn from a well-established working-class area of the city. The only country where the sample of religious activists could not be drawn was Kazakhstan because under the Soviet communist rule, practice of Islam was proscribed by the state. As a result of this, according to the local collaborators, there was no identifiable Muslim religious elite at the time of the fieldwork. In Kazakhstan, therefore, only two types of respondents, Muslim professionals and general public, were interviewed. However, in both these samples the respondents who lived in known religious regions of Kazakhstan were included.

The Indonesian respondents were drawn mostly from the province of Yogyakarta. In Pakistan, the majority of the respondents were selected from the city of Lahore, although some respondents from other cities were also included. In Kazakhstan, the respondents came from the regions of the cities of Almaty and Shymkent. In Egypt all respondents came from the Cairo metropolitan area. In Indonesia, 1472 respondents were interviewed. In Pakistan and Kazakhstan, 1162 and 1000 respondents respectively were interviewed. In Egypt, the target of 1000 interviews could not be met because political and media pressures caused the fieldwork to be stopped after only 766 interviews.

The interviewers in all countries were selected by the collaborating research centres. Almost all interviewers had social science degrees and were experienced in conducting field research. Each interview took between 60 to 90 minutes. As mentioned earlier, all samples were purposive and not random. The findings of the study, therefore, cannot be generalized to the whole populations of the countries. They only reflect the views of the respondents who were interviewed. But given the sizes of the samples, they provide a unique data set in the world to explore and investigate Muslim perceptions of religion and society. More details about the methodology, fieldwork and sampling are given in Appendix A. The social and demographic profiles of country samples are given in Table 1.1.

A Note on the Samples of Muslim Professionals, Religious Activists and General Public

As mentioned earlier, in all countries except Kazakhstan the sample consisted of three broad groups: Muslim professionals, religious activists and general public. In Kazakhstan, the sample consisted only of Muslim professionals and the general public. One of the aims of the study was to focus on the individuals and

Table 1.1 Social and Demographic Characteristics of the Country Samples (%)

Characteristics		Indonesia	Pakistan	Kazakhstan	Egypt
Gender	Male	74.3	79.1	53.8	75.8
	Female	25.7	20.9	46.2	24.2
Age (Lifecycle)	<25 years	20.3	11.5	17.0	16.0
	26-40	34.6	50.5	40.2	54.6
	41-55	31.7	23.7	26.1	19.1
	>56	13.3	14.6	16.7	10.3
Level of education (Human Capital)	Less than High School	10.7	4.4	12.9	7.6
	High school/Some College	48.7	25.8	85.4	15.4
	College/professional	40.6	69.8	2.4	77.0
Sample type (Social Location)	Religious activists	49.9	41.9	—	36.4
	Muslim professionals	15.9	26.1	49.3	50.2
	Public	34.2	32.0	49.3	13.4

groups that influenced the governance of society. The focus on Muslim professionals and religious activists was intended to assist in achieving this aim. It is therefore appropriate to ascertain the extent to which these groups were likely to be influential in the society. Two measures, namely, educational attainment and the number of people supervised at place of work, were used to make this assessment.[75] Muslim professionals and religious activists were significantly more educated and consisted of a larger proportion of people who occupied supervisory positions at their respective place of work compared with the respondents from the general public. The evidence would indicate that significant proportions of respondents interviewed in this study were drawn from middle- and upper middle-classes which play a significant role in the governance of modern society.

Muslim Conceptions of Islam and Society

The aim of the study was to undertake a comparative investigation of everyday beliefs of Muslims in contemporary Muslim societies. This focus was based on the assumption that moral consciousness is closely related to political and social conditions. The following three chapters explore Muslim conceptions of religion. These chapters focus on the nature and structure of Muslim piety, ummah consciousness and the self-image of Islam held by the respondents. The chapters that follow them focus on Muslim conceptions of three aspects of society. Chapter 5 on the Islamic State explores the relationship between politics and religion in Muslim societies; Chapters 6 and 7 are devoted to gender issues in contemporary Muslim societies, and Chapter 8 focuses on respondents' images of the 'other'. The final chapter provides an overview of the findings and their sociological implications for the future developments of Muslim social formations.

NOTES

1. World Bank 1998; Hassan 1992.
2. Thurow 1996, 1999.
3. Hassan and Effendi 1995.
4. Rahman 1982; Esposito 1995, 1983; Maududi 1960; Qutb 1953; Gellner 1992, 1994; Tibi 1988; Lewis 1993; Haddad and Esposito 1998; Hoodbhoy 1991; Bodman and Touhadi 1998; Watt 1988; Abu Sulayman 1997; Arkoun 1994; Hassan 1992.
5. Abu Sulayman 1997, p. xvi.
6. Tibi 1988, pp. 127-148.
7. Arkoun 1994.
8. Muhammad 1989, p. 19.
9. Gellner 1983, p. 7.
10. Gellner 1983, p. 65.
11. Rahman 1989.
12. Rahman 1982.
13. Rahman 1982, pp. 161-62.
14. Rahman 1982, p. 162.
15. Gul 1997, p. 17.

16. Gul 1997.
17. Rahman 1982.
18. Rahman 1982, p. 137.
19. Marty and Appleby 1991.
20. Marty and Appleby 1992, p. 34.
21. Marty and Appleby 1991, 1992; Beinin and Stork 1997; Esposito 1983.
22. Karawan 1992; Akhavi 1992; Deeb 1992; Muzaffar 1988; Marty and Appleby 1991.
23. Marty and Appleby 1991.
24. Watt 1988.
25. Gellner 1983.
26. Tamney 1980; Hassan 1985; Yap 1980; Rahman 1982; Marsot 1992.
27. Watt 1988.
28. Watt 1988, p. 2.
29. Ibn Khaldun 1958.
30. Weber 1964.
31. Hume 1976.
32. Hodgson 1975.
33. Gellner 1983, p. 89.
34. Mol 1972.
35. Folliet 1955.
36. Tamney 1980.
37. Hassan 1984, 1985 and 1987.
38. Irfani 1983.
39. Maududi 1960; Lewis 1993; Huntington; 1993; Rahman 1982; Watt 1988; Pipes 1981; Esposito 1992; Weber 1978; Turner 1974; Gellner 1983.
40. Lapidus 1992, 1996.
41. Lapidus 1996, p. 24.
42. Keddie 1994, p. 463.
43. Butterworth and Zartman 1992.
44. Zubaida 1989; Sadowski 1997; Ayubi 1991; Sivan 1985.
45. Esposito 1995, p. 5.
46. Levy 1972; Rahman 1966; Ali 1970.
47. Ali 1970, pp. 55-59.
48. Rahman 1966.
49. See Esposito 1982; Haddad & Esposito 1998.
50. Anderson 1976.
51. Haeri 1993; Esposito 1982.
52. Hardacre 1993; Haeri 1993.
53. Levy 1972.
54. Haeri 1993; Hardcore 1993; Levy 1972.
55. Levy 1972; Rahman 1982; Mernissi 1989; Rugh 1984.

56. World Bank 1997.
57. Hassan and Effendi 1995.
58. Hodgson 1975; Woodward 1989.
59. Geertz 1968.
60. Geertz 1960, 1968.
61. Wahid 1988; Abdullah 1988; Peacock 1978.
62. Binder 1963; Hassan 1987; Syed 1982.
63. Ahmad, M. 1991, 1995; Hassan 1985; Ahmad, R. 1994; Nasr 1994.
64. World Bank 1997; UNDP 1996.
65. Altoma 1994; Olcott 1995; Akiner 1990; Voll 1994.
66. Mustafina cited in Altoma 1994; Olcott 1987; Akiner 1990; Vakhabov 1980.
67. Olcott 1995; Altoma 1994.
68. World Bank 1997.
69. Ibrahim 1996.
70. Auda 1994; Esposito 1995.
71. Ibrahim 1996.
72. Esposito 1995.
73. Esposito 1995; Ibrahim 1996; Auda 1994.
74. Esposito 1995, p. 124.
75. Tables 2 a, b, c, d, and 3 a, b, c, d, in Appendix A report the educational attainment of the two groups and the number of people normally supervised by the respondents at work.

2

MUSLIM PIETY
Religious Commitment in Muslim Societies

Religion and Muslim Identity

Religion is the essence of Muslim identity. This applies to all Muslims whether they are devoutly religious and belong to religious organizations such as Muhammadiyah in Indonesia, Jamaat-i-Islami in Pakistan, or Al-Ikhwan al-Muslimin in Egypt or live in largely secular societies such as Kazakhstan and Turkey. It applies to Muslims living in Muslim-majority countries as well as to those in non-Muslim countries such as India, Thailand, Germany, Australia or the United States. Consequently, religious commitment is both the evidence and the expression of Muslim identity.

There is considerable debate among Muslims about the nature as well as the content of religious commitment (religiosity) which a Muslim must display and adhere to in order to be a true believer. One of the key claims in this debate is that, in order to be a Muslim, there must be evidence of religious piety at behavioural, ethical and cognitive levels. Islamic philosophy and theology contain a large body of expository literature dealing with this issue.[1] There are, however, no meaningful studies which explore sociologically the nature and content of Muslim piety.

Two plausible reasons account for this absence. First, sociological scholarship in Muslim societies, especially in the field of sociology of Islam, is relatively underdeveloped, which makes such studies difficult to undertake. Second, Islamic sectarianism makes such an undertaking fraught with intense controversy bordering on hostility. This, however, does not mean that Muslims shy away from making such judgements. At the level of common everyday experience, many Muslims make judgements about the religious piety of their fellow Muslims.

Sociology and common sense indicate that being 'religious' can mean different things to different people. This was evident in the reactions and comments evoked by the title 'Religiosity of the Elite' in the survey among the selected (Muslim) respondents interviewed in Australia, Pakistan and Indonesia as part of the process of developing and pre-testing the survey questionnaire used in the fieldwork. In these comments the meanings given to the words 'religious' and 'religiosity' by different, mostly highly educated, interviewees covered a broad spectrum of activities.

Field notes show that many people were very sceptical and sometimes disparaging of the 'religiosity' or religiousness of their fellow Muslims, particularly those who faithfully observed the mandatory Islamic rituals. In Pakistan, some respondents described them as 'Musallah Muslim' (prayer mat Muslim). For many, 'religiosity' was essentially a spiritual experience of a very intimate nature not amenable to objective empirical study. They contended that the only way to appreciate or comprehend it was to observe a person's behaviour over a long period not only in the religious domain but in other domains of life as well.

For them, being 'religious' entailed not only religious worship but an ethical commitment and conduct which covered all spheres of life. This, some argued, was too difficult to observe, document, study and analyse. The term 'religious', in other words, was seen as having a variety of meanings and multiple dimensions. They may well be an aspect of a single phenomenon but they were not simple synonyms. Just because people are religious in one way does not mean that they will be religious in other ways.

Muslim Piety

One of the objectives of this research was to investigate the nature and expression of Muslim piety. As there were no previous sociological studies on this subject which could be used as a possible model, an appropriate framework which could be used in such an investigation was looked for. The field observations described above confirmed an important insight of sociology of religion—that religious piety is a multi-dimensional phenomenon.[2]

In their seminal sociological studies of religious piety, Stark and Glock address the question of multi-dimensionality of religiosity or religiousness.[3] These scholars take up the challenge of identifying different dimensions of religiosity and also how to measure them methodologically. The core of religiosity for them is religious commitment. They also take up the task of defining and operationalizing it, and undertake a linguistic analysis in order to determine the different things that can be meant by the term and the different ways in which an individual can be religious. They then try to analyse whether religiousness manifested in one of these ways has anything to do with its being expressed in others.[4]

Table 2.1 Dimensions of Religiosity according to von Hugel, Pratt and Stark and Glock

von Hugel	Pratt	Stark and Glock
1. Traditional (historical)	1. Traditional	1. Ideological (belief)
		2. Ritualistic (practice)
		3. Intellectual (knowledge)
2. Rational	2. Rational	
3. Intuitive and volitional	3. Mystical	4. Experiential (feeling)
	4. Practical (moral)	5. Consequential (effects)

Source: Wulff 1997, p. 214.

Building on the earlier works of von Hugel and Pratt, Stark and Glock conceptualise religiosity as multi-dimensional rather than a uni-dimensional phenomenon. This conceptualisation can also be attributed to the Berkeley Research Programme in Religion and Society. The multi-dimensional conceptualisation takes into account distinctions in the way religion may be expressed, as well as in the degree of intensity with which it may be practised.

Any serious student of religion will acknowledge that expressions of religion vary greatly among world religions. Different religions expect quite different things from their followers. For example, regular participation in Holy Communion is obligatory for Christians, but it is alien to Muslims. Similarly, the Muslim imperative of performing *Hajj* (pilgrimage to Mecca) during one's life is alien to Christians. The expectations of Hinduism and Buddhism are again different from those of Islam and Christianity.

However, according to Stark and Glock,[5] although there is great variation in the religious expressions, there also exists a considerable consensus among the world's religions as to how religiosity ought to be manifested. As indicated in Table 2.1, Stark and Glock identify five core dimensions of religiosity within which all of the many and diverse manifestations of religiosity prescribed by the different religions of the world can be ordered. They label these dimensions the ideological, the ritualistic, the experiential, the intellectual and the consequential.[6]

The ideological dimension is constituted by the fundamental beliefs which a religious person is expected, and often required, to adhere to. The ritualistic dimension encompasses the specific acts of worship and devotion which people perform to express their religious commitment. Often, it comprises public or communal, as well as private or personal, acts of worship.

All religions have certain expectations, however imprecisely stated, that a religious person will at some time or the other achieve direct knowledge of the ultimate reality, or experience a religious emotion. This includes all those feelings, perceptions and sensations, felt by an individual or a religious group, that involve some type of communication with God or a transcendental being. Stark and Glock label this as the experiential dimension.

The intellectual dimension refers to the expectation that religious persons will possess some knowledge of the basic tenets of their faith and its sacred scriptures. This dimension is clearly related to the ideological dimension, since knowledge of a belief is a necessary condition for its acceptance. However, belief need not follow from knowledge, nor does all religious knowledge bear on belief.

The consequential dimension encompasses the secular effects of religious belief, practice, experience and knowledge on the individual. It includes all those religious prescriptions which specify what people ought to do and the attitudes they ought to hold as a consequence of their religion.

Validation and verification of the multi-dimensionality of religion have been achieved primarily through studies of intercorrelations of scales which seek to represent different dimensions. Most of these studies have found generally robust scale intercorrelations.[7] This has led to criticism about the independence of different dimensions. Such criticism is given further support by factor-analytic studies that report only one factor—ideological commitment—which is not only clearly defined but also explains most of the variance.[8] On the basis of such findings, these researchers have argued that 'religiosity is essentially a single-dimensional phenomenon composed primarily of Ideological Commitment whose strength is reflected in experience and practice'.[9]

Other studies, however, provide strong support for the multi-dimensionality of religiosity. The most sustained support has been offered by studies conducted by King and Hunt.[10] Dejong, Faulkner and Warland[11] found evidence of six dimensions of religion. Their evidence also showed a cluster of three dimensions encompassing belief, experience and practice which they labelled as 'generic religiosity'. The cumulative evidence from sociological and psychological studies of religious commitment continues to provide support for Stark and Glock's multi-dimensional conceptualisation of religiosity.[12]

On the basis of the evidence reviewed above, the study and analysis of Muslim piety was guided by Stark and Glock's conceptualisation of religious piety. This was then subjected to extended interviews with knowledgeable Muslim respondents in Australia, Pakistan and Indonesia. In addition, in all these countries, several focus group discussions were organized in which the participants were invited to review critically, and to evaluate, various dimensions of religiosity as part of the larger task of reviewing the draft of the survey questionnaire. The final version was to be used in a multi-country study of religiosity in Muslim countries.

As a result of these interviews and discussions five dimensions were identified which were purported to express and signify Muslim piety. These dimensions were the ideological, the ritualistic, the devotional, the experiential, and the consequential religious image dimension. Individual respondents, as well as the focus groups, were asked to indicate the appropriateness of various questions to be included in the survey questionnaire to gather data for the five stated dimensions. The following section provides a brief description of each dimension and the items used to gather data for each dimension.

Dimensions of Muslim Piety

The Ideological Dimension—Religious Beliefs

This dimension comprises the religious beliefs a Muslim is expected and, in fact, required to hold and adhere to. The belief structure of Islam, like other religions, can be divided into three types. The first type of beliefs warrants the existence of the divine and defines its character. The second explains the divine purpose and defines the believer's role with regard to that purpose. The third provides the ground for the ethical strictures of religion. In sociological discourse, these beliefs are generally described as warranting, purposive, and implementing beliefs.[13]

In Islam great emphasis is placed on warranting and purposive beliefs. Mere emphasis on the beliefs, however, avoids the issue of their salience and function in the life of a believer. These can be indirectly assessed through the believer's ritual behaviour which also relates to other dimensions of religiosity or piety. In this study the focus will be on the doctrinally inspired core beliefs Muslims hold and not on the meaning of these beliefs for them, since issues of meaning raise other complex questions and require a separate study.

A large number of doctrinally inspired core beliefs were identified from the sacred Islamic texts and were presented to the focus groups and to key selected informants. The following beliefs were most commonly mentioned and, therefore, were chosen to ascertain the magnitude and intensity of the ideological dimension: belief in Allah; belief in the Qur'anic miracles; belief in life after death; belief in the existence of the devil; and belief that only those who believe in Prophet Muhammad (PBUH) can go to heaven. All these are primarily warranting and purposive beliefs.

The Ritualistic Dimension

Rituals are an integral part of formal religion. They include acts of religious practice including worship, devotion and 'the things people do to carry out their religious commitment'.[14] All religions include rituals of praise, petition, penance and obedience, although emphasis on each of these varies among different formal religions. In sociological analysis, rituals are regarded as playing an extremely important role in the maintenance of religious institutions, the religious community and religious identity. Participation in collective religious rituals plays an important role in the socialization of the individual through unconscious appropriation of common values and common categories of knowledge and experience.[15]

Analysis of religious rituals can be approached in at least two ways. Firstly, it can focus on distinguishing individuals in terms of the frequency with which they engage in ritualistic activities and, secondly, it can focus on the meaning of ritual acts for the individuals who engage in them. The analysis undertaken here will focus primarily on the first perspective, but it will also attempt to explore the question of meaning as well. However, a deeper and proper study of the meaning of rituals for the individual Muslim must await a more appropriate future opportunity.

Islam is a religion rich in ritual. Muslims are required to perform specific rituals as an expression of their faith. Rituals such as *Salat* (daily prayers) and *Wudu* (the cleansing of hands, face and feet prior to performing the prayers) have always been and still remain significant in promoting a sense of religious community among Muslims. The frequency of observance of religious rituals is a useful and meaningful indicator of an individual's religiousness or religiosity. Thus, the following rituals were selected to ascertain this dimension: performance of Salat five times or more a day; recitation of the Holy Qur'an daily or several times a week; fasting in the month of Ramadan; and payment of the Zakat. The analysis focuses on the frequency and regularity of observance. One of the assumptions made was that these rituals are interrelated at both individual and collective levels.

The Devotional Dimension

This dimension is akin to the ritualistic dimension. Rituals are highly formalized aspects of religious expression and commitment. Often a religious person participates in personal and somewhat private acts of worship. Social pressure and other non-religious considerations can sometimes motivate people to participate in formal religious rituals. This is especially true in Islam given the pervasiveness of religious rituals in daily life and also the ease with which a person can participate in ubiquitous rituals like daily prayers. In other words, participation in religious rituals may, or may not, indicate religious commitment or piety. This, however, does not apply to acts of devotion which are private and often spontaneous. For these reasons devotionalism is a good and meaningful indicator of religious commitment. Two measures of devotionalism were used in this study: consulting the Qur'an to make daily decisions, and private prayers.

The Experiential Dimension

This is the cognitive dimension of religiosity. It includes feelings, knowledge and emotions arising from or related to some type of communication with, or experience of, ultimate divine reality. These experiences are generally ordered around notions of concern, cognition, trust, faith or fear.[16] Such expectations are found in all religions.[17] In Islam, Sufi traditions, as well as many traditions of 'folk' or 'popular' Islam, place great emphasis on personal religious experience or communication with the divine as an affirmation of individual piety.[18]

This dimension invariably involves subjective feelings, sensations or visions which arise out of an individual's presumed contact with supernatural consciousness. Religious experience constitutes occasions defined by those undergoing them as encounters, or contacts, between themselves and some supernatural consciousness. In this study five feelings were used to assess religious experience: a feeling of being in the presence of Allah; a sense of being saved by Prophet Muhammad (PBUH); a sense of being afraid of Allah; a feeling of being punished by Allah for some wrong done; a feeling of being tempted by the devil. Experiences of this nature can be described as confirming, responsive, salvational, sanctioning and temptational respectively.[19]

The Consequential Dimension

All religions concern themselves with the effects of religion on the believers and their daily lives. Some religions are more explicit about these effects than others. In Islam, submission to its religious teachings is seen as the certain way of achieving divine merit in this world and spiritual salvation in the other. Rewards sometimes are immediate and include such things as peace of mind, a sense of well being, personal happiness and even tangible success in activities of daily life. Islam also warns of the consequences of not subscribing to its fundamental religious beliefs and teachings.

In Islam, for example, great emphasis is placed on warranting beliefs about the existence of Allah and the divine creation of life. Disbelievers are declared to be *kafirs* who are condemned to eternal damnation. In this study two conceptions were identified in defiance of divine injunctions. These were formulated in the following questions: 'Would you agree that a person who says there is no Allah is likely to hold dangerous views'; and, a belief that, 'Darwin's theory of evolution could not possibly be true'.

Muslim Piety: International Comparisons

The Ideological Dimension—Religious Beliefs

Belief in Allah

Respondents in Indonesia, Pakistan, Kazakhstan and Egypt were asked, 'Which of the following statements comes closest to expressing what you believe about Allah?' The findings reported in Table 2.2 show that in Indonesia, Pakistan and Egypt, 97 per cent of the respondents agreed with the statement that: 'I know Allah really exists and I have no doubts about it'. The belief in Allah in these countries was almost universal.

In Kazakhstan, the response was strikingly different. Only about one-third (31 per cent) of the respondents believed in the existence of Allah without any doubt, and 25 per cent agreed with the statement that, 'while I have some doubts, I feel I do believe in Allah'. Fifteen per cent of Kazakhs said that, 'I find myself believing in Allah some of the time but not at other times' and the same proportion said that, 'I don't believe in a personal Allah, but do believe in a higher power of some kind'.

Table 2.2 Belief in Allah

	Indonesia	Pakistan	Kazakhstan	Egypt
Number	1472	1185	970	786
I know Allah really exists and I have no doubts about it	97%	97%	31%	97%
While I have doubts, I feel I do believe in Allah	0.5	0.9	25	2
I find myself believing in Allah some of the time but not at other times	0.3	0.3	15	0.4
I don't believe in a personal Allah, but do believe in a higher power of some kind	—	—	15	0.1
I don't know whether there is an Allah and I don't believe there is any way to find out	—	0.3	5	—
I don't believe in Allah	—	—	3	0.1
None of the above responses represents what I believe about Allah	2	0.2	3	0.1
Other responses	—	0.8	4	0.3

Belief in the Qur'anic Miracles

Respondents were asked: 'The Qur'an tells of many miracles, some credited to the Prophet Muhammad (PBUH), and some to other Prophets. Generally speaking, which of the following statements comes closest to what you believe about Islamic miracles?' The responses are given in Table 2.3. Almost all Pakistanis (98 per cent) believed that miracles happened the way the Qur'an says they did. Pakistanis were closely followed by Egyptians, of whom 94 per cent agreed with the statement.

Although a large majority of Indonesians (84 per cent) held the same belief, 14 per cent of them said that the miracles can be explained by natural causes. There was a small percentage of respondents, ranging from 1 to 4 per cent in these countries, who did not believe in miracles.

The response of Kazakh Muslims again followed a strikingly different pattern compared with those from the other three countries. Only 29 per cent of Kazakhs believed in the Qur'anic miracles, and almost the same percentage said that the miracles can be explained through natural causes. Nearly half of Kazakh respondents (44 per cent) did not believe in miracles.

Table 2.3 Belief in miracles

	Indonesia	Pakistan	Kazakhstan	Egypt
Number	1472	1139	962	782
I believe that miracles happened the way the Qur'an says they did	84%	98%	29%	94%
I believe that miracles can be explained by natural causes	14	0.5	28	2
I do not believe in miracles	2	1	44	4

Life after Death

Respondents were asked to indicate how certain they were that there is life after death. The results reported in Table 2.4 show that over 90 per cent of Indonesian, Pakistani and Egyptian respondents completely believed in life after death. Only a small percentage of Kazakhs, however, completely believed in life after death, but 34 per cent said that it is probably true that there is life after death. Unlike their fellow Muslims from the other three countries, 31 per cent of Kazakhs said that they did not know if there was an afterlife and another 17 per cent were not sure.

Table 2.4 There is life after death

	Indonesia	Pakistan	Kazakhstan	Egypt
Number	1472	1185	1000	786
Completely true	93%	95%	13%	91%
Probably true	5	1	34	5
Not sure	0.6	1	17	1
Probably not true	0.3	0.2	3	0.4
Definitely not true	0.2	0.7	2	1
Do not know	1	0.3	31	1

Belief in the Devil

The question about how certain they were that the devil really exists generated almost an identical pattern of response to that about belief in an afterlife (see Table 2.5). Over 90 per cent of Indonesian, Pakistani and Egyptian respondents believed that the devil really exists, but only 7 per cent of the Kazakhs expressed this belief. However, 29 per cent of Kazakhs said that the devil probably exists. Thirty per cent did not know and another 20 per cent were not sure.

Table 2.5 The devil actually exists

	Indonesia	Pakistan	Kazakhstan	Egypt
Number	1472	1185	1000	786
Completely true	91%	94%	7%	95%
Probably true	7	2	29	4
Not sure	1	0.8	20	0.5
Probably not true	0.1	0.3	5	0.1
Definitely not true	0.1	0.7	3	0.3
Do not know	0.9	0.6	35	0.1

Belief that only those who believe in Prophet Muhammad (PBUH) can go to Heaven

Muslim piety entails complete faith in the divine revelations and that these revelations will lead the faithful to the righteous path of salvation. One of the most significant acts of faith for a Muslim is to believe in Prophet Muhammad (PBUH) as a saviour.

Following his example—*Sunnah*—is the path for a pious Muslim life and hence salvation. For Muslims, Muhammad (PBUH) is the most revered human being and an object of their total devotion and affection.

The responses from different respondents are reported in Table 2.6 and these show that 77 per cent of respondents in Pakistan, 61 per cent in Indonesia and 47 per cent in Egypt believed that it was completely true that only those who believe in Muhammad (PBUH) would go to heaven. Only a small minority of the Kazakhs shared the same belief with their fellow Muslims from other countries. Surprisingly, in Egypt the respondents were not as certain as the Indonesian and Pakistani respondents were that only those who believed in Muhammad (PBUH) would go to heaven. These findings showed that the pattern of response to this belief among Muslims from different countries is significantly different compared with the other beliefs examined here.

Table 2.6 Only those who believe in Prophet Muhammad (PBUH) can go to Heaven

	Indonesia	Pakistan	Kazakhstan	Egypt
Number	1472	1185	1000	786
Completely true	61%	77%	9%	47%
Probably true	13	4	21	15
Not sure	7	8	21	17
Probably not true	4	2	4	9
Definitely not true	6	4	9	8
Do not know	9	4	36	4

Index of Orthodoxy

An index of orthodoxy was constructed using the following methodology. The response 'I know Allah really exists and I have no doubt about it' was given a score of one and all other responses were scored as zero. The score of one was given to the response 'I believe that miracles happened the way the Qur'an says they did', and other responses were scored as zero. Similarly, the response 'completely true' to 'Life after death', and 'the devil really exists' and 'Only those who believe in Prophet Muhammad (PBUH) can go to heaven', were scored as one and all other answers were scored as zero. Using these scores an Index of Ideological Orthodoxy was constructed. In this index the highest score of five signifies high orthodoxy and a score of zero signifies low orthodoxy.

Table 2.7 reports the results of the index of orthodoxy for the four countries. Pakistan, with 76 per cent of respondents scoring five, was the most orthodox country in terms of religious beliefs followed by Indonesia (49 per cent) and Egypt (39 per cent). Kazakh respondents were the least orthodox. If we combine the scores of four and five, then overwhelming proportions of Indonesian, Pakistani and Egyptian respondents are orthodox, but the Kazakh respondents are a mirror image of them, with a large majority (75 per cent) scoring zero and one.

Table 2.7 Index of Orthodoxy of Religious Beliefs

	Indonesia	Pakistan	Kazakhstan	Egypt
Number	1472	1111	950	780
High 5	49%	76%	1%	39%
4	34	20	3	50
3	11	2	6	7
2	5	0.8	14	3
1	1	0.4	24	0.8
Low 0	0.1	0.3	51	0.1

Further analysis of the evidence showed that the level of orthodoxy was influenced by socio-demographic factors. In general, gender had an effect on the level of orthodoxy in religious beliefs. Older persons were slightly more orthodox in their religious beliefs. In Egypt and Indonesia educational attainment was positively associated with orthodoxy, but not in Pakistan, where the trend was the opposite. In Egypt and Indonesia religious elites were more orthodox than the general public. However, in Pakistan, Muslim professional elites were less orthodox than the general public. In Kazakhstan the religious beliefs of the general public and the elite were more or less homogenous.

The Ritualistic Dimension—Religious Practice

Islam is a ritual-rich religion, and Muslims are required to perform specific rituals as a religious duty or as an expression of their faith. Four religious rituals commonly performed by Muslims were used to ascertain the ritual dimension in this study: performance of daily prayers; payment of Zakat; fasting in the month of Ramadan; and the recitation of the Holy Qur'an. The results of the investigation are reported in the following section.

Performance of Daily Prayers

All adult Muslims are required to observe prayers five times a day as a religious duty. Respondents were asked, 'How often do your perform Salat?' They were offered a number of responses which are listed in Table 2.8. Indonesian respondents observed their duty to pray most strictly, with 96 per cent of them praying five times or more daily. They were followed by the Egyptians, of whom 90 per cent prayed five times or more every day. Only 57 per cent of Pakistanis prayed five times or more. The Kazakhs were the least observant of the daily prayers, with only five per cent indicating that they prayed more than five times a day. In fact, an overwhelming percentage of Kazakhs either never prayed or only prayed sometimes. The evidence, therefore, reveals significant diversity in observing mandatory daily prayers among Muslims.

Table 2.8 Perform Salat

	Indonesia	Pakistan	Kazakhstan	Egypt
Number	1472	1185	1000	786
One to four times daily	1.4%	19%	3.7%	3.1%
Five times a day	47	46	4	70
More than five times a day	49	11	0.8	20
Only on Fridays	0.1	5	2	—
Only on special occasions	0.4	3	9	1
Never	0.1	10	67	3
Occasionally/Sometimes	2	5	14	2

Payment of Zakat and Fasting

Two other practices expected of a Muslim are the payment of *Zakat* (poor tax) and fasting in the month of Ramadan. Respondents were asked if they had paid Zakat and fasted during the previous twelve months. The results reported in Table 2.9a show that for Zakat the pattern was similar to the one observed in the case of prayers. Indonesians and Egyptians were significantly stricter observants of their Zakat duty than Pakistanis and Kazakhs. In relation to fasting, Indonesians, Egyptians and Pakistanis reported almost universal observance, whereas only 19 per cent of the Kazakhs reported having fasted during the past year (Table 2.9b).

Table 2.9a Paid Zakat

	Indonesia	Pakistan	Kazakhstan	Egypt
Number	1472	1185	1000	786
Yes	94%	58%	49%	87%
No	6	39	50	13

Note: Figures exclude 'no response'

Table 2.9b Fasted

	Indonesia	Pakistan	Kazakhstan	Egypt
Number	1472	1185	1000	786
Yes	99%	93%	19%	99%
No	1	5	81	1

Note: Figures exclude 'no response'

Recitation of the Holy Qur'an

All Muslims are required to read the Holy Qur'an since it is the most important sacred text of Islam. Its recitation alone is regarded as a source of merit for the individual. The recitation of the Qur'an, therefore, is a very common practice among Muslims. Respondents in the study were asked, 'How often do you read the Qur'an?' They were presented with several choices and asked to choose the one which most applied to them. The actual choices and the results are given in Table 2.10. The results show that about half of the Indonesians, Pakistanis and Egyptians read the Qur'an regularly once a day or several times a week. This was in sharp contrast to the Kazakhs, among whom only 5 per cent acknowledged reading the Qur'an regularly.

Table 2.10 Read the Qur'an

	Indonesia	Pakistan	Kazakhstan	Egypt
Number	1472	1185	1000	786
I read it regularly once a day or more	30%	32%	2%	23%
I read it regularly several times a week	16	15	3	26
I read it regularly once a week	2	3	3	9
I read it quite often but not at regular intervals	31	18	8	24
I read it once in a while	12	20	18	7
I read it only on special occasions	4	5	64	7
I never recite the Qur'an, or read it rarely	4	5	2	3

Index of Ritualistic Behaviour

Religious Practice

To obtain an overall estimate of the observance of religious practices, an index of ritual behaviour was constructed using the following methodology. Performance of prayers five times or more a day was scored as one and all other responses as zero; the yes response to having paid Zakat and fasted during the last year was scored as one and the no response as zero; the response indicating reading of the Qur'an once a day, or several times a week regularly, was scored as one and all other responses as zero.

The resulting index ranged from four, indicating high score to zero indicating low score. Table 2.11 shows the distribution of respondents in the various categories. The findings confirm the evidence presented for the individual items. The Indonesians and the Egyptians showed the highest commitment to Islamic rituals, followed by the Pakistanis. The Kazakhs had a strikingly different pattern. Only 4 per cent of them had scores of five and four and 84 per cent scored one and zero indicating very low commitment to religious rituals. These findings clearly indicate both similarities and differences between Muslim populations in their religious commitments as measured by the index of religious rituals.

There were some important variations in religious practice when data was analysed by the socio-demographic characteristics of respondents. In Egypt, Pakistan and Indonesia, women were more observant of religious rituals than men, and the difference was especially pronounced in Egypt and Indonesia. Kazakh men and women were least likely to observe religious practice. In these countries, age was also positively associated with observance. Educational attainment was also a major factor in making people stricter observers of religious rituals. The elites were significantly stricter in practising religious rituals than the general public or Muslim professionals. The Kazakhs practised religious rituals the least.

Table 2.11 Index of Religious Practice—Ritualism

	Indonesia	Pakistan	Kazakhstan	Egypt
Number	1472	1135	1000	785
High 4	44%	24%	0.9%	45%
3	49	31	3	40
2	7	28	12	10
1	0.7	15	41	4
Low 0	—	2	43	0.4

Religious Devotion

Stark and Glock[20] identify devotion as a dimension of religious commitment. The difference between devotion and ritual is that, whereas the ritual acts are highly formalized and typically public, acts of devotion are typically personal acts of worship and contemplation. All religions encourage such acts of devotionalism. In Islam, many Muslims pray privately, which is beyond their formal religious duties. One act of devotion which is both private and spontaneous for Muslims is their commitment to the Holy Qur'an, and the belief that its teaching is the best guide to behaviour. Consequently, many Muslims consult the Qur'an for guidance in their daily lives.

In this study the respondents were asked, 'Thinking now of your daily life and the decisions that you have to make about how to spend your time, how to act with other people, how to bring up your children, presuming you have them, and so on, to what extent does what you have read in the Qur'an help you in making everyday decisions?' The respondents were given a number of options and asked to indicate the one that applied to them most closely.

The responses, as well the distribution of respondents in the four countries, are given in Table 2.12. The findings show that if we combine the two response categories, 'I can remember specific times when it has helped me in a very direct way in making decisions' and 'I often consult the Qur'an to make specific decisions', then the Indonesians are the most devoted, followed by the Egyptians and Pakistanis. The Kazakhs once again are the least devoted. This finding is consistent with the findings reported above about ritualism.

Table 2.12 How the Qur'an helps you in making everyday decisions

	Indonesia	Pakistan	Kazakhstan	Egypt
Number	1472	1170	1000	786
I hardly think of the Qur'an as I go about my daily life	2%	33%	45%	13%
I can't think of specific examples, nevertheless I feel sure that the Qur'an is still of help in my daily life	34	17	20	33
I can remember specific times when it has helped me in a very direct way in making decisions	23	44	11	16
I often consult the Qur'an to make specific decisions	41	5	5	36
Other	1	1	19	2

Private Prayers

Information as to whether the respondents prayed privately was obtained only from Indonesia and Pakistan. The results showed that about half (48 per cent) of Indonesians and two-thirds (67 per cent) of Pakistanis performed private prayers. Women in both countries were more likely to pray privately than men, and age was also positively associated with the performance of private prayers. About half of the respondents from the elite and the general public in Indonesia said that they prayed privately. In Pakistan, the religious elite was most likely to pray privately (77 per cent) and the general public least likely to do so (56 per cent). In general, educational level did not influence the propensity to pray privately in both countries.

Since data for the performance of private prayers was available for Indonesia and Pakistan, an index of devotionalism was constructed only for these countries using the following methodology. Affirmative response to the question about private prayers was scored as one and the negative answer was scored as zero. The response categories three and four in the question about how the Qur'an helped the person in making everyday decisions were scored as one and all other responses were scored as zero. The index score, therefore, ranged from two (highly devoted) to zero (not devoted).

The index of devotionalism showed that 31 per cent of Pakistanis and 28 per cent of Indonesians were highly devoted, and 49 per cent of Indonesians and 59 per cent of Pakistanis were moderately devoted. These figures indicated that slightly more Indonesians were highly devoted than the Pakistanis, and more Pakistanis were moderately devoted than their Indonesian counterparts. The same pattern applied to those who scored zero on the devotionalism index. From this evidence, we can infer that in religious devotion, Indonesians were more polarized than Pakistanis.

The analysis of the evidence also showed that, unlike in Indonesia, women in Pakistan were significantly more devout than men. In both countries levels of religious devotion increased with educational attainment. The university educated were significantly more devoted. Twenty-seven per cent of respondents with high school education were highly devoted, and the corresponding figure for university educated was 38 per cent. The religious elites were more devoted than the general public. This tendency, however, was more pronounced in Indonesia than in Pakistan.

The overall conclusion which can be drawn from the evidence presented above about the expression of religious commitment through acts of ritual observance and religious devotion is that Indonesian and Egyptian Muslims were more religious, followed by the Pakistanis. The Kazakhs were the least likely to express their religiosity through ritual observance and acts of religious devotion.

Experiential Dimension

The experiential dimension relates to some kind of personal communication or experience of the ultimate divine reality. It is an expectation found in all religions. In Islam there are well-known Sufi and other religious traditions which place great emphasis on divine experience of some kind as an affirmation of an individual's religiosity. Data for experiential dimension was collected only from Indonesia, Pakistan and Egypt. The questions about this dimension were not answered by a significant number of Kazakh. The high non-response rate among the Kazakhs was due to the fact that during the communist era many Kazakhs were not exposed to any religious instructions and religious practice. As a result of this, their experience of religion was qualitatively different from the respondents from the other countries and, therefore, were not included in the analysis.

The responses to the experiential questions are reported in Tables 2.13 a, b, c, d and e. As the tables show, the five questions were: feeling you were in the presence of Allah; a sense of being saved by the Prophet (PBUH); a sense of being afraid of Allah; a

Table 2.13a Feeling you were in the presence of Allah

	Indonesia	Pakistan	Egypt
Number	1472	1128	786
Yes, I'm sure I have	63%	57%	35%
Yes, I think I have	20	25	26
No	16	18	39

Table 2.13b A sense of being saved by the Prophet (PBUH)

	Indonesia	Pakistan	Egypt
Number	1472	1099	786
Yes, I'm sure I have	29%	36%	33%
Yes, I think I have	29	27	12
No	42	37	55

Table 2.13c A sense of being afraid of Allah

	Indonesia	Pakistan	Egypt
Number	1472	1142	786
Yes, I'm sure I have	83%	82%	51%
Yes, I think I have	15	13	13
No	2	5	35

Table 2.13d A sense of being punished by Allah

	Indonesia	Pakistan	Egypt
Number	1472	1136	786
Yes, I'm sure I have	53%	66%	66%
Yes, I think I have	34	26	7
No	13	8	27

Table 2.13e A sense of being tempted by the devil

	Indonesia	Pakistan	Egypt
Number	1472	1128	786
Yes, I'm sure I have	63%	67%	51%
Yes, I think I have	29	24	17
No	8	9	32

sense of being punished by Allah; and, a sense of being tempted by the devil. The findings show some striking differences and similarities across countries. A large majority of Indonesian and Pakistani respondents reported that they were either sure, or thoughtthey were, that they were in the presence of Allah. The proportion of Egyptians with the same response was significantly less, but still 61 per cent of them have had the same experience. Only about one-third of the respondents, however, were certain that they had the sense of being saved by the Prophet (PBUH), and if the two positive responses are combined, then the proportion of persons having the same experience increased to 58 per cent in Pakistan, 63 per cent in Indonesia and 45 per cent in Egypt. A majority of the Egyptians had not experienced being saved by the Prophet (PBUH). Unlike the Indonesians and Pakistanis who almost universally reported being fearful of Allah, almost one-third of Egyptians reported not having the same experience. However, 64 per cent reported being afraid of Allah.

This evidence suggested that for an overwhelming numbers of Pakistanis and Indonesians and a majority of Egyptians, Allah was fearsome. Was this merely a function of the question? It may possibly be the case, but the differences between the Egyptians and Indonesians and Pakistanis suggest that there were some underlying sociological and psychological reasons producing this image of Allah, as the evidence from the next question will indicate.

The response to the question: 'A sense of being punished by Allah for something you had done?' showed a pattern similar to the one noted above. However, one significant difference was that, although relatively smaller proportions of respondents in Indonesia and Pakistan were sure of having been punished by Allah, a relatively larger proportion of Egyptians reported the divine punishment experience. However, compared with the other two countries a much larger percentage of Egyptians reported not having had the same experience.

The general conclusion that can be drawn from this evidence is that for a large majority of Muslims the sense of fear and punishment is an important part of their experience of the ultimate divine reality of Allah. At the same time there are significant differences among Muslims in terms of not having had such experiences. Both the similarities and differences point to the sociological and psychological foundations of these experiences of the divine which raises some important questions. These will be explored in the latter sections.

Finally, the response to the temptation question (sense of being tempted by the devil) shows that the general pattern is similar to the divine punishment question.

Index of Experiential Dimension

An index of experiential dimension was constructed using the following methodology. The response category, 'Yes, I am sure I have' was scored as one for all the five questions, and all other responses were scored as zero. This produced an index ranging from five to zero. The distribution of respondents on this index from the three countries is shown in Table 2.14. It confirms the general pattern revealed by the evidence reported above. The Indonesian and Pakistani respondents are more likely to have had a divine experience compared with the Egyptians. However, the index shows that a majority of Muslims from all countries have had some religious experiences of the divine reality.

Table 2.14 Experiential Dimension

	Indonesia	Pakistan	Egypt
Number	1472	1080	786
High 5	17%	22%	21%
4	22	23	13
3	22	22	12
2	20	16	16
1	12	9	11
Low 0	7	8	27

Analysis of the data also revealed that in general there were no significant gender differences in experiential religiosity. In Indonesia the younger respondents were more likely to have experienced high levels of religious experiences, whereas in Pakistan and Egypt the pattern was the opposite. More educated respondents were also likely to have greater religious experience. In all countries the religious elites were likely to score higher on the index of experiential religiosity. Muslim professionals (other elite) tended to have lower scores in all countries. A significant number among the general public also reported having had the religious experience but in most instances their proportions were lower than the elite.

The Consequential Dimension

The consequential dimension refers to the secular effect of religious belief, practice and experience. Religious beliefs and ideologies invariably compete with other beliefs and ideologies (i.e., magic, science) in society as explanations of questions dealing with the meanings and nature of the ultimate divine reality and the nature and purposes of human life, condition and destiny. In modern times science has become the major rival of religion in explaining the nature, purposes and meanings of human conditions and destiny. The beliefs and statements which counter some core religious beliefs usually evoke social and psychological pressures on the individual to reject such beliefs.

In this study two questions were used to investigate the consequential religiosity. The questions were 'Do you agree that a person who says there is no Allah is likely to hold dangerous political views?' and 'Do you agree or disagree with Darwin's theory of evolution?' These questions were chosen because they challenged two fundamental religious beliefs widely held by Muslims. For each question the respondents were offered multiple choice type responses which are indicated in Tables 2.15a and 2.15b.

Table 2.15a Would you agree that a person who says there is no Allah is likely to hold dangerous political views?

	Indonesia	Pakistan	Kazakhstan	Egypt
Number	1472	1167	1000	783
Agree	84%	74%	19%	89%
Disagree	7	14	50	11
Uncertain	9	12	31	0.1

Table 2.15b Do you agree or disagree with Darwin's theory of evolution?

	Indonesia	Pakistan	Kazakhstan	Egypt
Number	1472	1173	1000	785
The theory is almost certainly true	2%	5%	10%	3%
The theory is probably true	14	9	27	5
The theory is probably false	11	12	14	15
The theory could not possibly be true	61	60	14	52
I never thought about this before	12	14	35	25

The findings show that, with the exception of Kazakhstan, an overwhelming majority of people in Indonesia, Pakistan and Egypt agreed that a person who does not believe in Allah is likely to hold dangerous views. In Kazakhstan a majority of persons did not think so, or were uncertain about the consequences of disbelief in Allah. Similarly, Darwin's theory of evolution was held to be false by a majority of the respondents in Indonesia, Pakistan and Egypt. In Kazakhstan two or three times the respondents in the other three countries expressed qualified or unqualified support of the theory, and one-third of the Kazakh respondents said that they had never thought about the theory.

Index of Consequential Religiosity

An index of consequential religiosity was constructed using the following methodology. The agreement with the question that a person who says there is no Allah is likely to hold dangerous political views was scored as one and other responses as zero. For the Darwin theory, the response that the theory could not possibly be true was scored as one and all other responses were

Table 2.16 Index of Consequential Religiosity

	Indonesia	Pakistan	Kazakhstan	Egypt
Number	1472	1158	1000	782
High 2	53%	46%	3	48%
1	40	42	26	45
0	7	12	71	7

scored as zero. The findings reported in Table 2.16 confirm the observations made above. Almost half of the respondents in Pakistan, Indonesia and Egypt scored the highest possible score of two and about another 40 per cent scored one. The Kazakhs were the opposite with 71 per cent scoring zero.

Further analyses of the data showed that Indonesian, Pakistani and Egyptian men were likely to be more conservative than women and conservatism increased with age and level of education. Indonesian and Pakistani religious elite were more conservative compared with the public and Muslim professionals. In Egypt, all groups were equally conservative. In Kazakhstan, gender and age had no effect on consequential religiosity, but the more educated and the public were less conservative.

Tests of the Inter-relatedness of the Dimensions of Muslim Piety

Are different dimensions of Muslim piety interrelated? If they are, then it will further confirm the findings about the inter-relatedness of multiple dimensions of religiosity reported in the first part of this chapter. To assess the inter-relatedness, a correlational analysis between the indices of four dimensions of piety was carried out for each of the four countries. As data for devotional religiosity was not available, this dimension was not included in the correlational analysis.

The findings reported in Tables 2.16 a, b, c and d show that the four indexes were significantly correlated in Indonesia and Pakistan. In Kazakhstan, the correlations between the three dimensions was correlated because the data for the experiential dimensions was not available (see Table 2.16c). In Egypt, experiential dimension was found to be not significantly correlated.

Table 2.16 a, b, c, d Matrix of Correlations between the Indexes of Four Dimensions of Piety

a: Indonesia

		Index of orthodoxy	Index of religious practice	Index of experiential dimension	Index of consequential religiosity
Index of orthodoxy	Correlation coefficient	1.000	.172	.131	.143
	Sig.	.000	.000	.000	
	N	1472	1472	1472	1472
Index of religious practice	Correlation coefficient		1.000	.091	.098
	Sig.			.000	.000
	N		1472	1472	1472
Index of experiential dimension	Correlation coefficient			1.000	.086
	Sig.				.000
	N			1472	1472
Index of consequential religiosity	Correlation coefficientf				1.000
	Sig.				
	N				1472

b: Pakistan

		Index of orthodoxy	Index of religious practice	Index of experiential dimension	Index of consequential religiosity
Index of orthodoxy	Correlation coefficient	1.000	.176	.206	.286
	Sig.		.000	.000	.000
	N	1176	1143	1075	1151
Index of religious practice	Correlation coefficient		1.000	.164	.187
	Sig.			.000	.000
	N		1151	1051	1129
Index of experiential dimension	Correlation coefficient			1.000	.233
	Sig.				.000
	N			1080	1066
Index of consequential religiosity	Correlation coefficient				1.000
	Sig.				
	N				1158

c: Kazakhstan

		Index of orthodoxy	Index of religious practice	Index of experiential dimension	Index of consequential religiosity
Index of orthodoxy	Correlation coefficient	1.000	.287		.296
	Sig.		.000		.000
	N	950	950	5	950
Index of religious practice	Correlation coefficient		1.000		.100
	Sig.				.000
	N		1000	5	1000
Index of experiential dimension	Correlation coefficient				
	Sig.				
	N			5	5
Index of consequential religiosity	Correlation coefficient				1.000
	Sig.				
	N				1000

d: Egypt

		Index of orthodoxy	Index of religious practice	Index of experiential dimension	Index of consequential religiosity
Index of orthodoxy	Correlation coefficient	1.000	.207	.002	.189
	Sig.		.000	.956	.000
	N	781	774	781	778
Index of religious practice	Correlation coefficient		1.000	.015	.211
	Sig.			.675	.000
	N		779	779	775
Index of experiential dimension	Correlation coefficient			1.000	.038
	Sig.				.289
	N			786	782
Index of consequential religiosity	Correlation coefficient				1.000
	Sig.				
	N				782

Note: Significance test in these tables are two tailed. This test asserts that the two means are different.

The Religious Factor in Everyday Life

The evidence analysed in the preceding parts indicates that a majority of Indonesian, Pakistani and Egyptian respondents shared an orthodox religious piety, but most of the Kazakhs had an unorthodox religious piety. If this is the case, then one should expect that in countries of orthodox religious piety, religion will play a visible and prominent role in everyday life. This proposition was examined in some detail. The respondents in all countries were asked the strategies they followed when they were confused or frustrated while facing an important problem, and the actions they took while making an important decision. For the first question the respondents were asked to indicate a first and a second choice.

The evidence showed that as their first strategy over half of the respondents in Indonesia referred to religion and prayer and slightly less than 50 per cent tried to solve the problem on their own. Men were more likely to solve the problem on their own and women were more likely to refer to religion and prayer. This pattern was followed by young and old across all levels of education. The elite groups were more likely to refer to religion than the general public. The most common second strategy followed was once again religion and prayer followed by help from the family and trying to solve the problem on their own.

As for the actions taken to make an important decision, the three most common actions taken in terms of frequency were discussions with a family member, asking Allah for help and consulting a holy person. More men favoured discussions with a family member and consultation with a holy person, whereas women tended to rely more on help from the Almighty and prayers. Discussions with the family was the preferred method among older persons and the less educated, and asking Allah for help and praying were more common among younger persons and the more educated respondents. The religious elite, predictably, was more likely to rely on religion and Muslim professionals and the public more on family discussions.

In Pakistan, the preferred strategies followed when facing an important problem were broadly similar to the Indonesian pattern, except that there were more people who relied on family members. Men were more likely to solve the problem on their own, and younger persons and those with lower educational attainment were more likely to rely on religion and prayer. In terms of second choice, religion and prayer were the most common method followed by seeking help from the family.

When making an important decision, the Pakistanis were most in favour of asking Allah's help and praying. It was followed by discussions with a family member and with friends. Women were more likely to rely on the family, and men on friends. The religious elite and the general public respondents were significantly more likely to rely on religion, and the Muslim professionals were more likely to discuss the problem with family.

The role played by religion in everyday affairs in Egypt revealed patterns very similar to the ones displayed by the Indonesian and Pakistani data. The first strategy adopted by the Egyptians when they faced an important problem was to pray for divine help (40 per cent), followed by trying to solve the problem on their own (36 per cent). Like the Pakistanis, the Egyptians also tended to rely more on the family for resolution of the problem (14 per cent). The reliance on religion increased with age and educational attainment. The religious elite was more likely to refer to religion and the Egyptian public least likely to do the same. For the second choice, guidance from religion was once again mentioned as the most common medium, and it was closely followed by the family (women tended to rely most on the family; 39 per cent as compared with 21 per cent of men), help from friends and then trying to resolve problems on their own.

The role of religion in the decision-making process was the most commonly mentioned strategy. Forty per cent of men and 40 per cent of women said that they would ask for the Almighty's help by praying, and another 7 per cent of respondents mentioned guidance of a holy person. The second method was discussion with the family, which was mentioned by 24 per cent of men and 36 per cent of women. This was followed by discussions with friends, mentioned by about 14 per cent of respondents.

Seeking the help of Allah was significantly and positively related to educational attainment. Among the university educated 52 per cent chose it compared with only 19 per cent of people with less than high school education. As one would expect, the religious elite was more likely to rely on religious guidance. Sixty-five per cent of the religious elite relied on religion compared with 37 per cent of the Muslim professionals and 23 per cent of the public.

The role of religion in everyday life of the Kazakhs was strikingly different from the other three societies. The Kazakh Muslims overwhelmingly stated that their first choice to solve a difficult problem was to try to solve it on their own. Ninety per cent of men and 87 per cent of women chose this response. Only 1 per cent said that they would refer to religion, and only 2 per cent mentioned seeking help from the family. But if they failed then religion was the second choice of a large majority (81 per cent of men and 74 per cent of women). In other words, religion played a very important role but only when their own efforts had not borne the desired results. Another striking feature of the Kazakh approach was the absence of the other strategies in solving the problem.

When it came to decision making, the Kazakhs also displayed a very distinctive pattern. Religion, or guidance from Allah, was mentioned only by 8 per cent of men and 13 per cent of women. The Kazakhs mentioned discussions with family members as the most important strategy (48 per cent of men and 53 per cent of women mentioned family) followed by discussions with friends, mentioned by about 18 per cent of respondents. The role of the family in decision making increased with age and level of education. The elite and the public relied equally on the family, although the general public mentioned religious guidance more frequently than the elite. The role of religion tended to increase with age and decline with the level of education. The inverse relationship with education was in contrast with the role attributed to religion in the decision-making processes by the highly educated Egyptians, Indonesians and Pakistanis.

The overall conclusion which can be drawn from this evidence is that religion, and in particular, reliance on religion in the activities of everyday life, features significantly in the lives of significant numbers of Indonesians, Pakistanis and

Egyptians. It plays an important role in strategies to find solutions to life's problems and in the processes of everyday decision making. This evidence is consistent with findings about their religious piety. For the Kazakh Muslims, who displayed a relatively non-traditional type of religious piety, the role played by religion in everyday life was also consistent with this finding. Religion played only a marginal and insignificant role in their strategies to find solutions to their problems and in the decision-making processes.

Concluding Remarks and Discussion

This is probably the first attempt to 'map out' different aspects of Muslim religious commitment quantitatively. As such, it probably has several limitations; the most important of which is whether the analytical approach used is the appropriate way to study it. Sociological methodology relies on proxy variables to study and understand social reality. The proxy variables focus on the manifestations of social reality and not on its 'essence'. That task is left to the theorists with sociological imagination and serendipitous insights based on the evidence. This opens the quantitative approach to a legitimate criticism of whether the chosen variables are in fact the most appropriate ones.

The analytical approach adopted in the analysis of Muslim religious commitment discussed in this chapter has relied largely on the work of the Berkeley Research Program in Religion and Society and especially on the work undertaken by Charles Y. Glock and Rodney Stark. The research publications arising from this programme have made some of the seminal contributions to the Sociology of Religion. The Berkeley research, however, was devoted primarily to the study of Christianity. It can be argued that the dimensions of religious commitment used in the Berkeley Project may not be appropriate for the analysis of Muslim religious commitment.

In my view, such a characterization could not be valid for two reasons. Firstly, the analytical framework used in the

Berkeley studies[21] is distinctively sociological and generic and can be applied to the study of religious commitment in other religious contexts. Secondly, assuming that this objection has some theoretical validity in the sense that the framework developed by Stark and Glock, among others, is specifically predicated on some broad understanding of the key theological principles of Christianity, my response to this will be that, like Christianity and Judaism, Islam is also an Abrahamic religion and shares several theological and philosophical principles with them. In these conditions, it can be argued that it should be possible to study and analyse religious commitment in all Abrahamic religions using a common analytical framework.

These and other similar arguments may not satisfy the purists, but if sociological scholarship is to advance theoretically as a distinctive approach to the study of social reality, then comparative studies are a major imperative. I hope that at least in this respect the present study will make a modest contribution to the advancement of sociological scholarship. It is also likely that some of the severest criticisms of my analysis of Muslim piety will come from Muslim scholars. In response to such criticism it should be mentioned that the methodology was not used uncritically. A serious and time-intensive attempt was made to evaluate the methodology through focus group discussions and intensive interviews with informed Muslim respondents in two of the four Muslim countries studied—Indonesia and Pakistan. This evaluation led to several modifications of the analytical framework, including identification of additional distinctive dimensions of Muslim piety, which were incorporated in the methodology.

Notwithstanding some of its limitations, the findings of this study lend themselves to some important conclusions. Firstly, the findings indicate that in several major Muslim countries a religious renaissance is taking place or has taken place. The evidence shows a robust religious commitment among Muslims from all walks of life. This commitment is characterized by a strong commitment to Islamic beliefs, rituals, religious devotion and experiential religiosity. Muslims share a common self-image of Islam, which is grounded in the traditions of scripturalism. Religion also plays an active role in the everyday activities of large numbers of Muslims. In other words, religious commitment is characterized by Islamic theology and a pragmatic orientation which is usefully applied in everyday life.

The empirical evidence also suggests that Muslim piety is socially constructed. The social construction is influenced by several factors, which include the general religious conditions or climate at the global and societal levels, social and political conditions in the country and social structure. Since its origin Islam has been a universal religion. This fact is reflected in the size and composition of Muslims in the world. In the contemporary world Muslims generally reside in the developing countries, but Islam plays a visible role in global affairs. Islamic religious activism is an important political force in Muslim countries as well as in international affairs. Global inequalities have given impetus to search for the creation of a more just social order at the national and international levels. For many Muslims, Islam provides a powerful model for the establishment of such a social order.

These attributes of Islam find regular expressions in the national and international media. This global fascination with Islam is an important factor influencing the religious climate in Muslim countries. It also influences religious commitment among Muslims. That national, social and political conditions play a critical role is evident from the nature of religious commitment in the four countries studied in this research.

Unlike the other three countries, Kazakhstan was, until 1990, a communist country very hostile to Islam whose teaching and propagation were strictly controlled if not banned. The result is that the Kazakh Muslims' piety is very different from the Indonesian, Pakistani and Egyptian Muslims. Whereas piety is strongly grounded in the knowledge of sacred texts, religious rituals, devotion and religious experience in the three countries, in Kazakhstan Muslim piety appears to be influenced by the socioculturalist conditions. In Kazakhstan, Muslim consciousness is grounded in the historical identity of the

Kazakh nation as Muslim. This consciousness coexists with a very secular perspective and outlook evident in the data which has been presented and discussed.

The social structural factors which may influence religiosity primarily relate to the family. The recent research has shown that religiosity, like social class, is largely inherited from the family. In this respect, the first factor which influences religiosity is the religiosity of the family itself. This is contrary to previous research which indicated that with age the influence of parental religiosity declined;[22] more recent research has shown that it is not the case.[23]

Another factor which influences religiosity is the characteristics of the household. The research shows that people raised in traditional family households with both biological parents, who are happily married, are likely to resemble their parents in religious beliefs.[24] Empirical evidence shows that socialization in traditional family structures maximizes the transmission of religiosity. In short, since the majority of people inherit religiosity, parental religiosity, quality of family relationship and a traditional family structure play an important and positive role in the inter-generational transmission of religiosity.[25]

The pattern of religiosity which has been reported here offers some support for these findings. The family organization in Indonesia, Pakistan and Egypt tends to be characterized by traditional family structures and the presence of two parents. These features, therefore, possibly explain the existence of the high degree of traditional religiosity in these countries. Kazakhstan was communist for over a hundred years. Under communism family organizations were radically transformed, which had a major impact on the gender division of labour. The religious institutions were suppressed and devalued. This could partly explain the non-traditional religiosity of the Kazakh Muslims.

The empirical evidence that is reported in this chapter could also be used to develop a typology of Muslim piety. There appear to be two types of religious commitments. One type is characterized by ideological orthodoxy, strong emphasis on ritualism, devotionalism, the image of Islam grounded in traditional readings of sacred scriptures and personal religious experience. The other type is characterized by a lack of ideological orthodoxy, lack of emphasis on ritualism and devotionalism and a non-traditional image of Islam. We can call the first type traditional Muslim piety and the second non-traditional Muslim piety. The first type, as the evidence has shown, characterizes the majority of Muslims in Indonesia, Pakistan and Egypt and a small minority in Kazakhstan. The second type characterizes the majority of Kazakh Muslims and a minority of Muslims in the other three countries.

The design of the study has also provided evidence of the multidimensionality of religious commitment. The findings have revealed the two types of religious commitments which have been identified and described above. What makes this finding conceptually and methodologically interesting is that the two types of commitments are broadly segregated. The traditional type of religious commitment characterizes Indonesia, Pakistan and Egypt. The non-traditional type is largely a characteristic of the Kazakh Muslims. The evidence of multidimensionality inheres in the fact that in all dimensions the Kazakh Muslims display different patterns of responses compared to their fellow Muslims from Indonesia, Pakistan and Egypt. This finding also provides confirmation of the interrelatedness of various dimensions because of the pattern of their temporal clustering. In this respect this study makes a unique and useful contribution to the comparative study of religious commitment in the modern world.

The findings that a majority of Muslims in countries like Indonesia, Pakistan and Egypt display a high level religious commitment also challenge the validity of the criticisms levelled against Muslims about their religious commitment by some of the leading Islamicists. For example, Muslim scholars and activists like Sayyid Abul-Ala Al-Maududi and Syed Mohammad Qutb have vigorously argued that the Muslim masses and elites possess a superficial and weak sense of religious commitment because of their exposure to godless secular education. Consequently, they are incapable of thinking Islamically. Muslims, they have argued, are unable to wriggle themselves out of the Western modes of thinking and practice in spite of the fact that they are eager to establish the Islamic way of life. According to Maududi and Qutb, their secularism is also reinforced by the influence enjoyed by the Western thinkers and policy makers in the Muslim countries.[26] The evidence reported here clearly shows a strong Muslim piety across social classes and countries, especially in the three major Muslim countries. The question then arises about the nature and type of evidence used by Islamicists in the construction of their critical discourse.

Frequently, the Islamicists identify the absence of genuine Islamic education as the cause of growing westernization and secularization in Muslim societies. This was the position taken by the participants in the First World Conference on Muslim Education held at Mecca, Saudi Arabia, in April 1977. According to the participants, Muslims in the twentieth century are passing through a period of self-doubt which is threatening their religious identity. The main cause of this is the Western system of education adopted by Muslim-majority countries in order to gain intellectual and material advancement. This system of education was producing cultural duality in the Muslim world. The traditional Islamic education that still persisted was supporting the traditional Islamic groups, whereas the modern secular education was creating secularists who were indifferent to Islamic values or paid only lip service to them.

The conference participants shared the concerns of Muslim thinkers who argued that under the dominant influence of the secular education system, the Muslim world will lose its identity by losing its Islamic character. It will thus suffer from the same moral disintegration and confusion as the West. The Muslim world can preserve that identity and save the ummah from confusion and erosion of Islamic values if the Muslims receive a truly Islamic education.[27]

Interestingly, such criticisms are internalized by Muslims. For example, a majority of the Egyptian respondents agreed with the statement that 'all over the world Muslims of today are devoid of Islamic character and morals, ideas and ideology, and have lost the Islamic spirit'. The evidence of this study clearly contradicts such self-perceptions and shows emphatically a high and strong level of religious piety among them. In fact, the findings provide some support to Gellner's observation about Muslim identity. In his discussion of civil society and Islam, Gellner[28] argues that while one of the two rivals of the civil society idea, Marxism, has been defeated, the Muslim world, by contrast, is marked by the astonishing resilience of its formal faith and a merely weak striving for civil society. Gellner attributes the weakness of civil society in Muslim countries to the rise of what he calls 'High' puritanic and fundamentalist traditions of Islam, to which most modern and modernizing Muslims transfer their social allegiance for the establishment of a just and egalitarian social order. Gellner's observation about the incompatibility of 'High' puritanical Islam and the civil society in my opinion is uncharacteristically deterministic and pessimistic. However, his observation that modern or modernizing Muslims tend to transfer their allegiance to 'High' puritanical Islam is supported by the evidence of this study.

NOTES

1. Rahman 1989; Muslim 1980; Maududi 1973; Kotb Qutb 1953; Watt 1979; Esposito 1991; Ali 1950.
2. Glock 1962; von Hugel 1908; Pratt 1907; Faulkner and DeJong 1966; Stark and Glock 1968.
3. Glock and Stark 1965; Stark and Glock 1968.
4. Stark and Glock 1968, p. 11-21.
5. Stark and Glock 1968.
6. Stark and Glock 1968.
7. Cardwell 1969; Clayton 1971; Gibbs and Crader 1970; Rohrbaugh and Jessor 1975.
8. Clayton and Gladden 1974.

9. Clayton and Gladden 1974, p. 141.
10. King and Hunt 1969, 1972, 1975, 1990.
11. Dejong, Faulkner and Warland 1976.
12. Dejong, Faulkner and Warland 1976; Hilty and Stockman 1986; Himmelfarb 1975; Maranell 1968; Tapp 1971.
13. Glock and Stark 1965.
14. Stark and Glock 1968, p. 15.
15. Bell 1997.
16. Glock and Stark 1965, p. 31.
17. James 1902.
18. See Gellner 1968, 1981; Geertz 1965.
19. Stark and Glock 1968.
20. Stark and Glock 1968.
21. Glock and Stark 1965; Stark and Glock 1968.
22. Cornwall 1988; Erickson 1992;
23. Myers 1996.
24. Myers 1996.
25. Myers 1996.
26. Maududi 1960; Qutb 1953.
27. See Watt 1983; al-Attas 1979.
28. Gellner 1994.

APPENDICES

All indexes are by country by social demographic characteristics of respondents.

Appendix 1 Index of Orthodoxy

Indonesia	Male	Female	<25 years	26-40 years	41-55 years	>56 years	< High School	High School-some college	Completed college/uni	Religious Activists	Mus. Professionals	Public
Number	1094	378	299	510	467	196	158	717	597	734	234	504
High 5	50%	47%	48%	46%	52%	52%	40%	47%	53%	53%	53%	41%
4	34	36	36	37	32	32	28	37	33	35	30	36
3	10	11	12	11	9	10	13	12	8	9	10	12
2	5	5	3	5	6	7	18	3	4	2	6	9
1	1	1	1	2	1	—	2	1	1	0.3	1	2
Low 0	0.1	—	—	—	0.2	—	—	0.1	—	—	—	0.2

Pakistan	Male	Female	<25 years	26-40 years	41-55 years	>56 years	< High School	High School-some college	Completed college/uni	Religious Activists	Mus. Professionals	Public
Number	882	229	125	536	257	159	50	287	766	447	277	357
High 5	77%	72%	78%	76%	78%	72%	84%	81%	74%	85%	65%	73%
4	19	23	21	20	17	23	14	16	22	13	28	22
3	2	4	1	2	3	4	2	2	2	1	3	3
2	1	0.4	1	0.6	2	0.6	—	0.3	1	0.2	1	1
1	0.3	0.4	—	0.7	—	—	—	—	0.5	—	0.7	0.6
Low 0	0.2	0.4	—	0.4	—	0.6	—	—	0.4	—	1	—

Kazakhstan	Male	Female	<25 years	26-40 years	41-55 years	>56 years	< High School	High School-some college	Completed college/uni	Mus. Professionals	Public
Number	509	441	157	380	249	164	123	803	24	235	230
High 5	2%	1%	1%	2%	1%	0.6%	4%	1%	—	3%	2%
4	4	3	2	4	2	4	4	3	—	5	3
3	5	7	5	6	7	5	6	6	4%	8	9
2	13	14	13	9	13	24	19	12	21	12	20
1	24	24	26	21	24	31	27	24	33	25	26
Low 0	52	51	52	58	52	35	40	53	42	46	40

Egypt	Male	Female	<25 years	26-40 years	41-55 years	>56 years	< High School	High School-some college	Completed college/uni	Religious Activists	Mus. Professionals	Public
Number	590	190	93	438	166	83	50	183	516	284	391	104
High 5	39%	39%	35%	34%	44%	60%	36%	37%	40%	29%	48%	34
4	52	46	54	55	43	35	42	51	51	66	40	47
3	6	10	7	7	9	2	9	9	6	6	8	10
2	2	3	2	3	3	1	4	3	2	0.4	3	6
1	0.5	2	1	0.5	1	1	6	0.5	0.4	—	0.5	4
Low 0	—	0.5	1	—	—	—	—	—	0.2	—	0.3	

Appendix 2 Index of Ritualism

Indonesia	Male	Female	<25 years	26-40 years	41-55 years	>56 years	< High School	High School - some college	Completed college/uni	Religious Activists	Mus. Professionals	Public
Number	1094	378	299	510	467	196	158	717	597	734	234	504
High 4	42%	48%	50%	37	42%	55%	35%	42%	48%	56%	36%	29%
3	49	47	44	54	51	37	52	51	45	39	56	58
2	7	4	5	8	6	7	11	6	6	4	6	11
1	0.7	0.8	0.3	0.8	1	0.5	2	0.8	0.3	0.4	0.9	1
Low 0	—	—	—	—	—	—	—	—	—	—	—	—

Pakistan	Male	Female	<25 years	26-40 years	41-55 years	>56 years	< High School	High School - some college	Completed college/uni	Religious Activists	Mus. Professionals	Public
Number	911	224	120	563	262	162	48	292	787	486	297	370
High 4	24%	25%	10%	17%	39%	40%	31%	31%	21%	37%	17%	14%
3	29	28	30	29	32	33	46	33	29	37	26	27
2	28	27	32	32	20	18	15	25	29	18	34	33
1	17	9	27	19	9	7	6	11	18	8	19	22
Low 0	2	1	1	3	1	2	2	0.3	3	—	3	4

Kazakhstan	Male	Female	<25 years	26-40 years	41-55 years	>56 years	< High School	High School - some college	Completed college/uni	Mus. Professionals	Public
Number	538	462	170	402	261	167	129	847	24	246	246
High 4	0.6%	1%	-	1%	0.8%	2%	0.8%	0.7%	8%	—	1%
3	3	3	0.6%	2	4	8	6	3	4	3%	7
2	12	12	9	7	17	19	23	11	8	15	18
1	44	37	35	45	43	35	44	40	62	48	44
Low 0	40	47	56	45	36	36	26	46	17	35	29

Egypt	Male	Female	<25 years	26-40 years	41-55 years	>56 years	< High School	High School - some college	Completed college/uni	Religious Activists	Mus. Professionals	Public
Number	596	189	93	441	165	86	51	184	519	286	394	104
High 4	49%	30%	25%	43%	52%	62%	35%	47%	44%	66%	36%	23%
3	37	50	38	42	40	35	29	29	46	29	49	36
2	9	14	26	11	5	3	20	17	7	4	12	23
1	4	6	12	4	2	—	14	8	2	1	3	17
Low 0	0.5	—	—	0.5	0.6	—	2	—	0.4	—	0.5	1

Appendix 3 Experiential Index

Indonesia	Male	Female	<25 years	26-40 years	41-55 years	>56 years	< High School	High School - some college	Completed college/uni	Religious Activists	Mus. Professio- nals	Public
Number	1094	378	299	510	467	196	158	717	597	734	234	504
High 5	16%	21%	20%	19%	15%	14%	16%	18%	16%	19%	16%	15%
4	22	22	24	24	19	20	22	22	22	23	20	22
3	22	22	24	21	21	22	17	24	21	22	21	22
2	21	19	17	21	22	21	22	19	21	20	21	20
1	12	11	9	10	15	12	12	11	13	10	14	13
Low 0	8	5	5	6	8	10	11	6	7	5	8	8

Pakistan	Male	Female	<25 years	26-40 years	41-55 years	>56 years	< High School	High School - some college	Completed college/uni	Religious Activists	Mus. Professio- nals	Public
Number	855	225	120	538	251	141	49	286	738	450	267	363
High 5	23%	20%	18%	20%	26%	22%	18%	25%	21%	26%	15%	23%
4	23	21	23	21	25	28	26	28	21	26	17	24
3	21	23	22	23	17	25	24	18	23	20	26	21
2	14	24	23	17	15	7	14	13	18	17	18	14
1	9	9	8	9	7	11	8	7	9	7	12	8
Low 0	10	3	5	9	9	7	8	8	8	4	12	10

Egypt	Male	Female	<25 years	26-40 years	41-55 years	>56 years	< High School	High School - some college	Completed college/uni	Religious Activists	Mus. Professio- nals	Public
Number	596	190	93	441	166	86	52	184	519	286	394	105
High 5	22%	17%	18%	21%	21%	26%	17%	23%	21	21%	21%	18%
4	13	13	17	13	10	14	10	17	12	13	12	15
3	13	8	10	12	11	12	15	9	12	14	11	9
2	14	24	24	15	17	14	11	15	17	17	18	11
1	11	12	3	12	12	8	11	10	11	11	10	13
Low 0	27	26	28	26	29	27	35	27	26	23	28	33

Appendix 4 Consequential index

Indonesia	Male	Female	<25 years	26-40 years	41-55 years	>56 years	< High School	High School - some college	Completed college/uni	Religious Activists	Mus. Professionals	Public
Number	1094	378	299	425	404	196	158	717	597	734	234	504
High 2	54%	48%	52%	52%	52%	58%	41%	53%	55%	58%	51%	45%
1	39	43	41	41	41	35	47	40	39	36	41	46
0	7	9	7	7	7	7	12	7	6	6	8	9

Pakistan	Male	Female	<25 years	26-40 years	41-55 years	>56 years	< High School	High School - some college	Completed college/uni	Religious Activists	Mus. Professionals	Public
Number	919	239	126	572	268	160	52	298	801	483	298	377
High 2	48%	41%	48%	50%	43%	50%	63%	45%	46%	52%	36%	48%
1	40	46	43	39	43	41	31	48	40	41	41	43
0	12	13	9	12	14	9	8	7	14	7	23	9

Kazakhstan	Male	Female	<25 years	26-40 years	41-55 years	>56 years	< High School	High School - some college	Completed college/uni	Mus. Professionals	Public
Number	538	462	170	402	261	167	129	847	24	246	246
High 2	3%	3%	2%	3%	3%	5%	7%	3%	5%	2%	4%
1	25	28	27	23	31	26	30	25	37	23	30
0	72	69	71	75	66	69	63	72	58	75	66

Egypt	Male	Female	<25 years	26-40 years	41-55 years	>56 years	< High School	High School - some college	Completed college/uni	Religious Activists	Mus. Professionals	Public
Number	594	188	92	439	165	86	52	184	515	286	390	105
High 2	52%	35%	36%	50%	49%	44%	21%	46%	51%	51%	51%	28%
1	41	56	58	42	45	46	71	49	41	41	42	67
0	7	9	6	8	6	8	28	5	8	8	7	6

3

THE ISLAMIC UMMAH
Myth or Reality

Introduction

The concept of ummah is an important part of Islamic discourse. Muslim and Western scholars of Islam use it to describe and analyse the vicissitudes of the historical, as well as the contemporary, Muslim world. The term is used to denote a transnational community which encompasses all Muslims and whose cohesiveness and social integration is inspired by, and based on, the commonly shared faith of Islam.[1] In contemporary sociology, Gellner's observation that 'The Muslim World displays a strong tendency towards the establishment of an ummah, an overall community based on the shared faith and the implementation of its law',[2] is probably shared by most sociologists and anthropologists of Islam.

Historical analysis credits the notion of ummah as an important contributing factor in the rise of Islam and in the growth and development of Islamic civilization.[3] Some analysts who focus on the economic, social and political decline of the Islamic world use a 'flawed sense' of the ummah as its principal cause. For example, in his book titled *Crisis of the Muslim Mind*, Abu Sulayman contends that while the political elite used coercion and authoritarianism to achieve political and social stability, the intellectual leadership used emotional and psychological means to keep the masses in check:

The net result of such pressure was the creation of inhibitions within the Muslim mind, which caused the mentality of the ummah and its character to develop in such a way that it lacked initiative and the ability to innovate and think for itself.[4]

The book outlines a framework to set things right to revive the ummah's 'true' spirit. The gist of it is that political and intellectual leadership should be combined to revive the past glory of the ummah.

While there have been some notable attempts to describe and analyse the nature and the role of the ummah in Islamic history, there is virtually no discussion of it from a sociological perspective. Invariably, the existing analyses seek to discuss and discover ways of reviving the ummah's glorious past. Such analyses wittingly, or unwittingly, conceptualize ummah as a kind of static social organization which is unaffected by major historical developments, modernization and globalization. This chapter would provide a sociological analysis of the development and future evolution of the ummah using analytical insights drawn from social theory. The first part will provide an overview of the existing studies and the analysis. The second part will attempt to apply the analytical framework derived from the sociology of the community and, using empirical evidence, it will examine 'ummah consciousness' in four Muslim populations of the modern world. The third part will discuss the impact of modernity and globalization on the development and evolution of the Islamic ummah and their consequences for Islam and the social and political organization of Muslim social formations.

Islamic Ummah: An Overview

The concept of the ummah has inspired the imagination of Muslims, especially Muslim intellectuals, from the very early days of Islam. The term ummah appears sixty-four times in the Qur'an with multiple and diverse meanings ranging from followers of a prophet, of a divine plan of salvation, a religious group, a small group within a larger community of believers, misguided people and, an order of being.[5]

The vague nature of the term allows Muslim leaders and ideologues to manipulate its meaning and usage in order to conduct their affairs and the affairs of the society according to the appropriate political and social milieu of the time. The root of the term ummah is uncertain, but many believe that it could be derived from the Arabic root 'umm', meaning mother, or its verbal root 'amma'. Some also associate the term 'ummah' with the word '*imam*', or 'leader'. However, most believe that the word ummah was borrowed from the Hebrew (umma) or the Aramaic (umm tha). Some believe that the term ummah entered Arabic in order to denote the 'tribal confederation in Arabia'.[6] Before the advent of Islam, the word ummah was used in Arabic poetry to connote a 'religious community', but such uses were rare.

Over time the meaning of the term ummah underwent a significant change and from a comparatively simple Qur'anic concept it evolved into a complex one, fundamental to the religion of Islam. According to Watt,[7] ummah was the sort of concept that could be given a new shade of meaning, and it was capable of further development. From its multiple and sometimes vague meaning at the beginning of Islam, it came to symbolize and embody the very notion of the Islamic community.

The change in the social structure of society which accompanied the growth and development of the Islamic community played a defining role in this transformation. The Prophet Muhammad (PBUH) would not begin to differentiate between ummahs until the ummah that he envisioned had established itself safely and concretely. Therefore, the term ummah retained a universal application (while it only had a small following in Mecca) until, at least, the time of the *hijra*, when the Prophet (PBUH) was accepted into the geographical territory of Medina, and the ummah that the Prophet (PBUH) envisioned began to materialize. The Constitution of Medina was drawn up in order to incorporate the diaspora community of Medina into the already established geographical community of Mecca. Muhammad (PBUH) achieved this joining of separate communities by instituting the *mu'akhah*, or a brotherhood, that would create a bond between the displaced Meccan Muslims, the 'muhajirs', and the 'ansars' (locals) of Medina. The result was that the religious term of ummah that was to incorporate humanity by claiming that it is in fact the same revelation as those brought by previous prophets began to carry a more specific connotation of a Muslim ummah. Thus began the evolution of the term from a universal monotheistic religious term to a socio-religious one that would become even more specific with further political and sociological developments.

The establishment of an Islamic community in Medina in 622 AD—after Muhammad (PBUH) emigrated from Mecca—provided the sociological backdrop for the evolution of the concept from a purely theological one to a socio-religious concept.[8] The term ummah appeared twice in the Constitution of Medina promulgated by the Prophet (PBUH) and signified a type of intertribal association. The Constitution of Medina effectively broke the familial and tribal ties that had formerly defined the lives of individuals and in turn adopted the idea of an ummah or brotherhood as their defining element. Also, it addressed the role that Jews played in such a social construction, affording them a position within the ummah by acknowledging them as a separate ummah that resides alongside the developing ummah of Islam. Gradually the term acquired a legal connotation. The Muslim scholars of the classical period defined ummah as a spiritual, non-territorial community distinguished by the shared beliefs of its members.[9]

One of the greatest, and historically unique, achievements of the Prophet (PBUH) was his ability to provide his early Arabian followers with a new and unique identity. The tribe was the universal definer of Arab identity in pre-Islamic Arabia. The social organization of a tribe was based on kinship and blood ties. There were social and cultural mechanisms such as *hilf jiwar*, *wala*, and later, *mu'akhah* used by the tribes to confer fictive kinship status on outsiders in order to incorporate them

into the tribe.[10] The ummah became a framework for the fusion
of tribal identities into a new identity based on Islam. It
represented a community based on a commonly shared religion
and the values it professed and proclaimed. Historical evidence
indicates that it was from the very beginning a non-static
phenomenon and it evolved as the social and political conditions
of Muslims changed.

Sociologically, ummah became a transformative concept in
the sense that it played a significant role, first, in transforming
the Arab tribes into a community of Arabs, and later, as Islam
began to expand to non-Arab lands, it transformed different
groups of Muslims into a community of believers.[11] Although
the term ummah was not unknown in pre-Islamic Arabia, there
is no evidence to link its meaning to the Qur'anic usage. In
Medina, it became the foundational term for the establishment
of the Islamic community.[12]

Muhammad (PBUH) succeeded in providing a new basis of
social organisation and a new means to generate social cohesion
among his followers by offering them membership in the Islamic
community based on the consciousness of being Muslim which
transcended their other primordial identities. It was this that
made Islam one of the most powerful transformers of social
consciousness in human history and thus laid the foundation for
the expansion of Islam and the rise of Islamic civilizations.[13]

Ummah as a community of believers entailed a consciousness
of belonging to a community whose membership was open
equally and without any qualification or restriction, except that
of the faith, to all believers. In its essence, it implied equality
and a means of absorption of additional populations of newly
conquered or converted groups into the Islamic community. In
this sense it embodied the universalism of Islam. It became a
means of establishing a religious and cultural identity which
was independent of the Muslim state. This means of constructing
a religious and cultural identity made the spiritual development
and sense of cohesion independent of the transitory territorial
states. The life of the new ummah was marked by a pervasive
new moral tone, derived from the individual relationship to God

and not by old primordial loyalties and maintained by the expectations prevalent in the group as a whole and given form in their corporate life.[14]

Over time, ummah became a state of mind, a form of social consciousness, or an imagined community which united the faithful in order to lead a virtuous life and to safeguard and even to expand the boundaries of the autonomous ummah. It was both a source as well as a symbol of social cohesion. It facilitated the integration into the Muslim community of sometimes alien communities by allowing them to carry over their traditional ways of life into the fold of the new community. The cannon law thus became one of the strongest cementing factors among disparate communities which continued following their customary law.

Ummah became a framework for maintaining the religious unity and accommodating the cultural diversity of the believers. This generated a strong sense of unity which permeated the Muslim world and was instrumental in submerging, or overriding, the significant ethnic and cultural differences on the level of the ideal. It thus became a critical basis for expansion that allowed for a certain disregard of the realities of life. Psychologically speaking, the term ummah provided for an existence on two levels namely maintaining religious unity and accommodating the cultural diversity, an existence in a tension that, never completely to be relieved, is still an important element in the inner unrest besetting significant parts of the Muslim world.[15]

What is unique and remarkable is that the notion of ummah is able to generate in the Muslim mind a sense of community continuity through the undisturbed relatedness to the same spiritual authority. It thereby relieves the tensions which may exist in the objective reality of a community which is expansive and socially and ethnically heterogeneous. As a community, the ummah is not only a basis of social cohesion cementing social bonds among the believers but also a political body.[16] Although it has not functioned as a unified political organization for a significant period of time, it remains the only true 'nation' for

Muslims, whose distribution among a number of states is, in the last analysis, accidental and irrelevant. In the modern world which is dominated by nationalistic ideologies, there are several powerful movements in all major Muslim countries which idealise and seek to redeem Islamic unity and reinvigorate the ummah in the face of Western intrusion.[17]

Political Role of the Ummah

At its foundation the ummah was defined by Islam as an expression of the various aspects of Muslim Arab life. What Arabian customs were already satisfactory were accepted, and customs contrary to the new faith were replaced. The main problem in Prophet Muhammad's (PBUH) time was to replace a system of feuding within society in favour of a common life under a single arbiter. Within decades after its foundation, the world of Islam had expanded to non-Arab territories. Under Omar, the second Caliph, the problem had taken new expressions. The new challenge was in how to bring some common discipline among rather lawless occupiers of the conquered territories. Muhammad's (PBUH) solution, to provide a central distribution of funds to those at a disadvantage and a central settlement of disputes by a divinely sanctioned moral standard, was to be adopted and extended.

The problem for Omar was to define the nature of the authority at such a centre. He resolved this problem by defining authority as *Amir al-Muminin* (Commander of the Faithful) because the only binding authority the Arabs had recognized was that of a military commander on the march to a new position or at war. He also introduced the new institution of *Diwan*—a register of all the Muslims for distribution of the booty to them. The new social and political conditions had necessitated the introduction of new institutions and redefinition of the power at the centre in order to maintain and consolidate the identity and cohesiveness of the Muslim ummah.

As the Muslim community continued to expand through conquest and conversion, it became larger and more diverse. By the time of the Abbasids it had become necessary to respond to the challenges of the expanded ummah. This response included separation of religious and political functions. The ulama—the clerical class—led the prayers in the mosque and administered shariah law, but a new political class of police, tax collectors, *kātibs* and secretaries took over the task of ensuring that the mosque was kept in good condition, law and order was preserved, stability was maintained in the market place besides commanding the defence of the frontier. Gradually, as the fragmentation of the ummah continued in the later Abbasid times, the separation of the religious and political domains was institutionalized.[18]

This brief account of the formation and development of the ummah in its formative years illustrates that its expansion had changed the social conditions, and as a consequence, the basis of social cohesiveness included not only religious doctrine but also the management of the mundane domain of community life. How well and effectively these conditions were managed became the basis of the ummah's cohesiveness and fragmentation.

A respectable body of Islamic scholarship, which is based on the Qur'anic exegesis, claims that the ummah, as the Muslim community, has been explicitly charged by the Qur'an to perform certain global moral tasks. The Qur'anic injunctions established the ummah as the community of Muslims and assigned it certain tasks. It proclaims that the function of the ummah is to be a 'median community' so that it can be a 'witness upon mankind' to mediate extreme positions and balance these out: 'And even so have We appointed you as a median community that you may be witness over mankind and that the messenger may be a witness over you' (The Qur'an, 2:142).

The Qur'an also envisages the Muslim community to be egalitarian and open and based on goodwill and cooperation, without elitism and without the mentality that generates secret conspiracies.[19] The task of the ummah is to establish on earth an order by effectively 'prohibiting evil and commanding good' on the basis of the belief in a singular and unique God. According to Rahman,[20] the task of establishing such an order and the functioning of the community as a 'witness' over mankind are fundamentally interdependent, and neither is possible without the other.

In the modern Muslim world the notion of ummah is a psychological, political and ideological reality. Its foundation is constructed on the basis of the Qur'anic revelations and on the collective memories of political grandeur of Islamic history. In the Muslim imagination, the ummah lives under a divine law whose protector is the ummah itself. The temporal political authority is neither a source nor a guarantee of the law. Its legitimacy is recognized so long as it guarantees the preservation and expansion of religion.[21] While this type of volitional orientation is very much in tune with the contemporary globalization trends, it is also an inherent source of political instability and unrest in the modern Muslim world. This is reflected in several major modern Muslim social and political movements, like the Jamaat-i-Islami and the Muslim Brotherhood.

For organizations like the Jamaat-i-Islami, the Muslim ummah is a transnational suprageographical entity with its heart lying in the modern Arabic Middle East. According to its ideologues, the dignity and political authority of the ummah have been severely undermined by the last five centuries of Western political and military domination. The Western attempts at keeping the ummah ineffective forever are now being resisted by the new signs of Islamic revival. The Jamaat attributes this Islamic resurgence to the Divine plan, as stated in the Qur'an 'and the unbelievers plotted and planned, and Allah planned too, and Allah is the best of planners' (3:54).

From the point of view of the Jamaat-i-Islami, the enemies of Islam have effectively neutralized the power of the Muslim ummah by politically dominating the Muslims, dividing them into small states, nationalities and tribes and imposing secular systems through secular rulers, all with their Western political, economic, educational and cultural agendas. The modernist liberal West, however, could not liquidate the Muslim ummah's strong Islamic creed. Under the leadership of the great Muslim scholars, the Muslim ummah is now strongly resisting the West's hegemony by asking the followers of Islam to resist the West and to submit to the teachings of the Prophet (PBUH) and the will of Allah. The Muslim ummah is responding to this appeal and joining the Islamic movements that seek this Islamic revival.[22]

The Islamic revival movements like the Jamaat-i-Islami and the Muslim Brotherhood, unlike nationalist movements, are the driving forces which have provided the activist Muslims with the discipline, strength, and the desire for global Islamic revival. The Islamic movements and the overall revival of Islam as a global religion are the real forces which are shaping the future of the Muslim ummah. These movements characterize the West as anti-Islamic, bigoted, secular and inegalitarian. Despite its total domination and command of the world, the West is seen as having failed to provide a just world order for humanity. The industrial growth and increasing wealth have not promoted justice and peace for humanity. This is evident in the enormous global inequalities.[23]

The ideological position and orientation of most of the modern Islamic religio-political movements is summarized in the following observation of one of the chief ideologues of the Jamaat-i-Islami:

Islam is the only constructive force for the future. Indeed, much has yet to be done. It has to strengthen its moral values and gain intellectual credibility in order to motivate the masses. It is also utmost desirable to get rid of those rulers of the Muslim countries who are under the influence of the West. Once [the] masses and the leadership work for the same ideology and destination and instead of confrontation the energies are used for new and positive objectives, change is sure to come. In order to achieve this objective firm belief, determination and continuous efforts are essentially required. God willing, the ummah is going to have a new and bright future in the 21st Century.[24]

The above discussion is an illustration of the fact that, for many Islamic activists, the notion of ummah is an important and integral part of the modern Muslim consciousness. While the concept is part of the Qur'anic revelations, its meaning and usage has evolved with the changes and growth in the world of Islam. It manifests itself at the ideological, cognitive, behavioural and ethical levels. For Muslims, and especially Muslim activists and intellectuals, it is a sociological reality. It is a unique principle of social identity in Islam which acts as a basis of collective consciousness and community organization. There is a consensus among Muslim scholars that the ummah refers to a spiritual, non-territorial community distinguished by the shared beliefs of its members. Membership of the ummah can be regarded as a kind of citizenship that is available to all Muslims and, in theory at least, guarantees equality among all Muslims.[25]

The Islamic world is not immune from the ideology of nationalism. However, often in Muslim countries nationalism has incorporated the concept of the ummah. While most of the Muslim countries, like their counterparts elsewhere, have been strongly influenced by nationalism, the Islamic revivalist movements invariably make the existence of the Muslim ummah an important part of their political platform. These movements argue that loyalty to the Islamic ummah overrides any other ethnic, linguistic and geographical loyalties. The political reality, however, is that while most Muslims regard the idea of ummah as an important source of their collective identity, nationalism and nationalist movements are also an important part and parcel of most Muslim countries. As such, Muslims tend to have dual or multiple social identities comprised of national, or ethnic, and Islamic identities. In a sociological sense, the concept of ummah refers to an ideal state—an all encompassing unity of the Muslims that is often invoked but never completely realized.

Sociology of the Ummah

As a sociological phenomenon, the ummah can be viewed at least from two analytical perspectives. It can be viewed as a 'community' and as a 'collective identity'. Both are related, of course, but it may be useful to conceptualize the phenomenon from these two perspectives because both can contribute to the analysis of its future development and evolution. The following is a further elaboration of the two analytical perspectives.

The Ummah as a Community

The general characterization of the ummah in historical and contemporary Islamic discourse resembles what German sociologist Ferdinand Tonnies has called 'community' or *'gemeinschaft'*.[26] According to Tonnies, the community is a social group based on kinship and organic ties, and hence, a moral cohesion often founded on common religious sentiments. Tonnies' analysis was undertaken within an analytical framework which he used to describe, explain and analyse social transformation that had occurred under conditions of modernity; that is, capitalism, industrialization and urbanization in Europe. According to Tonnies (as well as other sociologists like Emile Durkheim, Max Weber, Talcott Parsons who also explored the same problem in their works), under the impact of modernity, social organizations undergo a fundamental transformation. They are transformed from a community or 'communal' (*Gemeinschaft*) to an 'associational' (*Gesellschaft*) type of organization.

Tonnies postulates that social relations are the products of human will. He identified two types of 'wills'—natural and rational. Natural will is the expression of instinctual needs, habits, convictions and inclinations. Rational will, on the other hand, involves instrumental rationality in the selection of means and ends. Natural will is organic and real and the basis of communal life, and rational will is conceptual and analytical and expresses itself in associational types of relationships.

Community types of social organizations are characterized by social homogeneity, and they are largely based on primordial and organic ties and have a moral cohesion, often founded on common religious sentiments. These types of social organizations are transformed and dissolved by the growing social differentiation caused by the increasingly complex division of labour, individualism and modern capitalistic competitiveness, which gives rise to a society based on associational types of relationships. The significance of the transformation is that the new and emerging society he labelled 'association' (*Gesellschaft*) relies on individualism, individual autonomy, institutional differentiation and contractual relationships as the bases of its social integration and social cohesion.[27]

From the second perspective, the ummah can be viewed as a collective identity. Collective identity is grounded in the socialization process in human societies. Individuals develop it by first identifying with the values, goals and purposes of their society and by internalizing them. This process, besides constructing the individual identity, also constructs the collective identity. Rituals and ritualized behaviours of society further reinforce it and give members a sense of similarity, especially against the 'others' whose collective identities are different.

The key role in the construction of collective identity is played by symbolic systems of shared religion, language and culture, which also act as boundary defining mechanisms of the collective identity. The boundaries can be crossed, or changed through incorporation, or shedding of symbolic domains such as those which are entailed in religious conversion or excommunication. Some sociologists have suggested that collective identity is constructed through major 'codes' of primordiality, civility and transcendence or sacredness. These codes are ideal types as real coding invariably combines different elements of these ideal types.[28] The construction of collective identity is not purely a symbolic affair unrelated to the division of labour, control of resources and social differentiation. Collective identity and social solidarity entail consequences for the allocation of resources and for structuring entitlements to members of the collectivity as against the outsider.

From this perspective ummah would constitute a collective identity of Muslims in the sense that it refers to identification with the sacred domain of Islam and its incorporation in their individual consciousness. The implication of viewing ummah as a frame for the collective identity of Muslims is that, since it is a result of social construction in which social structure and social processes play critical roles, as these framing devices change, they also produce changes in the nature of collective identity. In other words, Muslims, besides partaking in common faith, also live their lives in the contexts of their respective societies. As these societies change under the impact of modernization, industrialization, political development and globalization the process of change also impacts on Muslim collective identity. For example, the social, structural, and political contexts of the Muslims of the Indian subcontinent have undergone changes over the past fifty years through the partition of the subcontinent in 1947 and then again through the break-up of Pakistan in 1972. These changes have also affected the collective identities of Indian Muslims.

Ummah Consciousness

The usefulness of applying the sociological frameworks discussed above to the study of ummah is that these allow us to operationalize the concept. It should then be possible to identify its key dimensions in order to measure or assess the degree or magnitude of their presence in the collective consciousness of different groups of Muslims. This enables us to identify its different dimensions, which could then be empirically examined and measured for comparative or historical analysis. As ummah refers to a 'community of believers', this would suggest that 'religious consciousness' would constitute an integral part of ummah consciousness. One way to investigate it, therefore, will be to focus on Muslim piety which has been already explored in Chapter 2.

Muslim piety, like religious piety in general, was conceptualized as a multidimensional phenomenon consisting of the following five dimensions: the religious beliefs (the ideological dimension), ritual observance (the ritualistic dimension), the experiential dimension, the devotional dimension, and the consequential dimension. Among these, two dimensions—religious beliefs (the ideological dimension) and the consequential dimension—would appear to be particularly suitable as indicators of ummah consciousness. In other words, the believers must be aware of the key religious beliefs and display a confirmation of these beliefs in their behaviour. As a consequence of these beliefs, the followers must believe in certain prescriptions which indicate what people ought to do and the attitudes they ought to hold as a consequence of their religion. This is not to deny the alternative way to assess ummah consciousness, but in this study this assessment was confined to these two indicators.

The religious beliefs (ideological dimension) comprises of beliefs which Muslims are obliged and required to adhere to. These include warranting, purposive and implementing religious beliefs. The key Islamic beliefs included in the analysis were: belief in Allah; belief in the Qur'anic miracles; belief in life after death; belief in the existence of the devil; and belief that only those who believe in Prophet Muhammad (PBUH) can go to heaven. Islam, like other religions, warns its adherents of the consequences of not subscribing to its fundamental religious beliefs and teachings. For example, disbelievers in the existence of Allah and the divine creation of life are declared as *kafirs* who are condemned to eternal damnation. The two questions used to ascertain consequential religiosity in this study were: 'a person who says there is no Allah is likely to hold dangerous views' and 'Darwin's theory of evolution could not possibly be true'.

Ummah consciousness was ascertained through the indexes of ideological and consequential dimensions of Muslim piety.

The methodology of how these indexes were constructed has already been described in Chapter 2. To investigate ummah consciousness the values of the two indexes were classified into 'high', 'medium' and 'low' categories and their distribution by gender, age, level of educational attainment and sample type was investigated. The result of this analysis is reported in the following section.

Ummah Consciousness—The Empirical Evidence

Religious Beliefs (Religious Ideology) Dimension of Ummah Consciousness

This dimension of ummah consciousness sought to ascertain the knowledge of some of the core beliefs of Islamic faith to which adherence is a prerequisite for being a Muslim. Using the methodology already detailed and discussed in Chapter 2, an index of religious ideology was constructed and its distribution across gender, age, educational level and sample types was analysed. The result of the analysis reported in Table 2.1 shows that an overwhelming proportion of respondents from Indonesia, Pakistan and Egypt displayed a high level of adherence to the religious ideology in general. The evidence also shows that in Indonesia and Egypt the education level was positively related to religious ideology, and religious activists in these countries were also more religiously conscious than the general public and Muslim professionals. These differences were not evident among the Pakistani respondents.

Kazakhstan, once again, was an anomaly, with a significantly lower percentage displaying adherence to Islamic religious ideology. Unlike their fellow Muslims from the other three countries, a large majority of Kazakhs displayed a low level of commitment to religious ideology. The case of Kazakhstan shows that the competing ideology of communism until the 1990s was a significant factor in lowering religious consciousness among them. It is very likely that the Kazakhs would develop a greater

Table 3.1 Ummah Consciousness—Index of Religious Ideology (Religious Beliefs) (%)*

Indonesia	Male	Female	<25 years	26-40 years	41-55 years	>56 years	< High School	High School-some college	Completed college/uni	Religious Activists	Mus. Professionals	Public
Number	1094	378	299	510	467	196	158	717	597	734	234	504
High	84	83	84	83	84	84	68	84	86	88	83	77
Medium	15	16	15	16	15	17	31	15	12	11	16	21
Low	1	1	1	2	1	–	2	1	1	0.3	1	2

Pakistan	Male	Female	<25 years	26-40 years	41-55 years	>56 years	< High School	High School-some college	Completed college/uni	Religious Activists	Mus. Professionals	Public
Number	882	229	125	536	257	159	50	287	766	447	277	357
High	96	95	99	96	95	95	98	97	96	98	93	95
Medium	3	4	2	3	5	5	2	2	3	1	4	4
Low	1	1	–	1	–	1	–	–	1	–	1	1

Kazakhstan	Male	Female	<25 years	26-40 years	41-55 years	>56 years	< High School	High School-some college	Completed college/uni		Mus. Professionals	Public
Number	509	441	157	380	249	164	123	803	24		235	230
High	6	4	3	6	3	5	8	4	–		8	5
Medium	18	21	18	15	20	29	25	18	25		20	29
Low	76	75	78	79	76	66	67	77	75		71	66

Egypt	Male	Female	<25 years	26-40 years	41-55 years	>56 years	< High School	High School-some college	Completed college/uni	Religious Activists	Mus. Professionals	Public
Number	590	190	93	438	166	83	50	183	516	284	391	104
High	91	85	89	89	87	95	78	88	91	95	88	81
Medium	8	13	9	10	12	3	16	12	8	6	11	16
Low	1	3	2	1	1	1	6	1	1	–	1	4

* By country by social demographic characteristics of respondents.

Islamic consciousness after their independence from the former USSR. There is already some evidence that many are cultivating an Islamic religious identity. Whether this trend will continue remains to be seen. The general conclusion which can be drawn from the evidence is that all countries except Kazakhstan display a high level of ummah consciousness, as measured by the index of religious ideology.

Consequential Religiosity Dimension of Ummah Consciousness

This dimension assumes that deeply held religious beliefs have important consequences for shaping social attitudes and secular activities of the believers. In modern societies, religious beliefs and science compete for providing explanations of questions dealing with meanings and the nature of the ultimate divine reality and the purposes of human life and destiny. The beliefs, or explanations, which contradict some core religious beliefs usually evoke social and psychological pressure on the individual to reject such beliefs. The two questions dealing with the denial of the existence of Allah and the validity of Darwin's theory of human origin were used to ascertain consequential religiosity. An index of the consequential religiosity was constructed using the methodology described in Chapter 2. The distribution of the intensity of consequential religiosity was then analysed by gender, age, level of education and sample types.

The results of this analysis, in Table 3.2, indicate that in Indonesia, Pakistan and Egypt an overwhelming proportion of respondents had high to medium scores on the index. Once again the distribution of Kazakh respondents was the opposite of these countries. These patterns are consistent with the underlying logic of the two dimensions of ummah consciousness as well as its distributions in the four countries.

The evidence also shows that in Indonesia, Pakistan and Egypt men tended to have higher scores, meaning that they were more religiously conscious than women. In Indonesia and Egypt, older respondents had higher scores, but this was not so in Pakistan. In Pakistan, younger respondents had higher scores, which was the opposite of Indonesia and Egypt. The pattern of distribution of the scores by educational level in the three countries was identical to the age pattern noted above. In these three countries, religious activists were more religiously conscious than the general respondents. The pattern in Kazakhstan showed older respondents and the more educated

Table 3.2 Ummah Consciousness—Index of Consequential Religiosity (%)*

Indonesia	Male	Female	<25 years	26-40 years	41-55 years	>56 years	< High School	High School-some college	Completed college/uni	Religious Activists	Mus. Professionals	Public
Number	1094	378	299	425	404	196	158	717	597	734	234	504
High	54	48	52	52	52	58	41	53	55	58	51	45
Medium	39	43	41	41	41	35	47	40	39	36	41	46
Low	7	9	7	7	7	7	12	7	6	6	8	9

Pakistan	Male	Female	<25 years	26-40 years	41-55 years	>56 years	< High School	High School-some college	Completed college/uni	Religious Activists	Mus. Professionals	Public
Number	919	239	126	572	268	160	52	298	801	483	298	377
High	48	41	48	50	43	50	63	45	46	52	36	48
Medium	40	46	43	39	43	41	31	48	40	41	41	43
Low	12	13	9	12	14	9	8	7	14	7	23	9

Kazakhstan	Male	Female	<25 years	26-40 years	41-55 years	>56 years	< High School	High School-some college	Completed college/uni		Mus. Professionals	Public
Number	538	462	170	402	261	167	129	847	24		246	246
High	3	3	2	3	3	5	7	3	5		2	4
Medium	25	28	27	23	31	26	30	25	37		23	30
Low	72	69	71	75	66	69	63	72	58		75	66

Egypt	Male	Female	<25 years	26-40 years	41-55 years	>56 years	< High School	High School-some college	Completed college/uni	Religious Activists	Mus. Professionals	Public
Number	594	188	92	439	165	86	52	184	515	286	390	105
High	52	35	36	50	49	44	21	46	51	51	51	28
Medium	41	56	58	42	45	46	71	49	41	41	42	67
Low	7	9	6	8	6	8	28	5	8	8	7	6

* By country by social demographic characteristics of respondents.

were relatively more religiously conscious. The same was true for the public, compared with the Muslim professionals.

The general conclusion which can be drawn from the evidence about ummah consciousness is that it, at least as has been ascertained here, appears to have a strong presence in Indonesia, Pakistan and Egypt. The respondents in these countries displayed some strikingly similar patterns in the distribution of ummah consciousness. In Kazakhstan, the general pattern was the opposite of the other three countries. This would clearly suggest that the production of ummah consciousness is strongly influenced by the prevalent social, economic and political conditions in society. The evidence also indicates that the Islamic ummah is a social reality, consciousness of which acts as an important vehicle of shared collective identity and a sense of community among disparate communities of Muslims in the modern world.

Discussion

The empirical evidence about ummah consciousness upon examination leads to two possible conclusions: firstly, it reveals its presence in all the populations studied; secondly, it also shows significant differences in the intensity and pervasiveness of ummah consciousness. Given the diversity of populations surveyed, and an objective measurement of ummah consciousness, it can be argued that, on the whole, the empirical evidence indicates that a significant proportion of Indonesian, Pakistani, Egyptian, and to a lesser extent, the Kazakh Muslims display a shared ummah consciousness. It is clear that the Muslim ummah is more a reality than a myth.

On the other hand, how can we explain the differences which are displayed by the empirical evidence, as well as the broader reality of cultural and structural pluralism which characterize the modern Muslim world? Can we adequately explain the differences in ummah consciousness and pluralism of the Muslim world through the application of the sociological perspective? It may be possible to do so. The community-association typology described earlier may provide us with a useful analytical framework to do so.

As discussed in the first part the foundation of ummah was laid by the Prophet Muhammad (PBUH) in Mecca as an expression of a new socio-religious organization. A consciousness of belonging to a community was evolving among the Prophet's (PBUH) followers in Mecca. At this juncture, each man retained his loyalties to his inherited clan; but he came to possess overriding loyalties to this new grouping based not on the family and primordial ties but on individual acceptance of the faith which Muhammad (PBUH) preached.

The empirical reality of the contemporary Muslim world is that it is now in a highly fragmented state. Politically, at least, it is organized and divided into over forty-five independent states of various sizes, most of which are internally fragmented as well. Many are facing serious economic, social and political crises. How can the present state of the ummah be explained? The answer lies in the consequences of modernization and globalization and not in the decline of the intensity and commitment to Islam among the Muslim masses and the elite. The empirical evidence presented in Chapter 2 indicates that religious piety is an important part of the daily lives of the majority of Muslims. The following discussion attempts to examine and show that the present state of the Muslim ummah is, so to speak, a natural outcome of the two processes which have profoundly affected the human condition over the past hundred years or so.

Modernization and the Ummah

Modernization is a vague concept, but, in general, it refers to the processes of technological change, increasing institutional differentiation and bureaucratization. It is now a global phenomenon, which began with the Industrial Revolution in England and from there spread to other parts of the world. It also coincided with the emergence of the nation state, first in Europe and then globally, as the dominant political and economic organization to manage the internal and external affairs of the new polity. These conditions affected Muslim societies just as they did the rest of the world and resulted in the emergence of forty-five Muslim majority states.

Over time, a distinctive feature of national societies was the development of institutional differentiation and functional specialization. This gave rise to autonomous functional instrumentalities such as polity, law, economy, science, education, health, art, family and religion. An important consequence of the relative institutional autonomy was that the institutions became independent of religious norms and values. Luhmann[29] and Beyer[30] have labelled this development as 'secularization'. These modern conditions characterize all national societies, although, in terms of level, intensity and extent of modernity, there are significant differences between countries. Muslim countries are not the ones with high levels of modernity, but they, like other countries, nevertheless are influenced by institutional differentiation and functional specialization.

The conditions of modernity have far-reaching implications and impact on the relationship between religion and other political, social, economic and cultural institutions. This is owing to the fact that religion becomes just one of the many institutions in a modern state-society. Like other institutions, it vies for a public role and influence in society. It loses its role as the over-arching institution in the society. To understand the transformation that occurs under the conditions of modernity, we can use the analytical framework proposed by Luhmann.[31] According to Luhmann, under conditions of modernity, the degree of public influence that religious institutions enjoy depends on how they relate to other institutions within society. He uses a framework consisting of institutional 'function' and 'performance' to analyse this relationship.

The functional role refers to 'pure' religious communication, which includes devotion and worship, the care of souls and search for salvation, guidance and enlightenment. Function is the pure religious communication, involving the transcendental and the aspect that religious institutions claim for themselves as the basis of their autonomy in modern society. Religious performance, by contrast, refers to non-religious functions performed by religious institutions. It occurs when religion is 'applied' to problems generated in other institutional systems but not solved there or simply not addressed anywhere, such as poverty, corruption and political oppression.

Religious institutions in a modern society gain public influence and legitimacy through the performance role by addressing non-religious and profane problems. The functional problem of religion in modern society is a performance problem. Religious institutions gain public influence when they efficiently carry out the performance role. This in turn requires religious institutions to be autonomous of the state and other institutional sub-systems. The logical inference which follows from this is that religious institutions will gain greater public influence in institutional configurations in which they are autonomous of the state. If they are not, then they cannot carry out their performance functions effectively.

Given that modernization invariably entails institutional transformation leading to institutional differentiation, specialization and autonomy, these features have become an integral part of all modern state societies, including Muslim state societies. As Muslim societies go through advanced stages of modernization, these institutional changes will produce significant sociological problems in them. Religion has been historically a dominant institution in Muslim societies, influencing other institutional areas such as economy, law and politics. For much of the pre-modern period, this has been a condition shared by most Muslim societies. Modernization, therefore, has instigated a struggle in Muslim social formations over this new institutional configuration. One of the challenges faced by the political elite has been to accommodate conditions of modernity to the historical experience and development of Muslim societies. It is, therefore, no surprise that one of the major struggles in Muslim societies, continuing from the twentieth at least, has been to define and adjust to the structure of the institutional configuration of a modern state society. There have been major conflicts over this.

To date, there appear to be two types of institutional configurations of Muslim social formations—differentiated and undifferentiated. A differentiated social formation is one in which religion and politics occupy a separate space, and religious institutions largely perform specialized roles and are autonomous of the state. The undifferentiated social formation is one in which religion and politics are integrated, and religious institutions perform a more generalized role which extends beyond the purely religious domain. The undifferentiated social formation is also called the Islamic state. Under conditions of modernity, there is, one can say, a struggle over the role of Islam in society. By and large, this struggle has led to a general consolidation of the differentiated social formation model in Muslim countries. Nevertheless, there are major exceptions to this, and several states have sought the model of undifferentiated social formations—that is, Islamic state—for organizing and managing their political affairs. These include the Islamic Republics of Iran, Saudi Arabia, Afghanistan, and to some extent, Sudan and Pakistan. However, even these state-societies have not escaped the consequences of modernization. This struggle is likely to continue, although it appears to be declining in intensity in the political calculations of Muslim populations, as the results of the last presidential election in the Islamic Republic of Iran have shown.

Since the roles religious institutions perform have a direct bearing on their public influence and legitimacy, it follows from the logic of Luhmann's model that in differentiated Muslim social formations religious institutions will enjoy greater legitimacy and public influence because of their emphasis on the 'performance' role; whereas, in an undifferentiated Muslim social formation the opposite will occur, and religious institutions will lose public influence and legitimacy. This, however, raises other consequences. For example, when religious institutions begin to lose public influence and legitimacy in an undifferentiated social formation—that is, Islamic state—then the religious elite and its political allies begin to develop and follow strategies to stop the declining influence and legitimacy through 'innovative' Islamization policies. Perhaps one example of this may be the emergence of the Taliban movement in Afghanistan—which originated in the *madrasas* (religious schools) in Pakistan—a society in which religious institutions have been experiencing a decline in public influence and legitimacy (see Chapter 5). The success of the movement in Afghanistan can lead the Muslim elite to expand the movement to Pakistan and neighbouring Central Asian Muslim countries. This could have major and unpredictable social, cultural, political and demographic consequences for the Islamic ummah which resides in these countries.

The other possibility is that an Islamic state can also pave the way for the future secularization process in society. An example of this is the Islamic Republic of Iran in which the 1989 amendment to the constitution, which was sanctioned by Ayatollah Khomeini, empowered the government to disregard the Shariah provision in the legislation and policy. This amendment allows the Islamic government to abrogate Shariah principles—including the fundamental pillars of the faith, such as prayers and fasting—if it is in the general interests of the Muslim nation. The amendment gives the government far-reaching powers to decide when the provisions of Muslim law are, or are not, binding. Given that the 'tenets' of Islam are the ultimate constitutional limit on legislation and government power, their effective removal gives the government and parliament unlimited power. This kind of development could only occur in an Islamic state.[32] A conclusion which can be drawn from the Iranian situation is that Islamic states in fact can be viewed as a stage in the development of Muslim social formations.

Globalization and the Ummah

Another major influence on structural and cultural change in the modern world is globalization. Modern technology has resulted in rapid communication over unlimited space. This technology is now in existence nearly all over the world. The potential for worldwide rapid communication has been translated into actual practice. We now live in a globalizing social reality in which previous effective barriers to communication no longer exist. The world is fast becoming a global village and 'a single place'[33]. Therefore, in order to understand the major features of social life in contemporary Muslim societies, we need to go beyond local and national factors and situate the analysis in the global context. For example, in the pre-globalized world, the limitations of communication technology made 'knowing' of other cultures a very time-consuming, difficult, and at times, almost an impossible task. At best, only a small number of people were able to travel and thus exposed to other cultures and societies. The legendary travels of Ibn Batuta and Vasco de Gama are now an everyday reality for thousands of business and recreational travellers every year. In the early centuries of Islam, ummah consciousness was largely determined by the observance of the 'five pillars' of Islam and some key beliefs. The existence of the common ritualistic dimension of ummah consciousness was seen as if the whole culture had been Islamized; that is, come to resemble the Arabian culture—the foundational culture of Islam. It was believed that transforming the cultures of newly Islamized people into something which resembled the Arabian/Arabic Middle Eastern culture was an integral part of the 'Islamic' project. Furthermore, it was assumed that newly Islamized cultures are going to follow this trajectory in the development of their cultures. The limitations of communication technology made it easier to believe in this myth. But the reality was that Islamized cultures invariably added the Islamic layers on top of the various other cultural layers. The work of Clifford Geertz in Java provides an excellent illustration of this.[34] Similar conclusions can be drawn from the study of the customary laws of Muslim countries which still continue to play a significant role in social and cultural affairs of Muslim communities.[35]

In the pre-globalized world, a common Muslim belief is that Islam is not only a religion but a complete way of life was widely accepted. In Islamic discourse this refers to the 'one religion and one culture' paradigm. Globalization is prompting a reformulation of this belief. Communication links are now worldwide, rapid and increasingly dense. People, customs, societies and civilizations previously more or less isolated from one another are now in regular and almost unavoidable contact. This has had two consequences for the Muslim ummah. Firstly, it allows others to experience the reality of different Islamic cultures which are readily and commonly accessible. We can, for example, see the social exchanges and rituals surrounding the celebrations of Muslim festivals. This experience can demonstrate not only what is common among the Muslim ummah but also what is 'different'. Secondly, the experience of this difference can be unsettling if it is viewed as a deviation from 'the Islamic way'.

While the first consequence makes us conscious of the social and cultural diversity of the Muslim ummah, the second consequence produces a reaction of rejection of this cultural and social hybridity and a desire to replace it with the authentic 'Islamic way'. The struggle between 'hybridity' and 'authenticity' perhaps constitutes the most important challenge of globalization for the Muslim ummah and is one of the underlying causes of the emergence of Islamic fundamentalist movements. Islamic Fundamentalism refers to a religious way of being that manifests itself as a strategy by which Islamic 'purists' attempt to reassert their construction of religious identity and social order. They feel this identity is at risk and being eroded by cultural and religious hybridity. They try to fortify their interpretation of religious ways of being through selective retrieval of doctrines, beliefs and practices from a sacred past.

While there are differences between various fundamentalist movements in general, their endeavours to establish the 'new' political and social order rely on charismatic and authoritarian leadership. These movements also feature a disciplined inner core of the elite and the organization, as well as a large population of sympathizers, who may be called up in times of need. Fundamentalists often follow a rigorous socio-moral code and clear strategies to achieve their goals.[36] Religious fundamentalism is a problem produced by the encounter between modernity and religious community (ummah) in all its diversity and cultural hybridity. Its strength varies according to the intensity of attitudes towards diversity and cultural hybridity.

In a globalizing world, cultural mixing and crossovers are likely to become a routine part of social life. This may transform hybridity into an autonomous symbolic universe, which will pose a challenge to the conventional categorical oppositions of existing symbolic systems. Such a challenge will create the conditions for cultural reflexivity and change and may confer on hybridity its own symbolism with a unique character and powers which will claim coexistence and recognition along with the existing symbolic universes.[37]

For the Islamic world, it would have important implications as it may transform the Islamic regions as unique religious and cultural systems demanding recognition and acceptance as an authentic tradition of Islam. One outcome of this may be the 'decentring' of the world of Islam from a uni-centred cultural world, with the centre in the Arabic Middle East, to a world with multiple centres, ranging from Indonesian-Malaysian Islam, the non-Arabic Middle Eastern Islam, the African Islam and the Islam of the Muslim minorities in the West. The demographic pressures in the Muslim countries will further accentuate the movement towards decentring. Over time, these traditions may find strength and consolidate with the support of their followers. The decentring of the Muslim ummah will confer a kind of legitimacy on the regional ummahs, and this may lead them to chart their development—religious, political, economic, social and cultural—along distinctive lines appropriate to the history and temperament of their respective peoples. Such a scenario will offer new opportunities for the Muslim ummah to strive for achievment of ideological and material superiority once achieved by the ummah in the formative years.

Globalization, while corroding and challenging the inherited or constructed cultural identities, also encourages the creation and revitalization of particular identities as a way of competing for power and influence in the global system. This will be aided by a unique affinity of religion for particularistic identities. Since religion in a globalizing, modernizing world is marginalized, it uses new opportunities and ways to gain public influence and legitimacy. As pointed out earlier, under conditions of globalization, religion is confronted with two main routes to gain public influence. One, from the perspective of the sub-global, which I have called the regional perspective, and the other which focuses on the global or universal perspective. However, even the global and universal perspective paradoxically acquires particularistic characteristics. My point here is that, far from losing public influence, religion may gain public influence both in its transcendent and imminent forms under conditions of globalization. This influence, nevertheless, will be mediated by a sub-global religious tradition which can adapt and encourage the 'performance' role of religion with greater success than the inherited global tradition can. From the argument outlined here, it would appear that the 'performance' role of religion under conditions of modernity is the most effective avenue for religious institutions to gain public influence and legitimacy in a globalizing, modernizing world.

In the light of the above, the future Islamic ummah will gain strength not as a unified and unitary community but as a differentiated community consisting of ummahs representing different Islamic regions. Each regional ummah will embody the unique character moulded by history and the temperament of its people. It will chart its own course to gain material and ideological influence in a global system, and simultaneously, it will act as a supportive and effective constituent of Islamic civilization. This trend will also produce strong liberal and conservative movements, and each regional Islamic ummah would have to find its unique way to meet the challenge that these movements will pose.

The challenge for the Muslim world is not religious, but intellectual. At present, the Islamic ummah is in the doldrums not because of the weakness of commitment to the faith but because of its intellectual stagnation brought about by political, social and cultural conditions generated by colonialism, neo-colonialism and economic underdevelopment, some of which can be attributed to increasing devotional religiosity of the masses. This stagnation is most dramatically manifested in the scientific and technological backwardness of the Muslim world. According to a recent study, the total output of forty-five Muslim countries between 1990-94 was equal to the output of Switzerland (the scientific output was measured by the Science Citation Index [SCI] produced by the Institute for Scientific Information [ISI]).[38]

The real challenge for the differentiated Muslim ummah will be to find political, social and cultural ways to fuse a high degree of devotional religiosity and a high degree of intellectual activity for scientific advancement. There are examples of such pathways provided by Islamic and other civilizations. Most of these examples entail freedom of the individual to combine the two imperatives under socio-political conditions which accord autonomy to different institutions. Nevertheless, there is no reason to believe that the existing pathways exhaust all possibilities. The human condition and destiny are constantly evolving, and there may still be unimagined pathways to find creative interaction between the spiritual and the intellectual (rational) realms. The challenge for the Muslims is to explore these yet unimagined pathways with intellectual and scientific rigour. This task may be easier to undertake under conditions of a differentiated Islamic ummah, which, as argued above, is now evolving under conditions of modernization and globalization.

NOTES

1. Chaudhri 1994; Dallal 1995; Rahman 1989, 1982; von Grunebaum 1961; Ahmad 1997.
2. Gellner 1994, p. 26.
3. Khaldun 1958; Wolf 1951; Watt 1954, 1955; Chaudhri 1994.
4. Abu Sulayman 1997, p. xvi.
5. Dallal 1995; Von Grunebaum 1961, 1962; Rahman 1989; Nieuwenhuijze 1959; Denny 1975; Giannakis 1983.
6. Darrow 1987, p. 123.
7. Watt 1955.

8. Nieuwenhuijze 1959; Denny 1975; Giannakis 1983; Rahman 1984; Von Grunebaum 1962.

9. Dallal 1994.

10. Giannakis 1983; Wolf 1951; Watt 1954, 1955.

11. Denny 1975; Giannakis 1983; Rahman 1984; Watt 1955.

12. Denny 1975; Watt 1955.

13. Wolf 1951; Watt 1954, 1955; Rahman 1989; Khaldun 1958.

14. Hodgson 1977, pp. 172-206.

15. Von Grunebaum 1962.

16. Rahman 1989.

17. Von Grunebaum 1962.

18. Hodgson 1977.

19. Rahman 1982, 1989.

20. Rahman 1982.

21. Von Grunebaum 1962.

22. Ahmad 1997.

23. Ahmad 1997.

24. Ahmad 1997, pp. 8-9.

25. Dallal 1994.

26. Tonnies 1953.

27. Tonnies 1953.

28. Eisenstadt and Giessen 1995.

29. Luhmann 1982.

30. Beyer 1994.

31. Luhmann 1982.

32. Zubaida 1995; Malat 1993.

33. Robertson 1987.

34. Geertz 1960.

35. See, for example, Hooker 1984.

36. Marty and Appleby 1991.

37. Werbner and Modood 1997.

38. Anwar and Abu Bakar 1996.

4

THE SELF-IMAGE OF ISLAM

In modern Islamic discourse the self-images of Islam, held by
the believers and the observers, are frequently used descriptively
and analytically to explain the nature of Muslim religiosity and
the character of Islamic collective movements. These images
are taken as a kind of symbolic discourse which gives expression
to deeply held religious convictions and ideals that act as
primary texts for indexing social reality. Some of the key
contemporary Islamic discourses which have informed this study
will be examined first. The empirical evidence about the images
of Islam held by the respondents who were surveyed will be
then taken into account. One objective of this will be to assess
the validity of the characterizations of Islam in these discourses.
The chapter will conclude with a discussion of the findings and
their sociological significance and implications.

As discussed in the introductory chapter, the analysis of
religious reform and fundamentalism invariably invokes the
Islamic world-view and self-image as an explanatory variable.
This especially applies to the analytical contributions of
W. Montgomery Watt, Ernest Gellner, Fatima Mernissi and
Fazlur Rahman to name four influential contributors to the
sociology of contemporary Muslim societies. The central theme
of Watt's influential book *Islamic Fundamentalism and
Modernity* is that 'the thinking of fundamentalist Islamic
intellectuals and of great masses of ordinary Muslims is still
dominated by the standard traditional Islamic world-view and
the corresponding self-image of Islam'.[1]

Watt's Analysis of the Crisis of the Self-Image of Islam

Watt goes on to argue that this fact was of great importance since it significantly influences how contemporary problems in the Islamic world are seen by many Muslims, which may be very different from how they look to Western observers. For example, he argues that a key objective of many Islamic fundamentalist movements is the 'recovery of a truer self-image'.[2] This objective is predicated on the image of society many traditional Muslims held by and based on the belief that social conditions are unchanging and that return to the exact form of social life in the early Islamic period would solve all contemporary problems.

Western observers, however, see this supposition as based on a false assumption of 'unchangingness of the world'. While allowing that basic human nature has not changed, Western observers see the problem differently. They argue that Western science, technology and industry have so fundamentally transformed some of the material circumstances in which people live that changes of social structure have inevitably followed.[3] This means that a return to the social conditions which prevailed in the foundational period of Islam would be impossible. Many modern Muslim intellectuals also hold similar views.

Islamic fundamentalism, for Watt, is essentially an intellectual development in the Muslim world. He attributes its causation to the domination of the 'traditional Islamic world-view' and the corresponding 'self-image of Islam' in the thinking of Islamic intellectuals and great masses of ordinary Muslims. This development has also resulted in socio-religious divisions among Muslims. As he puts it, 'the important distinction is between those Muslims who fully accept the traditional world-view and want to maintain it intact and those who see it needs to be corrected in some respects. The former are fundamentalists... while the latter group will be referred to as liberals'.[4]

He argues that within the two groups there are significant divisions. The religious scholars, ulama, who are the primary bearers and transmitters of the traditional world-view, are mostly 'reactionary' in the sense that they tend to oppose religious and political reforms. Even among traditionalists, however, there are reformist elements, but, unlike liberals, the reforms they are interested in are largely social and political and leave the traditional world-view unchanged and unchallenged. The liberals are interested not only in changing the traditional world-view and self-image of Islam but also in broader political, social and religious reforms.

The Traditional Self-Image of Islam

After an extensive examination of the works of some of the leading Muslim intellectuals, Watt identifies the significant features of the traditional world-view and the self-images of Islam on which it is predicated. These include the following:

1. *The unchanging static world predicated on the complete absence of the idea of development.* For the traditionalists, unchangingness is both an ideal for human individuals and societies and a perception of the actual nature of humanity and its environment. This value orientation completely precludes the idea of development.
2. *The finality of Islam.* This characteristic refers to the claim by the traditionalists that Islam has all moral and religious truths necessary for all humanity, and therefore they do not expect human society to develop in any essential way.
3. *The self-sufficiency of Islam.* A key element of this self-image of Islam held by the traditionalists is that Islam owes nothing to any religious or philosophical system. This self-image has profound implications for the conception of knowledge which is reflected in the Muslim conception of knowledge. When a Muslim thinks of knowledge it is primarily knowledge for living, whereas when a Westerner thinks of knowledge it is mainly knowledge for power.[5] A similar view is expressed by Rahman when he describes the

medieval Islamic scholarship not as, 'an active pursuit, a creative reaching out of the mind to the unknown—as is the case today—but rather as the passive acquisition of already established knowledge.[6]

4. *Islam in History.* The essential feature of this self-image is the idea that Islam will be ultimately triumphant in changing the whole world into *dar-al-Islam* (the sphere of Islam) in which only the provisions of the Islamic Shariah are observed.

5. *The Idealization of Prophet Muhammad (PBUH) and early Islam.* This self-image idealizes the Prophet Muhammad (PBUH) as the perfect person in every respect and the early Islamic period as the perfect example of the social organization which must be emulated and followed in every respect by the modern Muslim states.

The traditional world-view of Islam, according to Watt, renders critical and historically objective scholarship highly problematic in Muslim consciousness, and deviation from the idealized and romanticized notions as a heresy and 'unthinkable'. These features of the Islamic world-view and the corresponding self-image are the basis of Islamic fundamentalism. The support for fundamentalism is embedded in the consciousness which fully accepts the traditionalistic world-view and wants to maintain it. The conditions of modernity and globalization which now characterize the world pose a serious threat to the traditional world-view, producing a 'crisis of self-image' among traditional Muslims which in turn contributes to a kind of' 'moral panic'.

The main reason for the resurgence of Islamic fundamentalism, according to Watt, is the feeling among ordinary Muslims, including some of the better educated, that they are in danger of losing their Islamic identity because of its erosion by Western intellectual attitudes. Many Muslims also feel that in the social upheaval caused by the impact of the West, Muslim societies are faring rather worse than many other societies. The modern Islamic fundamentalism is a collective response to this intellectual and emotional crisis because of its promise that a return to the 'true Islam' of the earliest period would solve all social problems facing Muslims and their societies.[7]

Watt's explanations of the causes of Islamic fundamentalism are echoed by Muslim intellectuals such as Hasan al-Banna, Syed Qutb and Sayyid Abul-Ala Al-Maududi and the Islamic political movements such as the Muslim Brotherhood (*Al-Ikhwan al-Muslimin*) and Jamaat-i-Islami founded by them. Their views are best expressed by Maududi, who argued that under the impact of Western civilization and its dominant atheistic and materialistic orientations, the Muslims have become devoid of Islamic character and morals, ideas and ideology, have lost the 'Islamic spirit' and are in danger of losing their identity.[8]

Ernest Gellner's Characterization of Islamic Traditions

Building on the previous historical and sociological analyses of Muslim society by Ibn Khaldun,[9] Hume,[10] Hodgson[11] and his own studies of Muslim societies of North Africa,[12] Gellner has developed a typology of Islamic traditions or styles which he has called 'High Islam' of the scholars and 'folk Islam' of the people. The boundary between these two traditions of Islam was not sharp but gradual and sometimes ambiguous. High Islam is carried by urban scholars recruited largely from the trading bourgeoisie and it reflects the natural tastes and values of the urban middle classes. High Islam is scripturalist, rule-oriented, puritanical, literal, sober, egalitarian, and anti-ecstatic. Folk Islam is the Islam of the masses, especially rural and tribal people, the large majority of whom are either illiterate or semi-literate. It is deeply influenced by their needs and proclivities. It is superstitious, ecstatic, hierarchical, mediationist and its characteristic institution is the saint cult.[13]

These two traditions or styles of Islam, in other words, correspond to the dominant and spatial features of the social structure of Muslim societies, namely the city and the countryside. High Islam may not be, as its adherents like to think, the perpetuation of the pristine practice of the Islam of the Prophet (PBUH) and his Companions, but as a tradition it has occupied a genuinely prestigious position in Muslim civilization. It possesses features which may have marked elective affinities with the virtues required to surmount the arduousness and strains of the long march to a disciplined, modern, industrial society.

Because of the structural needs, folk Islam has played a dominant role in historical Muslim societies. However, over the last century the trauma of the Western impact has forced Muslim thinkers to construct a response to this challenge. Their dominant and persuasive answer has been neither emulation of the West nor idealization of folk Islam but a return to a more rigorous observance of high Islam.

For Gellner, also, modern Islamic fundamentalism is the Muslim intellectual response to the challenge of Western modernity, and it constitutes the basic mechanism of the massive transfer of loyalties away from saint cults towards a scripturalist fundamentalist variant of Islam. This, according to Gellner, 'is the essence of the cultural history of Islam of the last hundred years. What had been a minority accomplishment or privilege, a form of the faith practiced by a cultural elite, has come to define the society as a whole'.[14] Gellner has called this 'A Pendulum Swing Theory of Islam'.[15]

Embedded in Gellner's analysis of the two traditions of Islam are the contrasting images. The high Islam is puritanical, scripturalist, rule oriented, literal, sober, egalitarian and anti-ecstatic. It is urban and lead by the Islamic scholars largely linked to the urban commercial classes. Its opposite is folk Islam. It is mystical, saint worshipping, mediationist, ecstatic, hierarchical, joyous and festival-worthy. Its ethic is one of loyalty, not rule observance. In its orientation it is closer to the Durkheimian religion, with its objective being maintenance of social order not social justice.

The two traditions by and large coexist in a kind of amiable symbiosis, but there is always a latent tension between them which surfaces from time to time, when social conditions change, in the form of puritanical revivalist movements aiming at transforming the folk tradition in the image of the high tradition. According to Gellner, Islam is the only Western religion with this built-in self-purifying and self-rectifying mechanism.[16] It is the dynamics of this system which can enable social scientists to chart the trajectories of Muslim social formations of past and present.

Self-Image of Islam in the Works of Fazlur Rahman and Fatima Mernissi

Fazlur Rahman's work also contains a typology of Islam which he has labelled folk Islam and modernist Islam. But unlike Watt he does not develop this typology fully. In its very essence folk Islam is similar to the traditional Islam of Watt and folk Islam of Gellner. For Rahman, the Indonesian Islamic tradition known as Nahdatul Ulama, whose leader Abdurrahman Wahid was elected in 1999 as the President of Indonesia in the recent elections, is an example of the folk Islamic tradition.

The modernist Islamic tradition in the Indonesian context is represented by the other major Indonesian Islamic organization Muhammadiyah.[17] Folk Islam is tradition-bound and rigid, whereas the modern Islam is 'intellectual' and amenable to change and reform by formulating general principles (normative Islam) embedded in the Qur'an. Modernist Islam is literate, intellectual and open to reformulation of the Qur'anic thought on the factual study of social conditions.[18]

Muslim feminist sociologist Fatima Mernissi has made some important, albeit controversial, contributions to the treatment and position of women in Islam.[19] The key question that has guided her work is why the Arab world is so hostile to women. She argues that petro-funded Islam, spearheaded by Saudi Arabia, has stifled democratic debate in the Arab world, stifled progressive forces and mutilated Muslim society. She sees this tendency as a continuation of the historical process of manipulation of sacred texts by powerful and dominant men to subordinate women and to control them. Implicit in her work are two images of Islam—an Islam embodying the Prophet Muhammad's (PBUH) social project to establish a just and ethical social order for humanity, and an Islam which is misogynist, male dominated, anti-democratic and blindly obeys traditional interpretations of Islam's sacred texts.

In the preceding discussion I have attempted to show that modern Islamic discourses explicitly or implicitly articulate certain self-images of Islam. These self-images are then used to explain prevalent social and cultural conditions in the contemporary Muslim countries. These images are a kind of symbolic discourse which give expression to deeply held ideals and values which act as definers of Muslim culture and identity. One of the objectives of this study was to investigate the validity of the self-images imputed to Islam by Muslim and Western scholars of Islam and Muslim society. The primary objective was to ascertain how far these images were also part of the Muslim consciousness. A secondary aim of the research was to examine whether or not the self-images of Islam can be employed to explain future religious and social trajectories of different Muslim societies. The following section reports the empirical findings obtained in this study.

Self-Image of Islam: The Empirical Evidence

Following Watt's analytical framework of the traditional self-image of Islam, which was outlined and discussed earlier, six statements were formulated which contained the essential points of his framework, namely the unchanging static world-view, the finality of Islam, the self-sufficiency of Islam, Islam in history and the idealization of the Prophet Muhammad (PBUH) and early Islam. These statements, in fact, were embedded in Watt's discussion. The statements were:

1. Human nature is unchanging and this is the reason for Muslim scholars asserting the finality of rules and laws for

human conduct which are expressed in the Qur'an and the Sunnah of the Prophet (PBUH);

2. In the ideal Muslim society there will be no need to foster change;
3. The Qur'an and Sunnah contain all the essential religious and moral truths required by the whole human race till the end of time;
4. The Qur'an and Sunnah are completely self-sufficient to meet the needs of present and future societies;
5. The ideal Muslim society must be based on the model of early Muslim society under the Prophet (PBUH) and the *Khulafa-e-Rashdeen* (pious Caliphs);
6. Muslim society must be based on the Qur'an and the Shariah law.

Each statement was presented to the respondents, and they were asked to indicate which one of the following responses came closest to their opinion: 'strongly agree', 'agree', 'not sure', 'disagree', 'strongly disagree' and 'do not know'. A composite index of 'agreement' with the statement was constructed by combining the 'strongly agree', 'agree' responses. Only those respondents who chose one of first five responses were included in the analysis. Between 85 to 95 per cent of respondents in Indonesia, Pakistan and Egypt responded to the questions in Table 4.1.

In Kazakhstan, the response rate for various items was around 60 per cent. One possible reason for the high non-response rate in Kazakhstan was that respondents had difficulty in understanding the meaning of the statements. This was probably because during the communist period people were largely untutored in Islam. My field notes indicate that this was not the case in the other three countries. The empirical findings are reported in Table 4.1. One interesting feature of the evidence is that once again the Kazakh response pattern was very different compared with the other countries. In fact, notwithstanding two striking differences, in general there was a remarkable

Table 4.1 Indicators of the traditional self-image (% agreeing)

	Indonesia	Pakistan	Kazakhstan	Egypt
Human nature is unchanging and this is the reason for Muslim scholars asserting the finality of rules and laws for human conduct which are expressed in the Qur'an and the Sunnah of the Prophet (PBUH)	84	86	41	71
In the ideal Muslim society there will be no need to foster change	15	70	37	59
The Qur'an and Sunnah contain all the essential religious and moral truths required by the whole human race from now until the end of time	97	92	45	93
The Qur'an and Sunnah are completely self-sufficient to meet the needs of present and future societies	96	91	40	85
The ideal Muslim society must be based on the model of early Muslim society under the Prophet (PBUH) and the Khulafa-e-Rashdeen	59	94	37	85
Muslim society must be based on the Qur'an and Shariah law	93	93	51	93

correspondence in the response pattern among the respondents from Indonesia, Pakistan and Egypt.

A large majority of respondents from Indonesia, Pakistan and Egypt accepted the finality of the Qur'anic and the Shariah rules for regulating human conduct. An even larger majority of respondents from these countries subscribed to the self-images which characterized Islam as self-sufficient and the Qur'an and the Sunnah as containing all the essential truths for humanity which are valid for eternity. A remarkably high 93 per cent of respondents from these countries agreed that Muslim society must be based on the Qur'an and the Shariah law.

There were strikingly different perceptions of the ideal Muslim society among the respondents from Indonesia, Pakistan and Egypt. Whereas 70 per cent of Pakistanis and 59 per cent of Egyptians perceived the ideal Muslim society as static and without any need to foster change, only 15 per cent of the Indonesians agreed with this perception. In this respect the

Indonesians were strikingly different from even the Kazakhs among whom the agreement rate was 37 per cent, almost two and a half times greater than the Indonesians.

Another different pattern also pertained to the self-image of Muslim society which idealized the Prophet (PBUH) and the *Khulafa-e-Rashdeen*. A large majority of the Pakistanis and Egyptians (94 and 85 per cent respectively) believed that the ideal Muslim society must be based on the model of the early Muslim society under the Prophet (PBUH) and the *Khulafa-e-Rashdeen*, only 59 per cent of the Indonesians and 37 per cent of the Kazakhs subscribed to this belief. In general, among the Kazakhs the agreement rates were much lower than the respondents from the other three countries. The evidence clearly showed that in general the Muslims from Indonesia, Pakistan and Egypt subscribed to what Watt has called the traditional self-image of Islam, but this was not so in the case of the Muslims from Kazakhstan. The evidence thus partially supports Watt's thesis that a large number of Muslims subscribe to the traditional self-image of Islam.

What are some of the sociological correlates of the traditional self-image of Islam is the subject of the following analysis.

Sociological Correlates of the Traditional Self-Image

An index of agreement with the traditional self-image of Islam using the following methodology was constructed for each country. The 'strongly agree' response was scored as five and 'strongly disagree' response was scored as one for each of the six questions about the traditional self-image (as in Table 4.1), and the score for each respondent was then calculated. A respondent, thus, could obtain a score of between 6 and 30. The distribution of the respondents in this range was calculated using the distribution pattern in Egypt as the norm (because it had the smallest range of scores, ranging from low of 12 to high of 30) the mid-point of the range (21) was used to classify the respondents as traditionalists and non-traditionalists.

The respondents with the score 21 and higher were classified as the traditionalists (i.e., who subscribed to the traditional self-image of Islam) and those with scores less than 21 were classified as non-traditionalists. In each country the distribution of the traditionalists was computed by gender, lifecycle (age), human capital (educational attainment) and social position (religious activists, Muslim professionals, and general public) of the respondents. The results of this analysis are presented in Table 4.2. The evidence shows that in general the Pakistanis and the Egyptians had the greatest proportion of the traditionalists, with around 90 per cent in both countries in this category. They were followed by the Indonesians, among whom around 70 per cent were traditionalist, and the Kazakh Muslims had the lowest proportion, with only around 40 per cent classified as traditionalists. This distribution is consistent with the evidence reported in Table 4.1.

In Indonesia, women, more educated and younger respondents were slightly more traditionalist. The religious activists were more traditionalist than Muslim professionals and the general public. There was no difference between Pakistani men and women, but the proportion of the traditionalists declined with age and educational attainment. Almost all Pakistani religious activists were traditionalists, and Muslim professionals comparatively were much less so. In Kazakhstan, men were more traditionalist than women, and respondents aged 26 to 40 and those with university education were more traditionalist than women and respondents aged 56 and above. The Kazakh Muslim professionals and general public had identical proportions of respondents who were traditionalists. In Egypt men, and those aged 26 to 55 were slightly more traditionalist. The proportion of traditionalists declined with educational attainment, and again, as in other countries, the religious activists were more traditionalist than the Muslim professionals.

Table 4.2 'Traditionalists'* (%)

	Male	Female	>25 years	26-40 years	41-55 years	>56 years	>high school
Indonesia	72	76	77	71	72	73	68
Pakistan	91	91	94	92	91	86	91
Kazakhstan	39	30	27	40	34	31	33
Egypt	92	84	87	91	91	83	98

	High school-some uni.	Completed uni.	Religious Activists	Muslim Professionals	Public
Indonesia	76	70	74	69	72
Pakistan	96	89	97	77	94
Kazakhstan	35	42	–	40	41
Egypt	93	89	94	86	93

* By selected characteristics and by countries.

Relationship between the Traditional Self-Image of Islam and Piety

Are those with the traditional self-image of Islam more likely to be religiously committed? This question was investigated through a correlational analysis between the index of traditional self-image and indexes of ideological (religious beliefs) and ritualistic (religious practice) dimensions of religious piety (see Chapter 1). The results of this analysis are reported in Table 4.3 and show that in Indonesia, Pakistan and Kazakhstan the index of the traditional self-image of Islam and the index of the ideological dimension of religious piety were highly and significantly correlated. Only in Egypt was the relationship not statistically correlated but it was still positive.

Table 4.3 Correlation of self-image with dimensions of piety

	Indonesia	Pakistan	Kazakhstan	Egypt
Ideological dimension of piety	.159**	.320**	.278**	.049
Ritualistic dimension of piety	.089**	.023	.205**	.117**

** Correlation is significant at the 0.01 level

The evidence reported in Table 4.3 also shows that there was a positive and statistically significant correlation between the index of traditional self-image of Islam and the ritualistic dimension of piety in Indonesia, Kazakhstan and Egypt.

Only in Pakistan was such a correlation, while still positive, not statistically significant. In general, the evidence presented in Table 4.3 indicates that those who hold the traditional self-image are likely to show significantly more religious commitment. The preceding analysis, therefore, offers some empirical support for Watt's theory.

'Liberal' Self-Image of Islam

In his typology of Muslims, Watt describes those Muslims who see the need for the traditional Islamic self-image 'to be corrected in some respects' as 'liberals'.[20] It was assumed that some Muslims could subscribe to some aspects of both 'traditional' and 'liberal' self-images of Islam. Rather than taking only those who did not hold the 'traditional self-image', a separate set of questions was used in the survey to identify those who held the characteristics of the 'liberal self-image'. These questions, again, were generated through the analysis of Watt's and Gellner's texts.

The key dimensions of the 'liberal self-image' were: need to interpret the Qur'an according to prevailing social conditions; the practical difficulties in basing a complex modern society on the Shariah law; the expressions of divine matters could only be expressed symbolically and not literally; the presence of the human element in the sacred texts; and, finally, the belief that knowledge came from human reason and not from divine revelations. The actual texts of statements are reported in Table 4.4.

Each respondent was asked to indicate which of the following responses came closest to expressing their opinion about the statement, 'strongly agree', 'agree', 'not sure', 'disagree', 'strongly disagree' and 'do not know'. A composite index of agreement was developed by combining 'strongly agree' and 'agree' responses. The response rates for the statements about the liberal Islamic self-image were much lower compared with those for the 'traditional self-image' statements. In Indonesia and Egypt, on average, the response rate was 85 per cent, in Pakistan it was around 70 per cent and in Kazakhstan it was only about 50 per cent. The Kazakh rates were low because many respondents simply did not understand the 'meaning' of the statement because of their lack of familiarity and knowledge of Islamic teachings. The response rates were generally lower among lesser educated respondents. The findings about the agreement rates are reported in Table 4.4. For the reasons mentioned above these findings need be interpreted with greater caution.

The findings show that a large majority of Pakistanis agreed that the message of the Qur'an should be interpreted according to the demands and conditions of the times, and around 60 per cent held the same opinion in Indonesia and Kazakhstan. In Egypt, the proportion agreeing was the lowest at only 44 per cent. The question that it was not realistic or practical to base a

Table 4.4 Liberal self-image of Islam (% agreeing)

	Indonesia	Pakistan	Kazakhstan	Egypt
The message of the Qur'an should be interpreted according to the demands and conditions of our times	58	90	63	44
It is not practical or realistic to base a complex modern society on the Shariah law	21	17	—	10
The truth about Allah cannot be fully comprehended by the human mind and cannot be fully expressed in human nature; statements about divine matters can be no more than evocative and symbolic	32	62	44	40
A human element is present in the messages from Allah contained in the sacred texts	92	56	51	60
Knowledge comes from human reason based on empirical evidence rather than from truths revealed to a select few by Allah	66	48	48	51

complex modern society on the Shariah law was not asked in Kazakhstan. In other countries the response rate for agreement ranged from 21 per cent to 10 per cent.

The agreement rate for the statement that the truth about Allah cannot be comprehended by the human mind and that statements about divine matters are only evocative and symbolic ranged from 62 per cent in Pakistan to 32 per cent in Indonesia. A majority of Indonesians agreed that there was a human element involved in the messages from Allah contained in the sacred texts. About half of the respondents held the same views in the other three countries. In response to the statement that knowledge came from human reason and not from truths revealed to a select few by Allah, the agreement was slightly higher in Indonesia (66 per cent) compared with the other three countries where it was around 50 per cent.

The Sociological Correlates of the Liberal Self-Image of Islam

The analysis was extended to an investigation of the sociological correlates of the liberal self-image of Islam. This investigation entailed the construction of an index of 'liberalism' for each country. This was done by scoring 'strongly agree' response as five and 'strongly disagree' response as one for each of the five questions in Table 4.4. The score for each respondent, therefore, could range from between 5 and 25 (except in Kazakhstan where the score ranged from 4 to 20 because one question, 'It is not practical or realistic to base a complex modern society on the Shariah law' was not asked). The distribution in this range once again was calculated using the mid-point of the range for the Egyptian data as the norm.

The respondents with scores of 17 and above were classified as 'liberal'. In each country the distribution of 'liberalism' was computed by gender, lifecycle, human capital and social position of the respondents. The results of this analysis, reported in Table 4.5, show that in Indonesia and Pakistan 43 and 53 per cent of

Table 4.5 'Liberals'* (%)

	Male	Female	>25 years	26-40 years	41-55 years	>56 years	>high school
Indonesia	43	42	40	41	47	41	49
Pakistan	53	55	53	53	46	62	61
Kazakhstan	37	31	33	39	33	29	40
Egypt	33	42	33	35	37	38	42

	High school-some uni.	Completed uni.	Religious Activists	Muslim Professio-nals	Public
Indonesia	41	43	41	44	45
Pakistan	62	49	48	55	57
Kazakhstan	33	42	–	41	45
Egypt	44	34	23	45	35

* By selected characteristics and by countries

males respectively were liberals and there was no difference between men and women. In Kazakhstan and Egypt there were significant differences between men and women. A larger proportion of men were liberal in Kazakhstan and in Egypt it was the opposite. The lower proportion of liberals in Kazakhstan was very likely a consequence of very high 'no answer' response rate because they did not understand the meanings of various statements. It is plausible that most of those who gave the 'no answer' response would have been liberals.

In Indonesia, Pakistan and Egypt older persons were slightly more liberal, whereas in Kazakhstan it was the opposite. In these countries the proportions of liberals declined with educational attainment, but in Kazakhstan it increased slightly. The religious activists were likely to be less liberal in Indonesia, Pakistan and Egypt compared with Muslim professionals and the general public. In all countries except Egypt, Muslim professionals and the general public had about the same proportion of persons with the liberal self-image. In Egypt, Muslim professionals were significantly more liberal compared with the religious activists and the general public.

Relationship between the Liberal Self-Image and Piety

The traditional self-image of Islam was found to be positively related to the two key dimensions of religious piety, namely the ideological dimension and the ritualistic dimension. Is the liberal self-image of Islam also related to these two dimensions of religiosity? To investigate, a correlational analysis was performed and the results of it are shown in Table 4.6.

The results indicate that in Pakistan and Indonesia there was a negative correlation between 'liberalism' and the ideological dimension of piety, but it was only statistically significant in Indonesia. In Egypt there was no correlation, and in Kazakhstan there was a positive correlation between the two variables. The ritualistic dimension, on the other hand, was negatively associated with 'liberalism', but the relationship was statistically significant only in Egypt and Indonesia. Again in Kazakhstan the relationship between the two variables was positive.

While the results of this analysis are not universally consistent, on balance one can argue that those who were very committed religiously at least at the ritualistic level were likely not to subscribe to the liberal-image of Islam. In this regard the results offer a qualified support for Watt's hypothesis. But the positive relationship between the two dimensions of piety and 'liberal-self-image of Islam' is puzzling. One possible reason for this pattern may be the fact reported earlier that the response rate for the liberal-self-image of Islam statements in Kazakhstan was very low. Only about 50 per cent of the Kazakhs responded

Table 4.6 Correlations of liberalism with ideological and ritualistic dimensions of piety

	Indonesia	Pakistan	Kazakhstan	Egypt
Ideological dimension of piety	-.076*	-.025	.159**	.021
Ritualistic dimension of piety	-.103**	-.056	.130*	-110*

* Correlation is significant at the 0.05 level
** Correlation is significant at the 0.01 level

to all 'liberal-self-image' questions. This means that the Kazakhs who participated in the survey were self-selected. In other words, those who did not respond to the questions were most likely the more secular Kazakhs as most of them did not even understand the question. This also means that those who did understand were also likely to be more religiously conscious. However, their responses are positively correlated with 'liberalism'. One possible explanation of this may be that in the post-communist period the Kazakhs, who had lived under the totalitarian governments, saw religion as part of a liberating and democratic transition which they credit for undermining communism, and therefore, subscribe to religion's positive as well as liberal world-view. This is an area which requires further examination of Kazakh religiosity.

A Note on the Fundamentalist Self-Image of Islam

According to the Fundamentalist Project of the American Academy of Arts and Sciences, fundamentalist movements are profoundly affecting the way we live. Religious fundamentalist movements are a common feature of all world religions and are found in all parts of the world. Over the past thirty years they have gained a great deal of prominence and influence, and there is no sign that this situation is likely to change in the foreseeable future.[21]

Fundamentalism is defined as 'a distinctive tendency—a habit of mind and a pattern of behaviour—found within modern religious communities and embodied in certain representative individuals and movements. Fundamentalism is, in other words, 'a religious way of being that manifests itself in a strategy by which the beleaguered believers attempt to preserve their distinctive identity as people or group'.[22] According to this definition, it is a kind of 'moral panic' brought about by a perceived threat to religious identity.

Similar conceptualization of Islamic fundamentalism is implicit in Watt's analysis[23] and in the works of some of the leading Muslim intellectuals like Muhammad Abduh, Hasan al-Banna and Sayyid Abul-Ala Al-Maududi.[24] A prominent American Islamicist, Esposito, also subscribes to a similar view when he argues that notwithstanding its complexity and plurality, Islamic revival is characterised by certain recurrent themes which include:

> a sense that existing political, economic, and social systems had failed; a disenchantment with, and at times a rejection of, the West; a quest for identity and greater authenticity; and the conviction that Islam provides a self-sufficient ideology for state and society, a valid alternative to secular nationalism, socialism and capitalism.[25]

He argues that the experience of failure triggers an identity crisis which feeds religious revival and fundamentalism.

Some of the questions included in the survey provided useful data not only to examine some of the above-mentioned assertions but also to investigate the fundamentalist self-image. Many Muslim intellectuals who were interviewed in this study regarded the term Islamic fundamentalism, as used in the popular discourse in the West, highly objectionable. They regarded it an offensive, pejorative and a deliberately anti-Islamic term. These observations are not baseless.

For most Muslims the term fundamentalism has very distinctive meanings. It connotes religious devotion. Many themselves are sometimes suspicious of fundamentalists (those who display a high degree of religious devotion) for reasons that their religious devotion was only for public display and a facade for their un-Islamic actions in public and private life. The questions which were included in this study sought to explore the meanings and purposes of Islamic fundamentalism. These questions were:

1. The main reason for the Islamic resurgence in the Muslim world is the feeling among Muslims that they are in danger of losing their Islamic identity;

2. Many fundamentalists are educated and sophisticated people who are genuinely concerned about the moral, social,

political and economic failures of their respective societies, and who believe that the answer lies in a return to religious values and lifestyles.

3. The spirit of fundamentalism is constructive rather than destructive.

4. Religious fundamentalist movements are movements that in a direct and self-conscious way fashion a response to modernity.

The respondents were asked to indicate which one of the following responses came closest to expressing their opinion: strongly agree, agree, not sure, disagree, strongly disagree and no answer. An index of agreement was constructed by combining 'strongly agree' and 'agree' responses. Table 4.7 reports the findings. Since a substantial number of these questions elicited a 'no answer' response from a substantial number of respondents, the figures in parenthesis signify the percentage of respondents who gave this response.

The data for the 'moral panic' hypothesis which links Islamic resurgence to the threat to Islamic identity was solicited through the first question in Table 4.7. This data was not available for

Table 4.7 Fundamental self-image (% agreement)

	Indonesia	Pakistan	Kazakhstan	Egypt
The main reason for the Islamic resurgence in the Muslim world is the feeling among Muslims that they are in danger of losing their Islamic identity	54 (8)	60 (14)	31 (29)	—
Many fundamentalists are educated and sophisticated people who are genuinely concerned about moral, social, political and economic failures of their respective societies, and who believe that the answer lies in a return to religious values and lifestyles	58 (26)	56 (29)	15 (50)	68 (9)
The spirit of fundamentalism is constructive rather than destructive	63 (20)	55 (29)	14 (52)	64 (7)
Religious fundamentalist movements are movements that in a direct and self-conscious way fashion a response to modernity	51 (26)	34 (37)	14 (51)	38 (9)

Egypt. In Indonesia and Pakistan over half of the respondents agreed with the statement. The respondents with higher education and those who were religious activists tended to agree more than the other respondents in both countries. In Kazakhstan, where the response rate was around 70 per cent, the agreement rate was 31 per cent suggesting the Kazakhs were less likely to link the threat to Islamic identity to Islamic resurgence like their fellow Muslims in Indonesia and Pakistan. The question that fundamentalists are educated and sophisticated people who are genuinely concerned about the moral, social, political and economic failures of their respective societies and believed that the solution was to return to religious values and life-styles was answered by between 70 to 90 per cent of respondents in Indonesia, Pakistan and Egypt and by only half in Kazakhstan. Over half of the Indonesian, Pakistani and Egyptian respondents agreed with the statement but only 15 per cent did so in Kazakhstan.

The absence of a religiously conscious class in Kazakhstan, a fact of Kazakh history, was obviously a major factor in their perception. The three other countries have a long history of religious activism and one reason for its presence and influence obviously had to do with its positive perception by the people as suggested by evidence. In Indonesia, Pakistan and Egypt education attainment and religious activism was positively correlated with the agreement.

The pattern of response for the statement that 'the spirit of fundamentalism was constructive rather than destructive' further reinforced the findings that for many Muslims religious fundamentalism and revival carried a positive connotation because they construct this phenomenon more in terms of religious devotion than their counterparts in the West tend to do. This is one reason why so often Muslim intellectuals take offence to the term Islamic fundamentalism as it is used in the Western discourse about Islam and the Muslim world.

The final statement that 'religious fundamentalism movements are movements that in a direct and self-conscious way fashion response to modernity' produced a different response pattern.

Only in Indonesia did a majority of the people agree with the statement, whereas in Egypt and Pakistan of those who responded only about one-third agreed with it. In Kazakhstan only a small minority expressed agreement with the statement. These findings suggest that while some Muslims may see religious fundamentalist movements as being shaped by resistance to modernization and globalization, many do not share this view.

This interpretation was further strengthened by the findings that the items discussed here were all positively and significantly correlated with the indexes of the traditional and liberal self-image of Islam discussed earlier in this chapter. The correlation between the fundamentalist image of Islam items and the traditional self-image was much stronger than the correlation between the fundamentalist self-image items and the liberal self-image of Islam.

Towards a Typology of Muslim Social Formations

As mentioned earlier, Gellner[26] has also proposed a typology of Muslim social formations he has called 'High Islam' and 'Folk Islam'. High Islam is characterized by 'scripturalist puritanism', representing the Islam of the ulama or Islamic scholars. It is essentially the Islam of cities because the urban environment has an elective affinity with scripturalist unitarian puritanism. Folk Islam is the Islam of the masses and is deeply influenced by their existential needs and proclivities. Its characteristic institution is the saint cult. The saint is the possessor of charisma with an aura and authority which knows no rules and is contrasted with authority bound by precedent or regulations. This strand of Islam dovetails neatly with the needs of rural and tribal society. It needs arbitrators and mediators who can claim autonomy from the local physical and social conditions in order to be effective. Saintly status makes mediators both viable and authoritative, standing as they do outside the web of alliance and feud. The scholars have the scripture, and the saints have the shrines and traditions. According to Gellner, the boundaries between these two traditions of Islam are not sharp but gradual and sometimes even ambiguous.[27]

If we use the empirical evidence presented in this chapter, we could use the traditional self-image of Islam (traditionalist) as a proxy for the religious orientation of Muslim social formations. The strong identification with the traditional self-image can be called 'High Islam' and the relative weak identification can be labelled as the 'Folk Islam' tradition. Alternatively, we could also use the liberal self-image of Islam as a proxy for the two Islamic traditions.

Gellner has also proposed that Muslim social formations are dominated by two types of elites. He calls them 'socially radical' and 'politically conservative/traditionalist' elites. The conservative/traditionalist elites are those who have their origins in one of those historical Ibn Kaldunian swings of the pendulum which had brought them to power in a fusion of religious enthusiasm and tribal aggression, like the Wahhabism which is now the defining religious symbol of Saudi Arabia and its ruling elite which came to power with it in the eighteenth century. Once in power they maintain their hold on society by claiming that they represent the pristine puritanical Islamic tradition.[28]

The radical elites prevail in those Muslim social formations where either colonialism has destroyed the old elite or a new one has come in from below claiming that it represents a purer and a more fundamentalist type of Islam and has overthrown the old traditional elite as in Iran and Afghanistan. Another route for social radicalism is where the new elite has overthrown the old traditional/ puritanical elite and successfully installed itself to promote radical political secularism as in Turkey or socialism as in Kazakhstan under Soviet rule.

If we contrast the traditionalists ranging from fundamentalist (religiously rigorist) to liberal (religiously lax) on one axis and political radicalism and conservatism along the other axis, we will get the following types of Muslim social formations: fundamentalist-socially radical; liberal-socially radical; fundamentalist-conservative and liberal-conservative. Figure 1 provides a schematic representation of this typology and

Fig. 1 A Typology of Muslim Societies

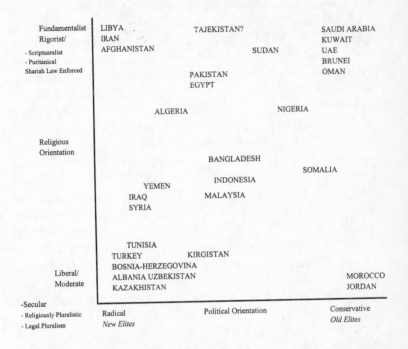

attempts to place the four countries included in this study, along with other major Muslim countries, on the basis of the religious orientation of their elites suggested by the evidence presented here for the four surveyed countries, and extended to other Muslim countries on the basis of understanding of their elites' religious and political orientations.

The fundamentalist-socially radical and the fundamentalist-conservative social formations are those in which 'High Islam' prevails. But they are also very different from each other in terms of social origins of their ruling elite and the type of the Islamic reform agenda of the elite. The elite of the fundamentalist-radical state have an Islamization agenda that involves radical restructuring of the institutional framework of the state and society. The fundamentalist-conservative social formations are largely committed to maintaining the status quo established by their ancestors. Saudi Arabia would be an example of the fundamentalist-conservative state, and Iran would be an example of the fundamentalist-radical state established by Ayatullah Khomeini after the 1979 Islamic revolution which overthrew the Pahlavi dynasty. The Iranian revolution took Iran out of the lower right hand corner and placed it in the upper left-hand corner in Figure 1.

Similarly, it should be possible to chart the political and religious trajectory of Afghanistan of the past fifty years. Until the late 1970s, Afghanistan was a liberal-conservative social formation under the rule of the Afghan King Zahir Shah and located in the lower right hand corner. After the communist coup of 1979, it became a radical-liberal social formation located in the lower left hand corner of Figure 1. After the Taliban took over in the mid-1990s its trajectory again changed radically and it became a fundamentalist-radical social formation.

The liberal-socially radical and liberal-conservative social formations are linked to Gellner's folk Islam. Again the two types of social formations are different from each other in terms of their political and Islamic agenda. The liberal-radical social formations are moderate, legally and religiously pluralistic. They have also come into existence as a result of the overthrow of the old conservative elite by a radical new elite which sought to restructure society and the state along liberal, secular lines. They tend to be self-expressly secular. Modern Turkey and Kazakhstan are examples of this type of social formation. The liberal-conservative social formations are those in which the old conservative elite still prevailed and maintained the historic status quo in the relationship between the state and politics and are largely religiously and politically moderate. Examples include states like Jordan and Morocco.

Gellner's conceptualization of the two traditions of Islam (i.e., two self-images of Islam) lends itself to a very useful typology of contemporary Muslim social formations. Not only that but it also provides an insightful framework to chart the future political and religious trajectory of a Muslim society. The framework described above makes it possible to follow Rahman's observation that, 'It is of the greatest importance to determine exactly where society is at present before deciding where it can go'.[29] It provides sociologists, anthropologists and political scientists interested in contemporary Muslim societies a framework which can be relatively easily applied to empirical study of the nature and direction of social change in them.

Conclusion

The evidence presented in this chapter displays both the plurality and unity of the images of Islam which dominate the intellectual orientation of modern Muslims. The traditional self-image appears to be a dominant feature of modern Muslim consciousness in societies with uninterrupted links to their Islamic heritage. In these societies it frequently co-exists with a liberal self-image. Even in a country like Kazakhstan where such links were ruptured under communism, the traditional self-image appears to be gaining ascendancy. In short, the traditional self-image is a powerful feature of the Muslim mind, and what is striking is that modern education appears to have little impact on bringing about any change in it.

One can almost argue that in some ways modern education appears to reinforce it. The American sociologist Joseph Tamney in his empirical work of Indonesian Islam had noted a similar tendency.[30] Social location does appear to have some impact since the evidence shows that the prevalence of traditional images declines among Muslim professionals.

If these findings validly reflect the social realities of the Muslim world then they also raise some important questions about its future. The new traditionalism that incorporates some of the elements of liberalism may in fact be a reflection of the search for the true faith. At the same time, the moral character it promotes has a powerful impact on the nature of the political and social conditions.

A near universal feature of the prevailing social conditions is the intellectual stagnation of the Muslim world. Anyone familiar with the conditions of the universities in the Muslim world will be aware of the intellectually stifling conditions which prevail in them, making the pursuit of creative and critical scholarship highly problematic. This is especially reflected in the state of science and technology in Muslim countries. According to the Pakistani Nobel Laureate, Dr Abdus Salam:

> There is no question but today, of all civilizations on this planet, science is weakest in the lands of Islam. The dangers of this weakness cannot be over-emphasized since honourable survival of a society depends directly on its strength in science and technology in the condition of the present age.[31]

Empirical evidence of scientific and technological backwardness and stagnation is revealed in a study carried out by two academics from the International Islamic University of Malaysia. Using data from the Science Citation Index produced by the Institute for Scientific Information, Anwar and Abu Bakar[32] show that the total contribution of forty-six Muslim-majority countries who were members of the Organization of Islamic Countries (OIC) to world science literature was a meagre 1.17 per cent of the total output between 1990 and 1994, as compared to 1.66 per cent by India and 1.48 per cent for Spain. The twenty Arab countries contributed only 0.55 per cent to the total scientific output, whereas Israel alone contributed 0.89 per cent in the same period. Some of the reasons for the scientific and technological backwardness are most certainly related to colonialism and the accompanying exploitation. Most Muslim countries went through a period of extended colonial rule, which severely limited opportunities for research and development. However, most of the causes of the present predicament in which Muslim countries find themselves must be attributed to the cultural features and practices which now prevail in them.

The problem of intellectual and scientific stagnation is further compounded by meagre resources allocated for science and development in most Muslim countries. On average Muslim countries spend 0.45 per cent of their GNP on research and development as compared to 2.30 per cent for the OECD (Organization for Economic Co-operation and Development). Muslim countries are also far behind in research and development manpower. On average, Muslim countries have 8.8 scientists, engineers and technicians per 1000 population as compared to 40.7 of world average and 139.3 for OECD countries.[33] A wider survey of this problem is given in an excellent book on science and Islam by Hoodbhoy.[34]

If Muslim countries are to succeed in improving the social and economic conditions of their citizens, they would need vibrant, free and intellectually challenging centres of learning to prepare their citizens for the 'knowledge economy' of the third industrial revolution which is now around us. The prevalence of the traditional self-image and the resulting religious orthodoxy and the spirit of intolerance are two major causes that can make the pursuit of objective scholarship highly problematic because of the kind of ideological control which the traditional world-view imposes. To borrow a concept from Mohammad Arkoun, the prevailing conditions in Muslim societies do not encourage Muslim intellectuals to think the 'unthinkable' and the 'unthought' but only what he calls the 'thinkable'.[35]

The evidence gathered in this study clearly shows that devotional religiosity is increasing among Muslims and this is happening at a time when the influence of Islam is also increasing in the world. Under these conditions, Muslims will be called upon to address problems of the modern age ranging from issues of equality for all citizens, including women and children, to ethical issues raised by the advancement in modern science and technology, management of human sexuality, environmental degradation, authoritarian state, rule of law, political and cultural freedom and new approaches to understanding and treating deviant behaviour. These and other modern problems would require a common understanding based on rational and scientific knowledge.

It would be absurd to argue that the Muslim approach should be based on some other principles. The prevalence of the traditional self-image only reflects the increase in devotional religiosity. But it can indirectly contribute to the rise of Islamic activism of all types, some of which may be contrary to the dictates of knowledge and common sense. One observation which has been made but which needs repeating is that for Muslims the notion of fundamentalism is something distinct from what is implied in the contemporary Western discourse on Islam.

For Muslims fundamentalism primarily refers to devotional religiosity and not to anti-Western political activism. Another implication of the findings is that in terms of the relationship between the West and the Islamic world, the religious developments in the Muslim world and the corresponding self-images may be contributing to a kind of moral polarization where Muslims see themselves as highly moral and others as the opposite. Such a development, besides being wrong, because of the over simplification it implies, would not be conducive to better international and inter-religious understanding.

The typology of Muslim social formations which has been developed by combining the theoretical insights of Gellner and the empirical evidence of this study can be a valuable tool for sociologists to undertake an empirical study of the social, political and religious trajectories of modern Muslim societies.

NOTES

1. Watt 1988, p. 1.
2. Watt 1988, pp. 71-77.
3. Watt 1988, p. 71.
4. Watt 1988, p. 2.
5. Watt 1988, pp. 8-14.
6. Rahman 1982, p. 38.
7. Watt 1988, p. 61.
8. Maududi 1960.
9. Ibn Khaldun 1958.
10. Hume 1976.
11. Hodgson 1975.
12. Gellner 1969; 1981.
13. Gellner 1981, 1992.

14. Gellner 1994, p. 22.
15. Gellner 1969.
16. Gellner 1981, 1992.
17. Rahman 1982, p. 46.
18. Rahman 1982, chapter 4.
19. Mernissi, 1988; 1996.
20. Watt 1982, p. 2.
21. Marty and Appleby 1991, 1992, 1994.
22. Marty and Appleby 1992, p. 34.
23. Watt 1988, chapter 3.
24. Abduh 1965; Maududi 1966.
25. Esposito 1995, p. 14.
26. Gellner 1981.
27. Gellner 1981, pp. 40-56.
28. Gellner 1981, pp. 62-69.
29. Rahman 1982, p. 162.
30. Tamney 1980.
31. Cited in Hoodbhoy 1991, p. 28.
32. Anwar and Abu Bakar 1996.
33. Anwar and Abu Bakar 1996.
34. Hoodbhoy 1991.
35. Arkoun 1994, chapter 1.

5

ISLAMIC STATE
Political Organization and Islamic Institutions

As stated in Chapter 1, the relationship between politics and religion in Muslim societies has been a focus of debate among scholars of Islam. A commonly stated view of many scholars of Islam is that Islam is not only a religion but also a blueprint for social order and therefore encompasses all domains of life, including law and the state.[1] It is further argued that this characterization sets Islamic societies apart from Western societies which are based upon the separation of state and religious institutions.

Lapidus[2] and Keddie[3] have pointed out that, notwithstanding several examples of state control of religion in Western societies, these differences are commonly used to account for the different developmental trajectories of Western and Islamic societies. Western societies, with their separation of church and state, of civil and religious law, are said to have promoted an autonomous domain for secular culture and civil society, which together form the bases of modernity. In Islamic societies, the lack of differentiation between the secular and the sacred has inhibited such development.[4]

After reviewing the evidence concerning the separation of state and religion in Islamic history, Lapidus[5] concluded that the history of the Muslim world revealed two main institutional configurations. The undifferentiated state-religious configuration characterized a small number of Middle Eastern societies. This configuration was characteristic of lineage or tribal societies. The historic norm for agro-urban Islamic societies was an institutional configuration that recognized the division between state and religious spheres:

> Despite the common statement (and the Muslim ideal) that the institutions of state and religion are unified, and that Islam is a total way of life which defines political as well as social and family matters, most Muslim societies did not conform to this ideal, but were built around separate institutions of state and religion.[6]

Keddie[7] has described the supposed near-identity of religion and the state in Islam as 'more a pious myth than reality for most of Islamic history.' Similar views of Islamic history have also been advanced by others.[8]

. The weight of historical scholarship indicates that the institutional configurations of Islamic societies can be classified into two types: a) differentiated social formations (i.e., societies in which religion and state occupy different space), and b) undifferentiated social formations (i.e., societies in which religion and state are integrated). While a majority of Islamic societies have been and are 'differentiated social formations,' a small but significant number have been and are societies which can be classified as 'undifferentiated social formations.' A label commonly used in contemporary discourse for undifferentiated Muslim social formations is 'Islamic State.'

Irrespective of the historical evidence, relations between the state and religion are an important issue in contemporary Muslim countries. Many Muslim countries are a product of the process of decolonization in this century, where nationalist movements were spearheaded by relatively secular leaders. These new states have defined their identities in nationalist terms and in many cases have preserved the secular legal, educational and political institutions inherited from the colonial era. Islamic revival movements have emerged in many Muslim countries, however, and in general they denounce the trend toward secularization, calling for the return to a state that represents and embodies Islam and enforces an Islamic way of life.[9] The Islamic way of

life they envisage will be based on the Shariah law and primacy
of religious institutions in social life.

Whereas in the past only Saudi Arabia defined itself as an
Islamic state, now countries like Iran, Libya, Afghanistan and
Sudan have become Islamic states, and while all of them define
themselves and function as Islamic states, they differ from one
another in many significant ways. Another major Muslim
country, Pakistan, is following the path of integrating Islam into
the state apparatus. A Constitutional Amendment Bill seeks to
make the Qur'an and Sunnah the supreme law of the land.
Algeria is currently enduring a bloody struggle for the
establishment of an Islamic state. In Turkey, the power of the
Kemalist secular state has come under muted challenge from
the Islamic Refah Party.

As argued in Chapter 4, the relationship between religion and
the state is influenced by the internal dynamics of Muslim
societies. These dynamics are grounded in the relationship
between the two traditions of Islam, namely the 'High Islam' of
the ulama and the 'folk' or 'popular Islam' of the masses. These
two styles or traditions of Islam provide a built-in mechanism
for self-rectification and purification which periodically
manifests in 'differentiation' and 'dedifferentiation' between
religion and politics in Muslim countries. The dynamics of the
relationship between these two traditions offer the possibility
for Muslim societies to move from one to the other.

Although relations between the state and religious institutions
are a significant concern of the Islamic world, there is no
empirical study of the attitudes of Muslims towards different
institutional configurations. The issue here is whether religious
institutions enjoy more or less trust in the public mind in
differentiated Muslim social formations, in which religion and
the state are separate, than in undifferentiated Muslim social
formations, in which religion and the state are closely integrated.
Assuming that the general character of a society is the reflection
of some kind of collective will of its people, it can be argued
that in an undifferentiated Muslim social formation (i.e., an
Islamic state), the religious institutions are likely to enjoy equal

or greater trust among the people compared with the same phenomena in differentiated Muslim social formations. Following this line of reasoning, we can hypothesize that:

> The level of trust in religious institutions in an undifferentiated Muslim social formation (i.e., Islamic state) will be higher than in a differentiated Muslim social formation.

The underlying logic of the relationship between the level of trust and the institutional configuration postulated in this hypothesis may also influence the relationship between trust in the religious institutions and trust in key institutions of the state. A likely expression of such an influence may be that the relationship between these institutions will be more positive in undifferentiated than in differentiated Muslim social formations. This relationship can be more formally stated in the following corollary hypothesis:

> The relationship between the level of trust in religious institutions and the level of trust in key institutions of the state will be stronger in an undifferentiated Muslim social formation than in a differentiated Muslim social formation.

Using the survey data gathered in this study these two hypotheses will be examined in this chapter. The four countries included in this study represent a significant cross-section of Muslim countries. They include three differentiated Muslim societies, Indonesia, Kazakhstan and Egypt, and one that is undifferentiated relative to the previous three, Pakistan. While Pakistan is not a theocratic state, there have been significant developments over the past twenty years that have resulted in the integration of Islam into the state apparatus.[10] (The most recent development in this regard was the introduction of the '15th Amendment Bill' by the government of the former Prime Minister Nawaz Sharif in August 1998). Countries like Saudi Arabia and Iran which at present are among the more striking examples of undifferentiated Muslim social formations could not be included in this study for logistical reasons but hopefully will be included in a future study.

A useful way to see the difference between the four countries is to focus on their respective state ideologies. The guiding political ideology of the Indonesian state is the Javanese concept of *Pancasila*, which, as a state doctrine, consists of five basic principles: belief in God, humanitarianism, national unity, democracy, and social justice. This state ideology was adopted in 1945 at the time of Indonesia's independence from the Dutch. At that time, the founding president of the Republic of Indonesia, President Sukarno, resisted the demands of Indonesian Islamic leaders who wanted a state based on Islam, and persuaded them to accept his broader, secular formulation.

Indonesian governments have maintained a steadfast commitment to *Pancasila* and have repeatedly stressed that it is rooted in Indonesian society and is the only ideology that can unite the country. The *Pancasila* is generally seen as a *perjanian luhur* (noble agreement) of the Indonesian Nation, and is expected to be honoured and respected by all Indonesians. Religion remains a private matter in Indonesia and is interpreted within the confines of *Pancasila*.[11] Civil servants are required to take *Pancasila* indoctrination courses, and all social, political and religious organizations are required to adopt it as their *azas tunggal* (sole fundamental principle).

Kazakhstan is also a secular society and its constitution contains no provision for the integration of religion in any organ of the state. Article 1:1 of the Constitution of the Republic of Kazakhstan states, 'The Republic of Kazakhstan is a democratic, modern state that respects the rule of law. The highest value of society is the human being: his or her life, rights and freedom'.[12] Similarly, the Constitution of the Arab Republic of Egypt also enunciates the state ideology. Article 1 states, 'The Arab Republic of Egypt is a Socialist Democratic State based on the alliance of the working forces of the people. The Egyptian people are part of the Arab Nation and work for the realization of its comprehensive unity.' Article 2 states that Islam is the religion of the state and that Shariah is the principal source of legislation. However, the Constitution categorically acknowledges that, 'Sovereignty is for the people alone who will practise and protect this sovereignty and safeguard national unity...'.[13]

Pakistan is the only country among the four studied whose constitution formally declares it to be an Islamic Republic and recognizes the sovereignty of Allah.[14] The first principle of the Preamble to the Constitution states, 'Whereas sovereignty over the entire Universe belongs to Almighty Allah alone, and the authority to be exercised by the people of Pakistan within the limits prescribed by Him is a sacred trust.' According to Part IX, Article 227:1, 'All existing laws shall be brought in conformity with the Injunctions of Islam as laid down in the Holy Quran and Sunnah... and no law shall be enacted which is repugnant to such Injunctions.' In view of the foregoing, we can say that among the four countries only Pakistan declares itself to be an Islamic State and makes clear-cut provisions for the integration of religion and the state.

Pakistan, therefore, can be used as a proxy for an undifferentiated Muslim society (i.e., a state society based on the integration of Islam and the state), and Indonesia, Egypt and Kazakhstan will be used as proxies for differentiated Muslim societies (i.e., state societies based on the separation of religion and the state). Another way to distinguish between these two types may be that the differentiated Muslim society is based on the notion of 'popular sovereignty,' whereas the undifferentiated Muslim society accepts 'divine sovereignty.' Such a classification will produce the same typology of Muslim societies as stated above.

Religious Institutions and the State

As mentioned earlier, relations between the state and religious institutions and communities are a central concern in the Islamic World. Notwithstanding the importance given to this issue, there have been no systematic empirical investigations of the subject.

This study is an attempt to fill this gap in our knowledge. The respondents in all four countries were asked how much trust they had in key institutions of the state and civil society. The analysis in this chapter is based on the response to that question, which was posed as follows: 'I am going to name a number of organizations. For each one, could you tell me how much you trust them to tell the truth and to do what is best for the country? Is it, a great deal of trust, quite a lot of trust, not very much trust, none at all, or do not know?'[15] The institutions about which the respondents' opinions were sought were the following:

Ulama[16]	Parliament	Press	Universities
Imam Masjid[17]	Courts	Television	Schools
Pirs/Kiyai[18]	Civil Service	Major Companies	Intellectuals
	Political Parties		
	Armed Forces		

In computing the trust scores from the data the two categories of 'a great deal of trust' and 'quite a lot of trust' were combined to arrive at a composite index of trust. Similarly, the 'do not trust' categories were combined, and the single score for this was generated by combining the two low trust categories with the 'do not know' category.

The findings of the survey data are reported in Table 5.1. They show that there are wide variations as well as similarities among respondents in the four countries in terms of their trust in core institutions of religion and the state. Kazakhstan stands out as a country in which Muslims universally have very low confidence in the key institutions of society. This is most likely a function of the dramatic changes that have occurred in Kazakhstan over the past decade. The impression gathered during the fieldwork was that most people were disoriented by the economic and social changes that followed the collapse of the former Soviet Union. These changes had reduced the total worth of Kazakhstan's Gross Domestic Product by half, thus

Table 5.1 Trust in Key Institutions (%)

Institution	Pakistan	Indonesia	Egypt	Kazakhstan
Ulama	48	96	90	24
Imam Masjid	44	94	83	22
Pirs / Kiyai	21	91	52	21
Parliament	22	53	34	19
Courts	55	55	76	16
Civil Service	26	58	44	11
Political Parties	12	35	28	12
Armed Forces	82	68	78	33
Press	38	84	54	33
Television	31	80	49	37
Major Companies	29	42	45	14
Universities	60	88	70	33
Schools	71	92	68	48
Intellectuals	66	92	81	37

adversely affecting the lives of ordinary citizens.[19] Many of them were disillusioned and very apprehensive about the future, and the data reflect this. In relative terms, roughly three out of ten respondents trusted the armed forces, press, television, universities and intellectuals. However, the religious institutions of the ulama, Imam masjid and pirs enjoyed much more trust than the key institutions of the state. This is rather surprising, given that most Kazakhs were not actively involved in religion during the Soviet era. As argued earlier Kazakhstan would need to be considered a special case. The other three countries can be compared with greater confidence, which is the strategy adopted in this paper.

Indonesia, Egypt and Pakistan, unlike Kazakhstan, are large, predominantly Muslim countries that have been ruled by the indigenous ruling classes for at least half a century. The key state institutions in these countries, namely the parliament, courts, civil service and political parties, enjoy moderate to low levels of trust in the public mind. The armed forces are trusted by a considerable majority of people, and in Pakistan in particular they are the most trusted institution of society. The most striking differences between the countries, however, relate to trust in the Islamic institutions. In Indonesia and Egypt, the ulama and the Imam masjid are the most trusted institutions of civil society. The institution of pirs/kiyai is very highly trusted in Indonesia, but less so in Egypt. In Pakistan, however, the situation is entirely different: all three Islamic institutions are trusted by less than half of the respondents.

Three other institutions that are trusted by a significant majority of the respondents in Indonesia, Egypt and Pakistan are the intellectuals, the universities and the schools. The level of trust in these three institutions is particularly high in Indonesia. The mass media is respected highly in Indonesia, moderately in Egypt, and not very highly in Pakistan and Kazakhstan. The empirical evidence presented in Table 5.1 does not support the hypothesis.

These findings are interesting because this is the first time such an empirical investigation has been carried out in four major Muslim communities in different regions of the world, and in different social formations. Intuitively, one would expect that since Pakistan is the only undifferentiated social formation of the four countries under study, the level of trust in the religious institutions should be relatively high. The results are the *exact opposite*. It is also worth mentioning that one does not expect religious institutions to be held in such high esteem in Indonesia and Egypt. During my field trips to these countries I never heard of any study which showed that the religious institutions were the most trusted institutions in these countries. In relative terms, even the trust shown in religious institutions in Kazakhstan as compared with state institutions was surprising, although, as said before, one must treat Kazakhstan as a special case, given its recent history. In view of the evidence reported in Table 5.1, we can say that the faithlines in contemporary Indonesian and Egyptian societies are very clearly delineated. The state institutions are held in low to moderate esteem, and the religious institutions are held in the highest esteem. In

Table 5.2 Results of Logistic Regression Analysis: Country Differences Controlling for Age, Gender, Education, Sample Group, Religiosity and Conservatism

	Ulama	Imam Masjid	Pirs/Kiyai	Parliament	Courts	Civil Service	Political Parties
Age	**1.01**	**1.01**	**1.01**	**1.01**	1.01	**1.02**	**1.02**
Male	1.00	1.00	1.00	1.00	1.00	1.00	1.00
Female	0.93	**0.76**	1.10	0.93	0.88	1.01	1.03
High School	1.00	1.00	1.00	1.00	1.00	1.00	1.00
HS/Some College	0.89	1.03	0.98	**1.35**	1.23	**1.42**	**1.69**
Coll/Univ/P-G	**0.65**	**0.61**	0.83	**1.24**	1.33	**1.64**	**1.42**
Religious	1.00	1.00	1.00	1.00	1.00	1.00	1.00
Not very religious	0.42	0.48	0.58	**0.79**	**0.73**	0.87	**0.75**
Pakistan	1.00	1.00	1.00	1.00	1.00	1.00	1.00
Indonesia	**26.69**	**17.28**	**39.00**	**3.80**	0.96	**4.09**	**3.97**
Egypt	**13.82**	**11.31**	**3.36**	**1.99**	**3.63**	**2.49**	**2.77**
Kazakhstan	**0.38**	**0.32**	**1.07**	0.83	**0.17**	**0.37**	1.02

	Armed Forces	Press	TV	Major Companies	Univ.	Schools	Intellectuals
Age	**1.02**	**1.00**	**1.01**	**1.01**	**1.01**	**1.01**	**1.00**
Male	1.00	1.00	1.00	1.00	1.00	1.00	1.00
Female	0.90	**1.22**	**1.42**	1.01	0.89	1.04	0.98
High School	1.00	1.00	1.00	1.00	1.00	1.00	1.00
HS/Some College	**1.64**	1.30	1.07	1.27	1.68	**1.85**	**2.10**
Coll/Univ/P-G	**1.51**	1.24	1.11	1.36	1.97	**1.69**	**2.23**
Religious	1.00	1.00	1.00	1.00	1.00	1.00	1.00
Not very religious	**0.66**	0.94	0.94	1.01	0.62	**0.64**	**0.77**
Pakistan	1.00	1.00	1.00	1.00	1.00	1.00	1.00
Indonesia	**0.40**	**7.75**	**8.46**	1.68	4.79	**4.44**	**5.56**
Egypt	1.03	2.09	**2.52**	2.09	1.73	1.01	**2.48**
Kazakhstan	**0.10**	**0.68**	1.18	0.37	0.42	**0.41**	**0.33**

Note: Bold numbers indicate a statistically significant relationship.

Pakistan, both state and religious institutions are held in low esteem, and a similar pattern prevails in Kazakhstan.

Are these differences an artifact of statistics or survey methodology? Indirect confirmation of the level of trust in religious institutions was provided by the findings of a 1996 Gallup Pakistan survey on Important Social Issues. A randomly selected sample of 821 urban respondents were asked how much they trusted the following institutions: military, religious scholars, industries, courts, newspapers, parliament, politicians, government officials and police. The results were: military 78 per cent, religious scholars 44 per cent, industries 38 per cent, courts 34 per cent, newspapers 29 per cent, parliament 21 per cent, politicians 19 per cent, government officials 17 per cent, police 10 per cent.[20] The results of the Gallup Survey are remarkably similar to the results of the present study, and provide an external validation of the findings reported here as they relate to Pakistan.

In order to investigate the possible effects of the demographic and sociological characteristics of the four samples, a logistic regression analysis was carried out. In this analysis, different controls were applied and the results are reported in Table 5.2 below. The most notable finding of the analysis was that after controlling for age, gender, educational attainment and self-reported religiosity, the level of trust in religious institutions in Indonesia and Egypt was significantly higher as compared with Pakistan. In Kazakhstan, however, the level of trust was significantly lower as compared with Pakistan. The findings of the logistic regression analysis clearly indicate that the differences in the levels of trust in religious institutions in the four countries are not an artifact of different sample compositions.

The results of logistic regression also indicate that the observed differences in the level of trust are not due to the cultural differences between the different countries being studied. By this is meant the propensity in some cultures for individuals to be more acquiescent in public. The variations in the logistic regression coefficients for the level of trust in different institutions would tend to counter arguments for such a bias. The results of the logistic regression show that Pakistani respondents are likely to distrust the religious institutions many times more as compared with the level of trust in the other institutions. This would suggest that in Pakistan, religious institutions are distrusted significantly more than in Indonesia or Egypt.

Relationship between Trust in Religious Institutions and Trust in Key State Institutions

Earlier it was hypothesized that, 'The relationship between the level of trust in religious institutions and the level of trust in key institutions of the state will be stronger in an undifferentiated Muslim social formation than in a differentiated Muslim social formation'. In order to test this proposition, the average percentages of trust in the three religious institutions, namely the ulama, Imam masjid and pirs/kiyai, and in the four state institutions, namely the parliament, political parties, civil service and courts, were computed. The findings of these calculations are reported in Tables 5.3 and 5.4. Table 5.3 reports the relationship between the level of trust in the key institutions of the state and the three religious institutions in each country. The figures in Table 5.4 provide a summary of the relationship between the average percentage of different levels of trust in the three religious institutions and the four institutions of the state.

These findings show that an increase in trust in religious institutions is associated with increased trust in the institutions of the state in Egypt, Indonesia and Pakistan. This association did not apply in Kazakhstan, and most likely this was due to the special historical conditions mentioned earlier. Another notable trend discernible from the evidence is that compared with respondents in Egypt and Indonesia, the average percentage of those in Kazakhstan who trusted the religious institutions and the key state institutions was significantly lower. This is

Table 5.3 Level of Trust in Ulama, Imam Masjid and Kiyai by Level of Trust in Key Institutions of the State

	Lot of Trust	Trust	No Trust
ULAMA			
Egypt	53	43	19
Indonesia	55	40	18
Pakistan	40	37	21
Kazakhstan	27	49	43
IMAM MASJID			
Egypt	54	46	20
Indonesia	58	43	25
Pakistan	44	34	23
Kazakhstan	20	37	37
KIYAI			
Egypt	56	50	42
Indonesia	57	42	33
Pakistan	42	39	26
Kazakhstan	21	47	33

Note: The figures are the average percentages of different levels of trust in the four institutions of the state, namely, parliament, political parties, civil service and courts and the three religious institutions.

Table 5.4. Level of Trust in Key Institutions of the State by Level of Trust in Religious Institutions

	A Lot of Trust	Trust	No Trust
Pakistan	42	37	23
Indonesia	57	42	25
Egypt	54	46	27
Kazakhstan	23	44	38

Note: The figures are the average percentage of trust in the three religious institutions, namely ulama, Imam masjid and pirs/kiyai, and the four state institutions, namely parliament, political parties, civil service and courts.

consistent with the findings reported earlier pertaining to the main hypothesis.

Based on the preceding examination of the data, we can now conclude that:

a) The differences in the levels of trust in Pakistan, Indonesia and Egypt are most likely to be produced by political and social dynamics, and not by cultural dynamics or methodological biases;

b) The same reasoning can be extended to explain the very low level of trust in political and religious institutions in Kazakhstan;

c) Low levels of trust in religious institutions in society negatively impact the level of trust in state institutions.

Interpretation and Discussion

What could be a possible explanation of these findings and what are their sociological implications? An explanatory hypothesis could be constructed in the following way. Given that in all of the societies under study there is a relatively low level of trust in key state institutions, we can hypothesize that a dialectical process is created by the social and political conditions within which key state institutions enjoy only low levels of esteem, and consequently legitimacy, among their citizens.

The main business of the state is to govern and manage the affairs of society in a fair and unbiased manner. When the state or its key institutions lack social/political legitimacy in the public mind, the state must use varying degrees of coercion to ensure compliance. This the citizens inevitably resist, which in turn produces a more authoritarian state response. This generates further resistance, and so a cycle of authoritarian response and resistance develops. The state ultimately comes to be seen as authoritarian, oppressive and unfair, and leads to political mobilization against the state. The institutions of civil society which act as the mobilizers of this resistance gain in public trust and consequently come to enjoy high levels of esteem and legitimacy among the public.

This model can explain the high level of trust in religious as well as other institutions of civil society—like the schools, universities and public intellectuals—in Indonesia and Egypt. Since both these societies are examples of differentiated Muslim social formations, the religious institutions play a public role in the mobilization of resistance to the state, thereby increasing their esteem in the public mind. Universities, schools and public intellectuals are also held in high esteem for the same reason. In Pakistan, however, the situation is different. Pakistan is an undifferentiated social formation and therefore the erosion of trust in state institutions also corrodes trust in the religious institutions which are perceived as part of the state. The schools, intellectuals and universities are probably trusted because of their role as mobilizers of resistance against a state perceived as weak, ineffectual and authoritarian. The low level of trust in religious institutions in Pakistan further reduces the trust in the state institutions. In the case of Kazakhstan, the disintegration of the former Soviet Union has resulted in unparalleled political, social and economic insecurity, and the low level of trust in all institutions is probably indicative of that insecurity, but again, the logic of the model applied in the case of Indonesia, Egypt and Pakistan can also be applicable to Kazakhstan.

The high level of trust in the armed forces could be a function of the underlying dynamics of the proposed model. The state's lack of legitimacy may create or aggravate an underlying sense of insecurity among the people. It may be that this sense of insecurity produces a positive perception of the armed forces as a compensatory force for the perceived sense of insecurity. In Pakistan the very high level of trust could also be due to the perception in the public mind of a military and political threat from India, which the Pakistan Government promotes as a matter of public policy to justify its huge allocations of public revenues to the armed forces. The recent military coup against the democratically elected government of Prime Minister Nawaz Sharif provoked no popular resistance from the public. On the contrary, it was largely welcomed by the Pakistani people. This public behaviour is consistent with our findings that the most trusted institution in Pakistan is the armed forces.

An alternative explanation of the findings can also be constructed by applying Luhmann's typology of the role of religion in modern society. According to Luhmann[21] a distinctive feature of modern society is institutional differentiation and functional specialization. This gives rise to autonomous 'functional instrumentalities' such as polity, law, economy, science, education, health, art, family and religion. One consequence of the relative institutional autonomy is that the major institutions become independent of religious norms and values, which Luhmann calls 'secularization.' In such conditions, the degree of public influence that religion enjoys depends on how it relates to other social systems in society. Luhmann uses the terms 'function' and 'performance' to analyse this relationship.

'Function' in this context refers to 'pure' religious communication, variously called devotion and worship, the care of souls, the search for salvation and enlightenment. 'Function' is the pure, social communication involving the transcendent and the aspect that religious institutions claim for themselves on the basis of their autonomy in modern society. Religious 'performance,' by contrast, occurs when religion is 'applied' to problems generated in other institutional systems but not solved there or simply not addressed anywhere else, such as economic poverty, corruption, political oppression, etc. Religious institutions gain public influence through the 'performance' role by addressing these non-religious or 'profane' problems. The functional problem of religion in modern society is a performance problem.

Religious institutions gain public influence when they efficiently carry out their performance role. This requires religious institutions to be autonomous *vis-à-vis* the state and other institutional sub-systems. A logical deduction of this is that religious institutions will gain greater public influence in institutional configurations in which they are autonomous from the state. If they are not, then they cannot carry out their performance role effectively. In the context of the present study, this means that religious institutions will enjoy, at least theoretically, greater public influence in a differentiated social formation than in an undifferentiated one. The findings of this study would appear to support Luhmann's analysis.

Viewed from this perspective, the findings may have important implications for the institutional configuration of the state in Muslim countries. An Islamic state that lacks trust, and consequently political legitimacy, in the public mind, may in fact cause an erosion of trust in Islamic institutions, thereby further weakening the fabric of civil society. For the religious elite in Muslim countries, the message of these findings is that an Islamic State may not always be in the best interest of Islamic institutions and religious elite. To promote a constructive socio-cultural, moral and religious role for religious institutions within a Muslim society, it may be prudent to keep faithlines separate from the state, and thereby prevent them from becoming the faultlines of the political terrain.

These findings also have implications for the ruling elite, particularly in differentiated Muslim societies. As we have noted, the findings show a feedback effect. The level of trust in religious institutions is directly related to the level of trust in the institutions of the state (see Table 5.4). This means that attempts to dis-establish Islam may have adverse consequences for the level of trust in and legitimacy of the state itself. The implication for the international community is that if an Islamic state were to come into existence through democratic and constitutional means, support for such a state could in the long run pave the way for the development of a kind of differentiated Muslim social formation.

As in the case of Pakistan, the Islamic elite may need to make some compromises with the state over time to ensure a stronger socio-cultural, moral and political role for religion in the society at large. This could be a type of 'secularization' of religion that manifests itself in calls to limit the political role of religion.

Recent political developments in the Islamic Republic of Iran provide a good example of this phenomenon. Since the late 1980s, the Mayor of Tehran, Gholamhosain Karbaschi, has been redesigning the city, and as a result of this, Tehran has assumed a new character. Instead of resembling an Islamic city in its spatial configurations and symbolism, it is more reminiscent of Madrid and Los Angeles, with its freeways, huge billboards and shopping malls, than Karbala or Qom.[22] At the intellectual level, the most dramatic evidence of the new Iran is the Alternative Thought Movement, led by philosopher Abdolkarim Soroush, a former ideologue of the Islamic state. The Alternative Thought Movement has gained widespread support in all sections of Iranian society, including theology students. They are concerned about the future of religion as an institution; they feel the basis of their legitimacy and prerogatives is being eroded amid the growing anti-clericalism in Iranian society.

The Alternative Thought Movement is neither anti-Islamic nor secular, but seeks to redefine the capacity of religion to address complex human needs in the modern age. It calls for a hermeneutic reading of the Qur'an, rejecting a 'single reading' or an exclusive 'expert reading' by the ulama. The movement seeks to end the professionalization of religious interpretation by clergy. It serves as an implicit critique of the idea of *velayat-i faqih*, the rule of the supreme jurist, which is the political basis of contemporary Iran. It advocates management of society not through religion but through scientific rationality. It calls for the establishment of a secular democratic state that accommodates Islam as a faith.[23]

Probably the most significant evidence of the Iranian State's pragmatic accommodation of the 'secular' domain of Iranian society was the 1989 amendment to the constitution, sanctioned by Ayatollah Khomeini, which empowered the government to disregard Shariah provisions in policy and legislation. This amendment allows the Islamic government to set aside Shariah principles, including the fundamental pillars of the faith such as prayers and fasting, if it is in the general interest of the Muslim nation. The amendment also gives the government far-reaching powers to decide when the provisions of Muslim law are, or are not, binding. Given that the 'tenets of Islam' are the ultimate constitutional limit on legislation and government power, their effective removal affords the government and parliament unlimited powers. This kind of development could only occur in an Islamic State.[24]

· The wide support for the Alternative Thought Movement in Iranian society was one of the reasons behind the recent election of the new and relatively moderate president of the Republic. This election and the support for the Alternative Thought Movement and other similar movements would suggest that important changes are taking place in Iranian society and that the ruling classes are making appropriate adjustments. This may be an indication that the political pendulum in Iran is gradually moving back to the centre, thus paving the way for the rise of at least a *de facto* differentiated Muslim social formation. It would also indicate the monumental misreading of the Algerian situation, which has resulted in protracted carnage and the loss of innocent human life.

In summary, the findings reported in this chapter show that the integration of religion and the state in Muslim countries may not always be in the best interests of Islamic institutions and the religious elite, because when a state carries a deficit of trust in the public mind, public trust in religious institutions can also be eroded. This could have serious social, cultural, political and religious implications. For example, if the public lacks trust in the institutions of the ulama and Imam masjid, this could significantly undermine their economic and social well-being and could lead them to create circumstances or support demands that might not be conducive to the profession and promotion of the universality of Islam. (Here one can speculate about the influence of the *madrasas* [religious schools] in Pakistan on the rise of the Taliban political and religious movement in neighbouring Afghanistan.)[25] This would also suggest that religious institutions within a Muslim society continue to play a constructive social, cultural and religious role when religion is kept separate from the state and when these institutions enjoy an appropriate place in the institutional configurations of the society. It may be prudent, therefore, to keep faith separate from the state.

Because of the feedback effect of the level of trust in religious institutions which has been noted earlier, the findings of this chapter may also have implications for the relationship between the state and religion in Muslim countries. As the level of trust in religious institutions is directly related to the level of trust in the institutions of the state, it follows that attempts to destabilize Islam may have adverse consequences for the level of trust as well as its legitimacy of the state. It has also been argued that the undifferentiated Muslim social formation tends to evolve over time towards a kind of differentiated Muslim social formation. An Islamic state, therefore, may also be a route to the social and political development of Muslim societies in which religion and state coexist in an autonomous but mutually cooperative relationship.

There is, of course, the logical possibility of a Muslim society which is characterized by high levels of trust in and esteem for the state, and in which there is also a high level of trust in religious institutions. However, as far as I know, there are no contemporary examples of such a situation that can be readily identified. This raises the interesting question of why this is so? Does it mean that such a situation is not possible, or could such a situation possibly come about under circumstances in which different political arrangements prevail between Islam and the state? It is hoped that this question as well as the findings of this chapter will stimulate further debate and discussion on the relationship between the state and religious institutions in Muslim countries.

NOTES

1. Maududi 1960, Lewis 1993, Rahman 1982, Watt 1988, Pipes 1981, Esposito 1992, Weber 1978, Turner 1974, Gellner 1981.
2. Lapidus 1996.
3. Keddie 1994.
4. Weber 1978, Crone 1980, Lewis 1993, Huntington 1996.
5. Lapidus 1996.
6. Lapidus 1996, p. 24.
7. Keddie 1994, p. 463.
8. Zubaida 1989, Sadowski 1997, Ayubi 1991, Sivan 1985.
9. Lapidus 1996, Beinin and Stork 1997, Esposito 1992, Marty and Appleby 1993.
10. Hassan 1985, Ahmad 1991, Weiss 1986.
11. Adnan 1990, Budiman 1990, Madjid 1980.
12. Constitution of the Republic of Kazakhstan, 1993.
13. Constitution of the Arab Republic of Egypt, 1990.
14. Constitution of the Islamic Republic of Pakistan, 1973.
15. Readers who are familiar with the World Value Survey will know that this is a modified version of the question posed there.
16. Ulama refers to scholars, jurists and teachers learned in the Islamic sciences. For a general discussion of the nature and functions of the Islamic institutions of Ulama, Imam Masjid and Pirs/Kiyai, see Keddie 1972.
17. Imam Masjid are the leaders of the daily mandatory prayers in Muslim mosques. See Keddie 1972.
18. Pirs and Kiyai are leaders of folk or popular Islam. The nomenclature used to describe or refer to this institution varies in different countries. See Keddie 1972, Mayer 1967, Gellner 1969 and Dhofier 1980.
19. UNDP 1996.
20. Gallup Pakistan 1996.
21. Luhmann 1977, 1982.
22. Hooglund 1995.
23. Bayat 1998, Beyer 1994.
24. Zubaida 1997.
25. For an elaboration and discussion of this, see Rashid 1998.

6

GENDER ROLES
Islamic Determinism or
Social Construction?

Gender Issues in Muslim Societies: Historical Context

For many Islamic and Western scholars of Islam, the status, role and position of women are important distinguishing features of Muslim societies which set them apart from their Western counterparts. Many people in the West regard Islam as an inherently misogynist religion and view the status of women in Muslim society as symptomatic of this.[1] Moreover, it is argued that gender relations in Islam have been primarily shaped by its Arabian origins. Nonetheless, while it is true that Islam has borne the mark of its Arabian origins, the Prophet Muhammad (PBUH) introduced a variety of reforms that would, in particular, alter the position of women within his community.[2]

Islam was instrumental in introducing wide-ranging legal-religious enactment to improve the position and status of women in Arabian society and to protect them from male excesses. In the pre-Islamic period Arabia had preserved the attitudes towards women which had prevailed before the Axial age. Polygamy was a common practice and while elite women enjoyed considerable power and prestige—for example, Muhammad's (PBUH) first wife Khadija was a successful and highly respected merchant—the majority were on par with slaves and had no political or human rights. Female infanticide was widely practised.

Women were among some of Muhammad's (PBUH) earliest converts and their emancipation was a central plank of his 'social project'. The Qur'an strictly forbade the killing of female children and gave women legal rights of inheritance and divorce: most Western women had nothing comparable until the nineteenth century. Several chapters of the Qur'an frequently addressed women explicitly, something that rarely happens in either the Jewish or Christian scriptures.[3] Numerous Qur'anic injunctions give effect to these changes in the public and private spheres, most importantly by recognizing a woman's fully fledged personality.[4] Rahman provides an overview of the reforms introduced by the Qur'an:

> The *Qur'an* immensely improved the status of the woman in several directions but the most basic is the fact that the woman was given a fully-[f]ledged personality. The spouses are declared to be each other's 'garments': the woman has been granted the same rights over man as man has over his wife, except that man, being the earning partner, is a degree higher. Unlimited polygamy was strictly regulated and the number of wives was limited to four, with the rider that if a husband feared that he could not do justice among several wives, he must marry only one wife. To all this was added a general principle that 'you shall never be able to do justice among wives no matter how desirous you are (to do so)' ([*Qur'an*] IV, 3, 128). The overall logical consequence of these pronouncements is a banning of polygamy under normal circumstances. Yet as an already existing institution polygamy was accepted on a legal plane, with the obvious guiding lines that when gradually social circumstances became more favourable, monogamy might be introduced. This is because no reformer who means to be effective can neglect the real situation and simply issue visionary statements. But the later Muslims did not watch the guidelines of the *Qur'an* and, in fact, thwarted its intentions.[5]

Other scholars have made similar observations. The Prophet (PBUH) sought to establish an Islamic movement based upon principles of humanitarianism, egalitarianism, social and political justice, righteousness, and solidarity. There is a general consensus among scholars of Islam that the protection and improvement of the status of women and children was an important plank in the Prophet's (PBUH) 'social project'.[6]

Yet through selective, literal, non-contextual and ahistorical interpretations of Qur'anic injunctions, a majority of Muslim scholars and rulers have chosen to thwart rather than to follow and promote these principles.[7] As in Christianity, the religion later was hijacked by the men, who interpreted the sacred texts in a way that was inimical to Muslim women.[8]

Baydawi, a thirteenth century Sunni scholar, reflected this tendency when he set out to classify the ways in which men stand superior to women. 'Allah has favoured the one sex over the other', according to Baydawi,

> In the matter of mental ability and good counsel, and in their power for the performance of duties and for the carrying out of (divine) commands. Hence to men have been confined prophecy, religious leadership, saintship, pilgrimage rites, the giving of evidence in the law-courts, the duties of the holy war, worship in the mosque on the day of assembly (Friday), etc. They also have the privilege of selecting chiefs, have a larger share of inheritance and discretion in the matter of divorce.[9]

Baydawi's observations and conclusions were based upon a selective reading and interpretation of the sacred texts that ignored the intellectual message of the Qur'an.[10]

Another Muslim scholar, Sheikh Muhammad Hasanayn Makhlouf, claiming the authority of Islamic law, issued a *fatwa* in June 1952 declaring that the Islamic social system lacked the authority to give women the right to vote or to be elected to parliament, given women's inherently unsuitable nature.[11]

The Islamic scholar Maududi made similar pronouncements about the role and position of women in Islamic society. He quoted a Hadith attributed to the Prophet Muhammad (PBUH), 'Those who entrust their affairs to a woman will never know prosperity',[12] and warned of catastrophes that will befall those who leave their affairs in the hands of a woman. Some nations have given woman the position of governor over man. But no instance is found of a nation that raised its womanhood to such a status and then attained any high position on the ladder of progress and civilization. History does not present the record of any nation that made a woman the ruler of its affairs and won honour and glory, or performed a work of distinction.[13]

The Moroccan sociologist Fatima Mernissi, in her recent work on women and Islam, disputes the authority of this Hadith and cogently argues that its use is a clear illustration of how Islamic scholars, who have almost always been male and have enjoyed close relations with the ruling classes, have manipulated the sacred texts to ensure male hegemony and control.[14]

The interpretations of these sacred texts by scholars like Baydawi, Makhlouf and Maududi have shaped the average Muslim's views and attitudes towards women. They express the commonly held Muslim view of women as beings who are incapable of and unfit for public duties. For them, as for other Islamic scholars, women's autonomy and independence pose a problem for the general functioning of society, particularly in regard to the family and marital relations. Female autonomy constitutes a deviation from the divinely ordained, legally upheld and historically enforced duties of a wife and can therefore only be construed as disobedience. Female autonomy threatens to infringe upon male prerogatives.[15]

For the nationalist leaders who spearheaded the independence movements in Indonesia, Pakistan and Egypt, 'woman issues' were a major dilemma. The questions raised by women about their role, status and function in these newly independent states generated highly emotive and divisive debates between nationalist leaders and Islamic scholars, centring around the issues of marriage and family law and the role and status of women in a modern independent Muslim state.

Notwithstanding strong resistance from Islamicists in several countries, the new nationalist leaders were able to overcome centuries of resistance and introduce modest changes to family and marriage law by providing women with a say if the husband should decide to take another wife, and by giving them opportunities for equal participation in political processes. These changes were introduced within an Islamic framework that did not expressly violate the relevant Qur'anic injunctions and Sunnah.[16]

The majority of the ulama and their followers have continued to criticise and oppose these reforms on the grounds that they violate Islamic law and commandments as codified in classical Islamic legal texts. Furthermore, they denounce the reforms as a thinly veiled attempt to provide an Islamic framework for an essentially Western approach to the issues of interpersonal relations.[17] This debate between Nationalists and Islamicists has not ceased, and, according to some evidence, it is becoming an important part of the political agenda of Islamic fundamentalists.[18]

Attitudes Towards Gender Roles in Muslim Countries: Empirical Evidence

The future direction of reforms seeking to improve the quality of economic, political and social citizenship of women will be strongly influenced by prevailing attitudes towards economic and social roles of Muslim women in society. More positive and 'modern' attitudes would not only facilitate reform but also considerably enhance the prospects of their successful implementation. For these reasons these attitudes were investigated in depth in this study. The respondents were presented with six statements about different aspects of women's role in society and asked to indicate their attitudes towards them. These statements were as follows:

1. A working mother can establish as warm and secure a relationship with her children as a mother who does not work.
2. Being a housewife is just as fulfilling as working for pay.
3. Both husband and wife should contribute to the household income.
4. On the whole, men make better political leaders than women.
5. If a woman earns more than her husband it is almost certain to cause problems.
6. Higher education is more important for a boy than for a girl.

To ascertain the respondents attitudes they were asked to indicate whether they 'strongly agreed', 'agreed', were 'not sure', 'disagreed' or 'strongly disagreed' with the statement. They could also register a 'don't know' response. For political and legal reasons statement number four was not included in the survey questionnaire in Kazakhstan. I was advised that this statement may violate Kazakhstan's strict sex discrimination law. An index of agreement was constructed by combining the 'strongly agreed' and 'agreed responses'.

Indonesia

Table 6.1 reports the degree of agreement with each statement in Indonesia. The evidence shows that 70 per cent of Indonesian women compared with 53 per cent Indonesian men, agreed that a working mother could have as warm and secure relations with her children as a mother who did not work. The age and educational levels were positively related to the agreement and Muslim professionals were more likely to agree than the religious activists and the general public respondents.

Table 6.1 Indonesia: Attitudes towards gender roles by gender, age, education and sample type (%)

	Male	Female	>25 years	26-40 years	41-55 years	>56 years	>High School	High School-some uni.	Completed university	Religious Activists	Muslim Profess-ionals	Public
A working mother can establish as warm and secure a relationship with her children as a mother who does not work	53	70	52	58	59	61	54	56	60	54	63	59
Being a housewife is just as fulfilling as working for pay	79	80	69	80	85	83	80	76	84	77	85	81
Both husband and wife should contribute to household income	69	73	53	70	79	73	77	67	72	65	74	76
On the whole, men make better political leaders than women	62	57	70	59	60	55	50	65	59	68	56	53
If a woman earns more than her husband it is almost certain to cause problems	33	33	46	32	28	29	25	38	29	37	27	30
Higher education is more important for a boy than for a girl	14	8	16	10	11	17	13	15	9	15	10	11

About 80 per cent of Indonesian men and women agreed that being a housewife was just as fulfilling as working for pay. The older respondents were more likely to agree with the statement. Religious activists were less likely to agree than the Muslim professional and general public. The same pattern was displayed by the responses to the statement that both husband and wife should contribute to household income. Significantly fewer respondents agreed with the statement and once again Muslim professionals and general public respondents were more likely agreeable than the religious activists.

Attitudes towards public roles of women varied widely in Indonesia. About 60 per cent of the respondents thought that men make better leaders than women. This attitude was positively related with educational level and negatively with lifecycle. Again religious activists were more supportive of the statement than other respondents from other walks of life. Only one-third of the Indonesians believed that a greater financial capacity of a wife would cause domestic discord. This attitude was negatively associated with age and positively associated with education. The religious activists were more prone to hold this view than respondents from the other walks of life.

The Indonesian respondents were unequivocal in not favouring male preference in higher education over females. A large majority from all sections of society held such opinions. In fact, as we will see in the following discussion, comparatively Indonesians were the least discriminatory in their attitudes towards giving access to higher education to women.

Pakistan

Table 6.2 reports attitudes towards gender roles in Pakistan. Only about half the respondents believed that a working mother could establish warm and secure relations with her children as a mother who was in paid work. Women were slightly more inclined to agree with the statement, and age appeared not to have any distinctive affect on the attitudes. Education, on the other hand, did effect the attitudes since the more educated had displayed more agreeable attitudes. The religious activists

Table 6.2 Pakistan: Attitudes towards gender roles by gender, age, education and sample type (%)

	Male	Female	>25 years	26-40 years	41-55 years	>56 years	>High school	High school-some uni.	Completed university	Religious Activists	Muslim Public Professionals	
A working mother can establish as warm and secure a relationship with her children as a mother who does not work	48	52	47	53	49	52	44	36	57	46	58	52
Being a housewife is just as fulfilling as working for pay	67	69	58	68	67	71	53	63	70	64	66	72
Both husband and wife should contribute to household income	48	53	55	53	46	52	43	42	56	40	59	61
On the whole, men make better political leaders than women	78	73	75	74	82	79	69	84	75	82	66	79
If a woman earns more than her husband it is almost certain to cause problems	56	44	52	50	59	58	48	65	49	56	46	54
Higher education is more important for a boy than for a girl	43	30	36	34	48	51	40	50	37	51	27	37

compared with the other two types of respondents were less likely to agree with the statement.

About seven out of ten respondents agreed that being a housewife was just as fulfilling as working for pay. Interestingly, this attitude was negatively associated with age and positively related to educational attainment. The religious activists were slightly less agreeable than Muslim professionals and the general public. Only about half of the Pakistani respondents agreed that husband and wife should equally contribute to household income. More educated persons were more likely to agree with the statement, and religious activists were least likely to do the same compared with the respondents from the other parts of society.

Over 70 per cent of Pakistani respondents believed that men make better political leaders than women, and this view was held more widely among the older and more educated persons and those who came from a religious activist background. About half of the Pakistanis saw inevitable family conflict if a wife earned more than her husband. Women were less likely than men to subscribe to this view. The older respondents and those who were religious activists tended to display higher agreement rates.

Only about one-third of the respondents agreed with the statement that higher education was more important for boys than girls, but women were more inclined to reject gender discrimination in education than men. The discriminatory attitude was positively associated with age and negatively with education. Religious activists were more likely to approve of gender preference for males in education than the other two types of respondents. On the whole, the evidence in Table 6.2 shows that Pakistani respondents tended to display less supportive attitudes towards gender equality than the Indonesian respondents

Egypt
The Egyptian attitudes towards gender roles follow a very distinctive pattern. The evidence reported in Table 6.3 shows that Egyptian women in general hold strikingly different attitudes than Egyptian males. Compared with men, of whom only 28 per cent believed that a working mother can establish a secure and warm relationship with her children just as a non-working mother can, 62 per cent of women respondents agreed that this can be done. Interestingly, younger respondents and those from religious backgrounds held views similar to those of the men. Slightly less than half of the respondents believed that being a housewife was just as meaningful as working for pay. The older respondents, religious activists and those with lower educational attainment were more likely to believe that being a housewife was just as fulfilling as working for pay.

There were striking differences between men and women in their attitudes towards household finance. Only 39 per cent of men agreed that husband and wife should contribute to household income, whereas 68 per cent of women expressed agreement with the statement. Older respondents and those who came from professional backgrounds were more likely to agree with the statement. Although a lower proportion of women subscribed to the attitude that men make better leaders than women, on the whole a large majority of Egyptians from all

Table 6.3 Egypt: Attitudes towards gender roles by gender, age, education and sample type (%)

	Male	Female	>25 years	26-40 years	41-55 years	>56 years	>High school	High school-some uni.	Completed uni.	Religious Activists	Muslim Professionals	Public
A working mother can establish as warm and secure a relationship with her children as a mother who does not work	28	62	28	31	52	41	40	25	38	16	51	34
Being a housewife is just as fulfilling as working for pay	44	47	39	43	51	51	53	35	46	41	47	47
Both husband and wife should contribute to household income	39	68	42	42	55	55	47	33	47	32	58	40
On the whole, men make better political leaders than women	88	73	76	87	84	84	83	87	85	86	85	81
If a woman earns more than her husband it is almost certain to cause problems	75	61	75	76	67	56	67	68	73	80	64	77
Higher education is more important for a boy than for a girl	57	31	46	53	55	38	50	70	47	59	45	51

walks of life subscribed to the view that men were superior to women in leadership potential.

A majority of Egyptians also agreed that if a wife earned more than her husband it would lead to family conflicts. Comparatively, women were less likely to hold this opinion than men. The tendency to agree with the statement was significantly more pronounced among respondents of younger age. Similarly, larger proportions of those with university education and who were religious activists were in agreement with the statement. Almost twice as many men than women displayed preference for boys to obtain university education. The evidence presented in Table 6.3 shows that the Egyptian respondents on the whole held more traditional attitudes towards gender roles than their counterparts from Indonesia and Pakistan.

Kazakhstan

In Kazakhstan the question that 'On the whole, men make better leaders than women' was not included in the survey because of legal and political reasons. In Kazakhstan the gender roles, therefore, were ascertained by the five remaining questions. The

Table 6.4 Kazakhstan: Attitudes towards gender roles by gender, age, education and sample type (%)

	Male	Female	>25 years	26-40 years	41-55 years	>56 years	>High school	High school-some uni.	Completed university	Muslim Profess-ionals	Public
A working mother can establish as warm and secure a relationship with her children as a mother who does not work	58	59	57	54	66	61	57	59	58	65	61
Being a housewife is just as fulfilling as working for pay	32	38	26	29	46	40	39	34	29	33	48
Both husband and wife should contribute to household income	55	59	54	55	63	56	51	58	46	63	61
If a woman earns more than her husband it is almost certain to cause problems	44	57	37	41	49	41	37	43	25	44	44
Higher education is more important for a boy than for a girl	43	57	32	40	43	31	36	39	29	40	47

empirical evidence presented in Table 6.4 shows that about six out of every ten respondents agreed that a working mother can establish as warm and secure a relationship with her children as a mother who does not work, and notwithstanding slight variations across different ages, this was the case generally.

A majority of the Kazakhs believe that housework is not as fulfilling as working for pay. Their attitude on this point is in sharp contrast to the attitudes of Indonesians, Pakistanis and Egyptians and clearly demonstrates the impact of the policies of the communist era. Interestingly, greater proportions of older respondents and general public respondents tended to agree with the statement. Over 50 per cent of respondents across all sections of Kazakh society favoured the view that husband and wife should jointly contribute to household income. Women, older persons and respondents from the professional classes as well as the general public held slightly more agreeable attitudes favouring joint contribution to family income.

While the majority of the women agreed with the statement that if wife earned more than her husband it would cause domestic discord, the majority of men believed that such a consequence was not inevitable. The educational level was

negatively associated and age was positively associated with
the agreement. A majority of women surprisingly agreed that
higher education is more important for males than females. The
positive attitudes favouring male preference for higher education
was negatively associated with age and education. On the whole
the evidence presented in Table 6.4 shows that while the
Kazakhs took a fairly modern view of gender roles, surprisingly
they were not as modern as the Indonesian respondents.

The effects of age, gender and educational level and countries
(national cultures) on the attitudes towards gender roles were
formally examined using logistic regression procedures. The
results of this exercise, which are presented in Table 6.5, show
that in general age and educational level were positively related
to modern attitudes towards gender roles. Compared with the
Pakistanis, the Indonesians held the most modern attitudes
towards gender roles which were more supportive of according
better quality of economic, political and social citizenships to
Muslim women. They were followed by the Kazakhs.
Surprisingly, the Egyptians on the whole were significantly more
conservative compared with respondents from the other three
countries. In general, the Indonesians and Kazakhs were
significantly more modern in their attitudes towards Muslim
women's public and private domain roles, and the Pakistanis
and the Egyptians were comparatively more traditional in this
respect.

Index of Attitudes Towards Gender Roles

An index of gender attitudes for each country was constructed
in order to compare their overall ideological orientations. The
'strongly agree' response was scored as five and 'strongly
disagree' response was given the score of one. In order to be
consistent in ascertaining modern and traditional attitudes gender
items one to three (see Table 6.5) were scored 'strongly agree'
to 'strongly disagree', and items four to six were reversed in
order to obtain a logically consistent orientation. Using this

Table 6.5 Odds ratios by selected demographic characteristics of respondents and country for those who strongly agreed and agreed with the statements on gender roles

Statements** Characteristics	1	2	3	4	5	6
			Odds Ratios			
Age	1.01*	1.02*	1.01*	0.99*	0.99*	1.00
Female	2.12*	1.09*	1.85*	0.62	0.80	0.45*
High School/Some University	1.07	0.93	0.87*	0.80	1.32*	1.11
University/Professional	1.60*	1.36*	1.20	0.56*	0.81*	0.66*
Indonesia	1.42*	2.23*	2.30*	0.55*	0.39*	0.20*
Egypt	0.52*	0.44*	0.70*	1.92*	2.65*	1.76*
Kazakhstan	1.82*	0.45*	1.59*	—	0.62*	1.15

Notes: * indicates significant at .05 level or above
Reference category for female was male, for educational level was 'less than High School' and for countries was Pakistan.

**Statements on Gender Roles
1. A working mother can establish as warm and secure a relationship with her children as a mother who does not work.
2. Being a housewife is just as fulfilling as working for pay.
3. Both husband and wife should contribute to household income.
4. On the whole, men make better political leaders than women do.
5. If a woman earns more money than her husband, it is almost certain to cause problems.
6. A higher/university education is more important for a boy than a girl.

methodology the score for each respondent was ascertained. The scores in Indonesia, Pakistan and Egypt ranged from 30 to 6 and in Kazakhstan these ranged from 25 to 5, since item four was not used in the Kazakhstan survey.

Using the mid-point of the scoring range each respondent was classified as 'modern' or 'traditional'. The modern score corresponds to high scores in this classification. The result of this exercise is reported in Table 6.6, and these confirm the trends already reported above that Indonesian respondents, both male and female, were significantly more modern in their attitudes towards gender roles compared with respondents from

Table 6.6 Index of attitudes towards gender roles (%) with 'modern' attitudes towards gender roles by selected characteristics and by countries

	Male	Female	>25 years	26-40 years	41-55 years	>56 years	>High school	High school-some uni.	Completed university	Religious Activists	Muslim Professionals	Public
Indonesia	65	78	54	71	73	72	76	65	71	62	74	75
Pakistan	27	45	30	35	25	27	25	18	36	21	45	32
Kazakhstan	42	48	50	44	42	47	49	44	53	–	49	42
Egypt	12	49	24	16	27	28	11	12	23	14	27	12

the other countries. They were followed by the Kazakhs, Pakistanis and Egyptians respectively. The male proportions varied from 65 per cent for Indonesians to only 12 per cent for the Egyptians. The female proportions were less spread out. Seventy-eight per cent of Indonesian women were modern and about half from the other three countries were similarly classified.

In Indonesia, the proportion of 'modern' respondents increased with age and declined slightly with education. The Indonesian religious activists were comparatively more traditional, although even among them 65 per cent were classified as modern. The Kazakhs were equally divided between modern and traditional across all groupings. In Pakistan, 45 per cent of women were modern compared with 27 per cent of men. Younger respondents and those with university education were slightly more modern. Compared with religious activists, the Muslim professionals in Pakistan were more modern.

In Egypt about half of the women were modern compared with only 12 per cent of their male counterparts. The males and females in Egypt were the most polarized respondents in terms of their attitudes towards gender roles. Neither age nor education appeared to make a big difference in Egypt, although, like Pakistan, university educated respondents were comparatively more modern even though among them only 23 per cent were classified as modern. This traditionalism was equally marked among respondents from different sections of society. Compared with their counterparts from other countries the religious activists, Muslim professionals and the general public in Egypt were significantly more traditional.

Attitudes Towards Gender Roles: Islamic Determinism or Social Construction

The evidence presented and reviewed above signifies a complex pattern of attitudes towards gender roles in each of the four Muslim societies. Two dimensions stand out in this complex pattern. These are a societal dimension and a gender dimension. The societal dimension refers to the variations in attitudes across countries. This begs the question that if Islamic values and norms are the sole determinants of Muslim attitudes towards gender issues, we should expect a reasonable correspondence in the attitudes among Muslims. The evidence, however, shows a significant degree of variations in attitudes across countries. It counters the arguments about 'Islamic determinism' and supports the theoretical arguments presented in a recent volume on women in Muslim countries which reject the widely held perceptions in the West and among some groups of Islamic activists which characterize Islam as an essentialist, monolithic, and static phenomenon. The evidence presented in this chapter provides insights into the complex ways in which religious beliefs and social reality interact in constructing social attitudes, including attitudes towards gender roles.[19]

The statistical analysis, especially the logistic regressions analysis, showed that the differences in the attitudes are not a methodological construct arising from the sample compositions. These differences are most likely a function of the local milieu which mediates between Islamic norms and their *in-situ* expression. The more 'modern' attitudes of the Indonesians are a function of the history and temperament of Indonesian people. Indonesians are generally socialized in a cultural milieu which has historically shunned some of the norms and practices of the

Middle Eastern Islam related to gender issues. This is evident in the religious practices followed by the members of the two largest Indonesian Muslim organizations, Muhammadiyah and Nahdatul Ulama which together claim to have over fifty million members.

The modernity of the Kazakh attitudes towards gender issues have been largely shaped by the predominant ideology of socialism during the Soviet era which prohibited gender discrimination and promoted gender equality in the public and private domains of Kazakh society. One can argue that the Kazakhs were basically 'de-Islamized' during the Soviet period and firmly socialized into an 'egalitarian' socialist ideology, which they internalized. Of course, the fact that the Soviet rulers treated their Central Asian Muslim peoples as second-class citizens was a fact not fully appreciated or widely known under the authoritarian communist political rule. One likely explanation, or part explanation, of very traditionalistic attitudes exhibited by the Pakistani and Egyptian respondents is that these attitudes have been shaped by centuries of practice of the Middle Eastern Islamic values centred around veiling, exclusion and patriarchy.

As for the gender dimension, in all countries surveyed, women have displayed comparatively more 'modern' attitudes than men. The differences between men's and women's attitudes tended to be the greatest in countries in which men's attitudes were comparatively more 'traditionalistic'. In other words, the degree of modernity of women's attitudes appeared to be positively related to the traditionalistic attitudes of men. The sociological significance of this is that while women have different opinions about gender issues, they have limited voice in changing the dominant male attitudes. Consequently, they suffer from varying degrees of oppression in the sense that they are not free to act out their views because of existing institutional arrangements that reflect both male domination and male social control.

The evidence also suggested another dimension of social division on gender issues. In general, the attitudes of religious activists in all countries are more traditionalistic than Muslim professionals and the general public. A significantly larger proportion of Muslim professionals exhibits modern attitudes in all countries. It is difficult to ascertain from the evidence whether the religious activists reflected the broader public opinion or whether they influenced public attitudes. I think one conclusion we can draw from the data is that the attitudes towards gender roles are a product of historical interaction between Islamic values and norms and unique social arrangements or institutional frameworks within which they are expressed.

The concept as well as the phenomenon of the 'working mother' is of relatively recent origin in most societies. It is only within this century that women have started entering the paid workforce in any significant numbers. This role challenges the traditional views of Muslim women. There is surprisingly remarkable uniformity of attitudes among female respondents. A majority of them in all countries agree that a working mother can be equally caring and nurturing towards her children as a mother who does not work. This phenomenon is most likely a reflection of their ability to realistically assess the capacity of a working mother to carry out her responsibilities towards her children. Men, on the other hand, differ significantly, and this also reflects the social reality of different societies.

Both Kazakh and Indonesian societies have been shaped by the political and cultural histories which have been conducive to the promotion of institutional equality for women, and this experience has obviously reflected in greater acceptance of women's participation in the labour market. The traditionalism of the Egyptian men is difficult to explain. In fact, this finding was counter-intuitive. It is possible that their attitudes have been more profoundly influenced by Egyptian scholars such as Baydawi and Shiekh Muhammad Hasanayn Makhlouf mentioned earlier who have propagated the views that Allah did not favour public roles for women because of their physical abilities.[20]

The widely prevalent perception in major Muslim countries that housework is fulfilling and rewarding will continue to act as a barrier to Muslim women's participation in the labour force. The prevalence of such views, as suggested by the data, would indicate that working Muslim mothers are likely to encounter considerable resistance, and this may in fact lead them to actively avoid entering the labour market. This in itself would be tantamount to huge wastage of a large reservoir of human resources for social and economic development of Muslim societies. The prospect of both husband and wife contributing to household income found favour among the majority of women in all countries. The juxtaposition of attitudes towards the housewife and the desirability of both husband and wife contributing to household income display the inherent complexity of attitudes towards gender roles. While men are, on the whole, more conservative in their attitudes, the evidence reviewed in this chapter indicates that women tend to be more flexible.

Asymmetry in the position and power of men and women in the family is largely predicated on the male role as the principle provider and income earner in the family. In traditional Muslim societies men largely continue to play this role and thereby ensure their status and power in the family. Women are socialized into playing a role secondary to men. In modern societies, including some more progressive Muslim societies like Indonesia, women are entering the paid workforce in increasing numbers, and a two-income family is no longer an isolated phenomenon. In these circumstances, it is likely that women will become more successful in the labour market and experience greater occupational mobility. Within the framework of traditional Islamic norms for defining the family roles, a higher mobility rate of women in the workforce may create conflicting situations in the family.

The perception of family discord in case the wife earns more than her husband appears to be associated with the objective conditions experienced by men and women in relation to the contribution they make to the household income. According to the Human Development Reports published by the World Bank, there are considerable differences in the 'earned income share' of men and women in the four countries surveyed in this study. Women's contribution to the 'earned household income' in 1996 was 39 per cent in Kazakhstan, 32 per cent in Indonesia, 23 per cent in Egypt and 19 per cent in Pakistan.[21] These proportions broadly correspond to the differences in the perceptions of family discord arising from greater earning capacity of the wife compared with her husband. In the two countries with smaller female contribution to the household income, the proportion of men agreeing with the statement that if a woman earned more than her husband it is almost certain to cause problems was significantly higher.

The attitudes towards public political roles of women were most conservative in Egypt and Pakistan, and this would again appear to suggest that the norms and beliefs entrenched in the Arab Middle Eastern Islam and their continuous reinforcement through the attitudes of the ulama play an important role in the production of such attitudes. Surprisingly, even in Pakistan, which has had two terms of Benazir Bhutto as Prime Minister, attitudes favour men as political leaders. Nonetheless, it is possible to override these as demonstrated by Benazir Bhutto's election in Pakistan.

The attitudes expressed towards preferential treatment for males in higher education also reflect the influence of the local social and cultural milieu. In Egypt and Pakistan, the two countries in which traditional Islamic norms about male and female roles are more prominent, the attitudes towards male preference are significantly higher compared with Indonesia and Kazakhstan. In these two countries, Muslims do not subscribe to the traditional Middle Eastern Islamic norms about gender roles. The effect of the local social and cultural milieu is further reflected in the more egalitarian views of female respondents compared with their countrymen.

In conclusion, the evidence about gender roles discussed in this chapter indicates that attitudes towards them are an outcome of complex and dynamic processes. These processes include the prevalent social, economic and political conditions in the country which mediate the practice of traditional Islamic norms in the local milieu. Material conditions of the country have greater influence in shaping the attitudes towards gender roles than does the traditional Islamic ideology. The perception of Islam as an essentialist, monolithic, and static phenomenon is clearly not supported by the evidence. The attitudes about women's roles and status in Muslim society are diverse and fluid and a product of complex interaction of local institutions and the Shariah. The Soviet system, notwithstanding its many undesirable attributes, did promote gender equality in employment, education, health and legal rights. These policies clearly shaped the attitudes of Kazakh men and women. On the basis of this achievement, one can argue that a supportive state committed to an egalitarian ideology does improve the quality of citizenship for women. The relatively modern Indonesian attitudes towards gender roles also suggest that a synthesis of the Shariah norms and local customary laws can also be a positive influence in promoting gender equality in contemporary Muslim societies.

NOTES

1. Esposito 1995, p. 5; Armstrong 1993, p. 184.
2. Levy 1957, p. 91; Rahman 1966; Ali 1970.
3. Armstrong 1993, p. 184.
4. Ali 1970, pp. 55-59; Armstrong 1993, chapter 5.
5. Rahman 1966, p. 38.
6. Rahman 1966; Levy 1957; Watt 1955; Mernissi 1989; Armstrong 1993.
7. Rahman 1966; Mernissi 1989.
8. Armstrong 1993, p. 184.
9. Baydawi as cited in Levy 1957, p. 99.
10. Rahman 1982.
11. *Islamic Review* [August 1952] as cited in Levy 1957, p. 99.
12. Sahih al-Bukhari 9, p. 18, as cited in Maududi 1987, pp. 170-71.
13. Maududi 1987, p. 111.
14. Mernissi 1989, chapter 3.
15. Haeri 1993.
16. Anderson 1976.
17. Haeri 1993; Esposito 1982.

18. Hardacre 1993; Haeri 1993.
19. Bodman and Tohidi 1998.
20. Levy 1957, p. 99.
21. United Nations Development Programme 1996.

7

ATTITUDES TOWARDS VEILING AND PATRIARCHY

Issues related to patriarchy, veiling and seclusion of women are the focus of much debate in Muslim countries. These have been important features of Islamic societies that have attracted much criticism from Muslim and Western feminist scholars in recent years. This chapter will examine the attitudes of Muslims towards patriarchy, veiling and seclusion of women and also investigate the social correlates of these attitudes.

The tradition and custom of veiling in Islam can be attributed to Islamic history and texts as well as to the traditional role of men in positions of power and authority in Muslim society. Historically, veiling became a customary practice of the Islamic community as a result of its presence in pre-Islamic Mecca. It was generally observed in the urban areas of pre-Islamic Arabia but not among the Bedouin women who lived in the desert. The women of the Prophet Muhammad's (PBUH) own tribe observed veiling. In pre-Islamic Mecca, it was the custom for unmarried daughters to dress in fine clothes once a year and walk about unveiled in order to attract suitable suitors, but once a husband was found, the woman resumed veiling.[1]

Furthermore, in the early years when Muhammad (PBUH) and his followers were subjected to insults and harassment, he commanded his own wives and daughters to identify and protect themselves by wearing long veils whenever they went out in public.[2] He also commanded his followers not to enter his home freely and asked his wives to talk from behind a veil to strangers. Muhammad (PBUH) also enacted rules for proper conduct in the public and private domains, which included exhortations to women not to display their beauty and charm except in the presence of their husband or close kin. This was reflected in the following Qur'anic edicts:

> Say to the believing men that they should lower their gaze and guard their modesty... And say to the believing women that they should lower their gaze and guard their modesty; that they should not display their beauty and ornaments except what (ordinarily) appear thereof; that they should draw their veils over their bosoms and not display their beauty except to their husbands, their fathers...[3]

Evidence from the first two centuries of Islam indicates that Qur'anic injunctions did not prevent women from praying in the mosque with men, and while they were expected to dress modestly, they were not required to veil. But towards the end of the second century, women were forbidden to pray in public assembly, and, over time, mosque attendance became a male prerogative. This came about despite evidence that the Qur'an does not discriminate between men and women regarding public prayer. It is most likely that the veiling and seclusion of women became a common Islamic practice under the influence of Muslims from Persia, where its practice was widespread. By the third century of Islam, veiling and seclusion of women had become a widely established custom. Even then, the practice varied according to economic conditions, so that in rural and tribal areas observance was less than universal.

The tendency to veil and seclude women and therefore limit their role and function in society is intertwined with the management of sexuality in Islam. Unlike Christianity, which idealizes and strongly sanctions celibacy, Islam explicitly prohibits celibacy and enjoins its followers to enjoy sexual pleasures as long as they do so within the limits prescribed by the sacred texts. In fact, as Mernissi[4] suggests, the lives of the most sacred personae of Christianity and Islam, namely Jesus Christ and Muhammad (PBUH), clearly demonstrate the attitudes of their respective religions toward sexuality and its management.

In Islam, women are seen not only as sexual beings but as the very embodiment of sex. In this sense, veiling explicitly conceals sexuality.[5] The underlying concern is that women may excite men's sexuality through immodest dress or exposure of their bodies.[6] For many Muslims, the sexual conduct of males is not dependent upon that of females because sexual relations are a matter of male discretion. Female sexuality exists in service to male sexuality and for reproductive purposes.[7] According to a respected Islamic commentator,

> The whole of the body of a free woman is to be regarded as pudendal and no part of her may lawfully be seen by anyone but her husband or close kin, except in case of need, as when she is undergoing medical treatment or giving evidence.[8]

Consequently, men view women as objects that exist and retain value only in relation to themselves. Women are to be owned and controlled. They are objects of desire, to be veiled and secluded. They exist as an indispensable commodity that adds to a man's sense of power and virility.[9]

The interpretations and expressions of religious injunctions change under the influence of prevailing social conditions in society and Islam has not been immune from this. As mentioned earlier, Islamic rules have been selectively applied, emphasized, ignored or circumvented in accordance with the social and political realities of Muslim societies through its history.

Over the centuries, the ulama issued decisions on veiling and seclusion of women that grew ever more elaborate and rigid than what is required by the Qur'an. They extended the veiling requirements that were once imposed on the Prophet's (PBUH) wives and daughters to all women. They justified these decisions on the grounds that since it was laudable for Muslims to follow the *Sunnah* (practice) of the Prophet (PBUH) in all matters, it was also commendable for women to follow the custom of the Prophet's (PBUH) womenfolk.[10]

The cumulative effect of the ulama's decisions on veiling as an Islamic requirement for Muslim women has resulted in a normative requirement of veiling and seclusion that, by and large, is universally accepted throughout the Islamic world. However, observance of the requirement varies according to economic conditions. In rural and tribal areas where women are actively engaged in economic activities, veiling is less universal. In most South-East Asian Islamic communities, the practice of veiling is generally not observed, although in recent decades it has gradually been increasing in the urban areas.[11]

With some notable exceptions, the general practice of veiling and seclusion has become a potent symbol in the Islamic world. The practice is in keeping with the supremacy of the male over the female as postulated by the Qur'an. The vagueness of these provisions has allowed the ulama greater authority in interpreting the religious texts and sayings, thus providing them with the opportunity to influence or to reinforce local customs and thereby gain favour with the dominant male elite. Some ulama have apparently even invented 'traditions' which may in fact be in conflict with Qur'anic statements and with the intellectual message of the Qur'an, in order to bolster their own interpretations.[12]

The efforts of Muslim women activists to interpret Islam from a feminist perspective have not been very successful in Muslim countries because they pose a threat to the way Islam has historically been interpreted. Women in the Muslim world are not in a position of power or authority to popularize their interpretations of the Islamic texts. According to Muslim feminists, the interpretations of the male Muslim clergy threaten the status and potential of Muslim women who want to challenge oppressive patriarchal traditions. Women are seen as the marker of identity in Muslim communities, and it is therefore critical for patriarchal states to safeguard women's morality and ensure that women conduct themselves in the manner prescribed by the traditional interpretations of Islam.[13]

Issues related to patriarchy and the veiling and seclusion of women have now become an important focus of debate among women, Islamicists, and secularists, not only in Islamic countries but internationally as well.[14] As noted at the outset, one of the most common Western stereotypes of Islam is that it oppresses women.[15] Because of this general prejudice, the Islamic religious fundamentalist movements which often advocate the veiling and seclusion of women are given wide media coverage in the West. This helps to confirm Islam's unequal treatment of the sexes. Little attempt is made to investigate the underlying factors responsible for the rise of the so-called fundamentalist movements. These factors are often related to delegitimizing oppressive regimes, failure of secular leaders to deliver an equitable government, uneven socio-economic consequences of capitalist development, disempowerment, identity crisis, alienation, fear of the future and moral panic arising from globalization and structural change. It includes a growing perception of Western economic and cultural imperialism.[16]

The veil has traditionally evoked images of seclusion, passivity and subordination of women. While this is by and large true, an overemphasis on its denouncement has not been conducive to understanding the complex reasons behind it and the paradoxical functions of the recent 're-veiling' phenomenon in many Muslim societies. This patronizing preoccupation with the veil has not been helpful in altering the obsession of Muslim males over covering the female body.[17]

While women in general have experienced lower citizenship status compared to men, in this century at least a number of Muslim countries have made concerted efforts to remove or at least reduce the obstacles to gender equality. Reforms in Turkey, Egypt, Iran, Iraq, Pakistan, Malaysia and Indonesia have sought to remove some of these obstacles as they relate to veiling and patriarchy. The former Soviet Republics of Central Asia that are now independent states have maintained the former socialist policies banning veiling and discrimination based on gender while promoting equal rights for women in marriage and the family. Some of these reforms have been moderately successful, but in some cases, such as in Iran and Pakistan, the pendulum has swung back to more traditionalist views of the role, status and function of women, and these views have gained favour with the current ruling elites. In general, however, the reforms are having a positive effect in most Muslim countries, even while the obstacles still remain. They will continue to exist until such time as the dominant ulama change their rigid attitudes or lose relevance to the general body of Muslims through a decline in their religious authority.

In summary, Islam recognizes sexual desire as a natural endowment of the human body and enjoins Muslims to satisfy and even enjoy its fulfillment, and provides a framework enunciated in the sacred texts to do so. Unlike Christianity, Islam does not sanction or idealize celibacy. Over the centuries, interpretations of the sacred texts by the ulama have led to the development of an institutional framework for the management and satisfaction of human sexuality by the imposition of control over women. Since women are seen not only as sexual beings but as the embodiment of sex itself, the social framework that has evolved has tended to view a woman's body as pudendal. This conceptualization has led to the development and observance of strict dress codes for women, including veiling and seclusion, in order to prevent them from displaying their bodily charm and beauty.

Other features of the institutional framework arose from the stipulation of woman as the principal actor responsible for preserving the sanctity of the family and social reproduction. This concept led to strict injunctions on the types of roles that women could play in the public sphere. Strong social and cultural traditions evolved which placed serious obstacles in the way of women seeking to succeed in public roles. Men, on the other hand, were assigned all public roles as providers, protectors and arbiters, and this reinforced their power in the domestic domain as well. Patriarchal family structures and their sociological correlates—honour, shame, virginity, *hijab*—thus became more functionally suited to ensuring the perpetuation of the institutional framework for the satisfaction and management of the family.

There now exists a respectable body of historical, ethnographic and sociological scholarship documenting the universality of norms for gender roles, veiling and patriarchy in

Muslim countries.[18] Given the significance of these practices
for future social and political developments, it is rather
surprising that there have been no systematic comparative
sociological studies documenting the attitudes of Muslims
toward these practices in different countries. In addition to
providing valuable empirical evidence, such information could
be useful in the formulation of social policy. Most importantly,
comparative studies can provide data on the variations, if any,
in attitudes towards these practices across Muslim countries and
can be useful in developing plausible sociological explanations
of these variations.

One objective of this study was to undertake a systematic and
comparative investigation of Muslim attitudes towards patriarchy,
veiling and seclusion of women in contemporary Muslim societies
and their sociological correlates. In order to ascertain attitudes
towards veiling and the seclusion of women each respondent was
asked to respond to the following two statements:

- In my opinion, women are sexually attractive, and segregation
  and veiling are necessary for male protection.[19]
- Women should observe the Islamic dress code.

As mentioned earlier, patriarchy was conceptualized as male
domination over women. To ascertain their attitudes towards
patriarchy, all respondents in the survey were asked to respond
to the statement: 'If men were not in charge of women, women
would lose sight of all human values and the family unit would
disintegrate'.

These statements were formulated to capture the underlying
rationale for veiling and seclusion of women and patriarchy and
Muslim attitudes towards these social practices. The respondents
were asked to indicate whether she/he strongly agreed, agreed,
was not sure, disagreed or strongly disagreed with the
statements. The respondents also had the option of choosing a
'do not know' response. In the analyses, a composite index for
'agreement' was constructed by combining the 'strongly agreed'

and 'agreed' responses. The analysis reported in the following section is based on this composite index.

Attitudes

Veiling and the Seclusion of Women

The percentages of respondents who agreed with the statement, 'Women are sexually attractive, and segregation and veiling are necessary for male protection' are reported in Table 7.1 by country.

The data offer some interesting comparisons regarding attitudes towards veiling in the four countries. Indonesian respondents expressed the most positive attitudes on this question. Eighty-one per cent of men and 80 per cent of women agreed that women should be segregated and veiled in order to protect men from female sexual provocation. In Egypt and Pakistan, the approval rate among men was 74 per cent and 72

Table 7.1 'Women are sexually attractive, and segregation and veiling are necessary for male protection' (% agreeing)

Countries		Pakistan	Indonesia	Egypt	Kazakhstan
Gender	Male	72	81	74	23
	Female	59	80	69	28
Age	< 25	68	75	70	26
	26 – 40	66	81	75	26
	41 – 55	76	83	66	22
	> 56	70	83	77	31
Education	< High School	77	82	78	30
	High School	76	79	82	25
	Univ/ Professional	67	83	70	25
Sample	Religious Activists	76	77	80	–
	Muslim Professionals	55	82	64	26
	Public	72	83	87	21

per cent respectively, and in both countries female approval
rates were significantly lower than for men. In Kazakhstan, the
situation was the reverse of that of the other three countries,
with only about one-quarter of the respondents agreeing with
the statement. The case of Kazakhstan provides a clear example
of the overriding influence of ideological indoctrination. While
in Indonesia, Pakistan and Egypt the attitudes being investigated
here were shaped by religious and cultural indoctrination, in
Kazakhstan they were shaped by the state socialist ideology.

Further analysis of the data shows that older respondents
were more approving of veiling and segregation compared with
younger respondents. In Indonesia, support for the statement
was widespread across different educational levels and sample
types, and among those who regarded themselves as very
religious and those who considered themselves modern. In
Pakistan, Kazakhstan and Egypt, those with tertiary education
were less inclined to agree with the statement. In general,
support for veiling and segregation of women was high among
respondents from the religious elites and the general public in
all countries except Kazakhstan. The logistic regression analysis
reported in Table 7.2 confirms the trends described above. In
addition, country comparisons show that women are significantly
less supportive of female segregation and veiling. Those who
label themselves as very religious and conservative are
significantly more approving as compared to their counterparts.

The country comparisons also show that compared to the
respondents in Pakistan, the Indonesians are significantly more
approving of veiling, and the Kazakhs are significantly less
approving; the Egyptian respondents are also less approving,
but the difference is not statistically significant. The major
finding of this analysis is that Indonesians, who generally do
not practice segregation and veiling, appear to be more
supportive of the practice than the respondents in Pakistan,
where veiling and segregation are widely practised. Predictably,
significantly fewer Kazakhs agree with the statement. Compared
with the Kazakhs, the Egyptian respondents are more supportive

Table 7.2 'Women are sexually attractive, and segregation and veiling are necessary for male protection' (odd ratios agreeing)

	Pakistan	Indonesia	Egypt	Kazakhstan	All Countries
Age	1.00	1.02	0.98	1.00	1.00
Male	1.00	1.00	1.00	1.00	1.00
Female	**0.48**	1.00	**0.40**	1.99	**0.77**
< High School	1.00	1.00	1.00	1.00	1.00
High School	1.07	1.37	0.80	1.20	1.21
Univ/ Professional	0.94	1.13	**0.24**	0.68	0.80
Religious Activists	1.00	1.00	1.00	–	–
Muslim Professionals	**0.33**	0.84	**0.20**	–	–
Public	0.71	1.15	**0.14**	–	–
Pakistan	–	–	–	–	1.00
Indonesia	–	–	–	–	**1.71**
Egypt	–	–	–	–	0.81
Kazakhstan	–	–	–	–	**0.19**

Note: Odds ratio figures in **boldface** are significant at $p = .05$.

in their attitudes towards veiling and segregation but less so than the Indonesian respondents.

Observance of Islamic Dress Codes

Related to veiling and seclusion of women is the belief that women should observe Islamic dress code. In fact, one can argue that the objective of veiling and social and physical seclusion is best achieved through the observance of dress codes. Implied in the Islamic dress code norm is the objective of preventing women from expressing or displaying their sexuality, which is considered inherently provocative for men. A secondary objective is to promote a moral code that accords respect to women and enables them to interact with men with 'honour'. The respondents in this study were therefore specifically asked

about their attitudes regarding women's observance of the
Islamic dress code.

Attitudes toward the Islamic dress code were ascertained by
the statement, 'Women should observe Islamic dress codes'.
The results, reported in Table 7.3, show that there was almost
universal agreement in Pakistan, Indonesia and Egypt that
women should observe Islamic dress codes. Only about 12 per
cent of the respondents in Kazakhstan expressed similar
opinions. Perhaps the most striking feature of the data is the
close correspondence in the attitudes of women and men. Age
had only a minor effect on attitudes in all countries. In Pakistan
and Kazakhstan, less-educated respondents were more likely to
agree with the statement. There was also a close correspondence
in the attitudes of the elites and the public in Indonesia and
Egypt. In Pakistan, the public was more supportive of Islamic
dress codes than the religious or other elites, and respondents
who regarded themselves as conservative and religious were
also more supportive than those who described themselves as

Table 7.3 'Women should observe Islamic dress codes' (% agreeing)

Countries		Pakistan	Indonesia	Egypt	Kazakhstan
Gender	Male	85	95	96	12
	Female	80	93	98	10
Age	< 25	83	95	96	12
	26 – 40	83	94	96	11
	41 – 55	87	96	98	11
	> 56	82	93	99	11
Education	< High School	92	93	98	18
	High School	88	94	99	10
	Univ / Professional	82	95	96	13
Sample	Religious Activists	83	95	97	–
	Muslim Professionals	78	94	96	5
	Public	90	95	100	13

Table 7.4 'Women should observe Islamic dress codes' (odds ratios agreeing)

	Pakistan	Indonesia	Egypt	Kazakhstan	All Countries
Age	0.99	0.98	0.97	1.00	0.99
Male	1.00	1.00	1.00	1.00	1.00
Female	0.85	0.76	0.65	1.19	0.90
<High School	1.00	1.00	1.00	1.00	1.00
High School	0.38	1.38	0.59	0.92	1.09
Univ/ Professional	0.27	1.22	**2.07**	0.68	0.83
Religious Activists	1.00	1.00	1.00	–	–
Muslim Professionals	**0.43**	**0.43**	0.00	–	–
Public	0.70	0.51	0.00	–	–
Pakistan	–	–	–	–	1.00
Indonesia	–	–	–	–	1.84
Egypt	–	–	–	–	4.06
Kazakhstan	–	–	–	–	0.02

Note: Odds ratio figures in **boldface** are significant at $p = .05$.

modern and not religious. In Indonesia and Egypt, there was almost universal support among respondents, irrespective of their level of religiosity or modernity.

Results of the logistic regression analysis, reported in Table 7.4, confirm the trends reported in Table 7.3. Perhaps the most significant finding revealed by logistic regression analysis after controlling for age, gender and education is that, compared with respondents in Pakistan, those in Indonesia and Egypt were two to four times more likely to agree with the statement. The Kazakhs, on the other hand, were the least supportive of these attitudes.

Attitudes Towards Patriarchy

Attitudes toward patriarchy were ascertained by the responses to the statement, 'If men are not in charge of women, women will lose sight of all human values and the family will disintegrate'. The findings reported in Table 7.5 show that patriarchal attitudes varied significantly among the four countries.

In Egypt, there was near-universal agreement with the statement, and surprisingly, there was practically no difference in male and female attitudes. Kazakhstan had the lowest rate of agreement, and here again there was no real difference between male and female respondents. In Indonesia, 68 per cent of men and 70 per cent of women expressed pro-patriarchal attitudes, while in Pakistan the corresponding rates were 62 per cent and 44 per cent. The much lower agreement rates in Kazakhstan probably reflect the influence of ideological socialization under the former Soviet regime. If this is the case, then the data appear to indicate the effectiveness of socialist ideology in reducing patriarchal attitudes. The near-universal agreement and correspondence in the attitudes of men and women in Egypt is very surprising and unexpected. Compared with women in Egypt and Indonesia, only 44 per cent of women in Pakistan expressed agreement with the statement, despite Pakistan being a much more patriarchal society than either Egypt or Indonesia.

The Egyptian respondents were the most patriarchal in their attitudes. An overwhelming majority of them agreed that men should be in charge of women. In Kazakhstan and Indonesia, the more educated were less patriarchal. The religious activists in Pakistan were markedly more traditional than the professionals, and public attitudes tended to be similar to those of the religious elite in all countries except Kazakhstan (where there was no religious elite). In Egypt, however, the public held firmer views about men being in charge of women than did the elites. Religiosity was found to be positively associated with patriarchal attitudes in Kazakhstan and Pakistan only.

Table 7.5 'If men are not in charge of women, women will lose sight of all human values and the family will disintegrate' (% agreeing)

Countries		Pakistan	Indonesia	Egypt	Kazakhstan
Gender	Male	62	68	86	24
	Female	44	70	86	27
Age	< 25	59	72	83	31
	26 – 40	54	67	87	22
	41 – 55	66	68	87	21
	> 56	61	67	85	34
Education	< High School	62	73	90	33
	High School	70	67	90	24
	Univ/ Professional	55	69	85	29
Sample	Religious Activists	64	66	87	–
	Muslim Professionals	44	69	82	20
	Public	62	64	95	20

Table 7.6 'If men are not in charge of women, women will lose sight of all human values and the family will disintegrate' (odds ratios agreeing)

	Pakistan	Indonesia	Egypt	Kazakhstan	All Countries
Age	1.01	1.00	0.99	0.99	1.00
Male	1.00	1.00	1.00	1.00	1.00
Female	**0.47**	**0.48**	**0.34**	1.19	**0.53**
< High School	1.00	1.00	1.00	1.00	1.00
High School	1.53	0.68	2.11	1.23	1.13
Univ/ Professional	0.92	**0.52**	1.14	0.55	**0.73**
Religious Activists	1.00	1.00	1.00	–	–
Muslim Professionals	**0.45**	0.79	**0.46**	–	–
Public	0.86	0.82	**0.35**	–	–
Pakistan	–	–	–	–	1.00
Indonesia	–	–	–	–	**1.36**
Egypt	–	–	–	–	**3.96**
Kazakhstan	–	–	–	–	**0.40**

Note: Odds ratio figures in **boldface** are significant at p = .05.

The logistic regression analysis reported in Table 7.6 confirms the general trends noted above. It also reveals that respondents in Indonesia and Egypt are significantly more patriarchal than respondents in Pakistan. The Kazakhs, on the other hand, are significantly less patriarchal compared with the other three countries. The most significant finding of the logistic regression analysis after controlling for age, gender and education is that, compared to Pakistan, the Egyptian and Indonesian respondents were significantly more approving of women observing veiling and Islamic dress codes, as well as being significantly more patriarchal in their attitudes. The Kazakhs, on the other hand, were the reverse in all these respects compared with Pakistani, Indonesian and Egyptian respondents.

Discussion

The evidence concerning female veiling and seclusion and patriarchy indicates that attitudes towards these issues are an outcome of complex interaction between the prevalent social, economic and political conditions in each country, and traditional Islamic norms. Material and social conditions in the country influence the shaping of attitudes towards these issues more strongly than traditional Islamic ideology.

The question on veiling specifically investigated whether women are perceived as sexually provocative and capable of alluring men and whether the veiling and seclusion of women is seen as necessary and desirable in order to avoid the possibility of sexual misconduct by men. The statement was deliberately phrased so as not to raise questions concerning men's role in arousing sexual desire. It implied that only women have the responsibility for maintaining appropriate sexual conduct. The question about women observing Islamic dress codes was essentially an extension of the question of veiling and secluding women as a means of ensuring appropriate social and sexual conduct between men and women. The results reveal overwhelming support among men in Indonesia, Egypt and

Pakistan for the veiling and segregation of women, and surprisingly, among women as well in Egypt and Indonesia. In Pakistan, support among women declines significantly, although a majority of them still express support for it. The low level of support for veiling and segregation in Kazakhstan is once again probably a function of the former socialist ideology which prohibited the veiling and seclusion of women, and discrimination against women in general.

Similarly, the question concerning patriarchy sought to explore the attitude that women need the guidance of men to conduct themselves in an appropriate manner in order to ensure the stability of the family and society. If this were so, the domination of men over women would be justifiable. Given that the underlying logic of patriarchy is gender domination, responses to the question directly reflect the prevalence of patriarchal ideology. Support for patriarchy was highest in Egypt and Indonesia, moderately high in Pakistan, and very low in Kazakhstan. Unlike their response on the issue of veiling and seclusion, only a minority of women in Pakistan expressed support on this issue.

These findings are somewhat counter-intuitive. If we compare Egypt, Indonesia and Pakistan, women in Indonesia and Egypt enjoy a higher quality of citizenship than women in Pakistan. Why is it then that attitudes are more conservative in those countries where women have relatively more freedom? Data from the United Nations *Human Development Report* (1996) show that the Gender Empowerment Index, an index constructed for the purpose of assessing whether women and men are able to actively participate in economic and political life and decision-making, is higher for Indonesia and Egypt than for Pakistan.[20] The Gender Empowerment Measure (GEM) focuses on the relative degree of empowerment or enfranchisement of women in aspects of public life in relation to their male counterparts. In short, the GEM can be regarded as a proxy summary measure of the quality of women's citizenship. The GEM value for the advanced industrial countries is 0.569; for the world it is 0.391. The value for Indonesia is 0.367, for

Egypt 0.280, and for Pakistan only 0.165. Unfortunately, the GEM value for Kazakhstan is not available in the report. It can, however, be roughly deduced from the GEM ranking of 174 countries, where Kazakhstan ranks 72, Indonesia 102, Egypt 106 and Pakistan 134.[21]

The question raised by the comparison of countries in terms of their GEM values concerns why the support for patriarchy and the veiling and seclusion of women is lower in Pakistan than in Egypt and Indonesia? One possible explanation of this disparity is the relationship between gender equality and the status of men. The GEM values cited above clearly indicate that the quality of female citizenship in Egypt and Indonesia is significantly superior to that of Pakistan. This means that, relative to men, women in Egypt and Indonesia have achieved greater equality. One sociological consequence of this is that, relative to women, men have experienced a loss of status in Egypt and Indonesia. In Pakistan, the quality of women's citizenship is relatively underdeveloped, and men have therefore not suffered the same degree of loss in status as men in Egypt and Indonesia.

One plausible conclusion we can draw from this is that the degree of status loss experienced by men is related to attitudes towards veiling, seclusion and patriarchy. In Muslim societies where men have experienced greater status loss relative to women, they have compensated for that loss by developing more conservative attitudes toward women, including support for veiling, seclusion and patriarchy. This would explain the attitudes of men in Egypt, Indonesia and Pakistan. The implication is that as the status and position of women in Muslim countries further improves as a result of government policies, Muslim women can expect to encounter new forms of social resistance.

One form this resistance may take is the emergence of fundamentalist Islamic movements which seek to establish Islamic norms, including the regulation of gender relations along the lines prescribed by traditional norms. It is rather paradoxical that the progressive trends in relation to gender equality coincide with politicization and ideologization of Islam. The objective of these developments is the Islamization of social protest movements which are nostalgic for the conservative patriarchal family and gender relations, and seclusion and segregation of women.

This model, however, does not explain the prevalence of relatively traditional views among female respondents. The most likely explanation for this is that the conditions that favour male domination and control act as powerful socializing influences on women's world views, and therefore women do not regard their own views on veiling and patriarchy as problematic. The data also suggests another possible explanation. In general, individual loyalty to social groups tends to vary according to the perceived ability of the group to meet and satisfy the individual's needs and aspirations. The individual's loyalty and identification with the group increase if the group is seen as satisfying the individual's needs. This would suggest that societies which are more successful in promoting conditions of institutional equality for women would also generate greater identification with the society and its dominant values among women. In other words, paradoxically, Muslim societies that attempt to ensure institutional equality for women and the quality of their citizenship may elicit a greater degree of conformity to traditional Islamic values of patriarchy, veiling and the segregation of women. The data from this study provide some support for this explanation when we compare women's attitudes towards these values and the quality of female citizenship in Indonesia, Pakistan and Egypt. This observation may not be applicable in the case of Kazakhstan, because of the role played by the state socialist ideology rather than by Islamic values in shaping individual and collective identities in the country until recently.

Finally, the overall findings regarding attitudes in the four countries to veiling, the seclusion of women and patriarchy also bears out the proposition presented here that socially enforced cultural practices may be an effective means of managing human sexuality. It has been argued that Islam, unlike Christianity, does not sanction or approve of celibacy. In fact, Islam regards sexual desire as 'natural' and enjoins its followers to satisfy and enjoy sexual desires within the framework of marriage and family. Over the centuries, interpretations of the sacred texts have developed a conceptualization of human sexuality which stipulates that women are not only sexual beings but also the embodiment of sexuality. It is women who are sexually provocative and capable of alluring men. The veiling and seclusion of women is seen as desirable in order to avoid the possibility of misconduct by men, as well as to ensure the stability of the family. Related to this is the domination of men in the private sphere of the family to ensure its proper functioning.

The evidence reported in this chapter provides very strong support for the hypothesis that attitudes towards veiling, the seclusion of women and patriarchy are related to the management of human sexuality. In societies such as Egypt, Pakistan and Indonesia, in which there are strong sanctions against any sexual contact between men and women outside of marriage and the family, attitudes towards veiling and patriarchy are the strongest and most conservative. In Kazakh society, where there are fewer socially enforced restrictions on premarital sexual contact between men and women, the attitudes toward veiling and patriarchy were the opposite of those expressed by respondents in Egypt, Pakistan and Indonesia. We need more focused evidence to explore these issues further, which unfortunately is not available in this study. I hope that the hypothesis postulating the link between attitudes toward sexuality, veiling and patriarchy will stimulate further debate on the problem. The sociological implication of the argument I have presented here is that as attitudes toward human sexuality change, attitudes to veiling, the seclusion of women and patriarchy will also undergo transformation.

NOTES

1. Levy 1957.
2. Mernissi 1989.
3. Qur'an, 24, pp. 30-31.
4. Mernissi 1989
5. Haeri 1993.
6. Hardacre 1993; Higgins 1985.
7. Hardacre 1993; Bullough 1973; Rugh 1986.
8. Baydawi as cited in Levy 1957, p. 126.
9. Haeri 1993.
10. Levy 1957.
11. Nash 1991.
12. Levy 1957; Rahman 1982; Mernissi 1989; Rugh 1986.
13. Bari 1998.
14. The veiling and seclusion of women in society is a vital issue among Muslim communities in the West as well. A recent issue of the *Muslim Women's National Network of Australia Newsletter*, vol. 16, March 1998 carried the following report under the heading, 'Sisters Refused Entry to Auburn Mosque at Eid':

    MWNNA has received two separate complaints from members that they and their sisters were barred from attending Eid prayers at Auburn Mosque. Men at the entry told them that women were not allowed and that 'Turkish women do not go to Mosque'. The sisters were very upset since attendance at Eid celebrations is a duty for both males and females and there are clear Hadith in which the Prophet (PBUH) indicated that men should not prevent women from attending the Mosques. Both our sisters were quite upset, and said that the incident ruined Eid day for them.

    Similar observations about attitudes among the Muslim Community in North America were discussed in a thoughtful article by Hathout (1998).
15. Esposito 1995; Armstrong 1994.
16. Tohidi 1998; Keddie 1999.
17. Mernissi 1991; Ahmad 1992; Tohidi 1998.
18. See collection of papers in Bodman and Tohidi 1998.
19. In attitudinal research it is highly desirable to use statements which refer to a single dimension of the phenomenon or social reality being investigated. This approach enhances the validity and the reliability of the data gathered from respondents. Given the sensitivity and the length of the survey questionnaire in the study this was not always possible. The questions on veiling and patriarchy had more than one dimension. It would have been ideal to split the questions in such a way that each ensuing statement dealt with only a single dimension. But this was not

done for logistical and theoretical reasons. The logistical reason was related to constraints of time and resources. In pre-tests of the survey instrument it was found that many respondents found single dimension statements like 'women are sexually attractive' meaningless and, therefore, objected to them. The theoretical reason for including the multidimensional statements in the study was that in the Islamic discourse the multiple dimensions are inextricably linked. Their separation, therefore, was considered to be contrary to the theoretical objective of the study that was to chart or identify attitudes of respondents to sensitive religious and social issues which are often not accessible to sociological investigation. The statements put to the respondents were formulated in such a way that they conveyed the inquiry or the question so that it corresponded to their, i.e., Muslim understanding of the social reality being investigated.

20. UNDP 1996, Table 1.12.
21. UNDP 1996, Table 3.

8

MUSLIM PERCEPTIONS OF THE 'OTHER'

This chapter will focus on two questions that broadly relate to Muslim attitudes towards the 'Other'. Firstly, it will explore the respondents' perceptions of how influential Islam, Christianity, Judaism and Atheism will be in the future. Secondly, it will examine Muslim perceptions of the attitudes of the governments of some of the major non-Muslim countries in the world towards Islam. The focus on Christianity, Judaism and Atheism was prompted by their historical as well as contemporary relevance to the debates about the present and future civilizational and political conflicts in the world.

The Muslim perceptions of the attitudes toward Islam of some of the major non-Muslim countries indirectly expands the discussion by including other religions such as Hinduism and Buddhism which are practised in some of the countries included in this investigation. A secondary reason for undertaking this analysis was to explore the phenomenon that can be described as 'moral polarization'. Moral polarization here refers to the widespread view held by many Muslims that in the modern world only Islam offers and promotes a real moral and ethical alternative to permissiveness, consumerism, hedonism, moral relativism and individualism associated with and promoted by the modern Western cultures. Indirectly, therefore, this chapter will seek to ascertain the extent of this moral polarization from the empirical evidence. The perception of the existence of moral polarization has important consequences for the relationship between the West and the Islamic world.

The data about the perception of the 'Other' was collected from each respondent surveyed in the study. The respondents were asked how they felt about the future of Islam, Christianity, Judaism and atheistic beliefs. They were asked to indicate which one of the following responses came closest to expressing their opinion:

1. It (Islam) will probably gain more and more influence;
2. It will continue about the way it is;
3. It will probably lose some influence;
4. It will probably grow rather weak;
5. Do not know.

In the analysis response categories three and four were collapsed together. There were very few 'Do not know' responses. Only those who had chosen the reconstituted response categories one to three were included in the analysis.

For ascertaining whether respondents perceived some of the non-Muslim countries as pro-Islamic or anti-Islamic the respondents were asked the following question: What kind of attitudes do you think the governments of the following countries have towards Islam? The list of countries included the following: the United States, the United Kingdom, Germany, France, Russia, China, Australia, Singapore, Japan and India. They were asked to indicate which one of the following responses came closest to expressing their views: pro-Islamic, anti-Islamic, do not know. The following discussion will first focus on the findings pertaining to the respondents perceptions of the future of Islam, Christianity, Judaism and Atheism followed by the findings pertaining to the perception of the attitudes of the governments of different countries towards Islam.

The findings about the perception of the future of Islam, Christianity, Judaism and Atheism are reported in Table 8.1. In Indonesia and Pakistan, an overwhelming majority of the respondents saw the influence of Islam increasing in the future. In Kazakhstan and Egypt, comparatively smaller proportions expressed the same view. The reason was that a much higher

Table 8.1 Respondents' perceptions of the future of Islam, Christianity, Judaism, and Atheism (%)

	Islam	Christianity	Judaism	Atheism
Indonesia				
Lose influence	2	37	68	83
Stay the same	5	51	29	12
Gain influence	93	12	4	5
Pakistan				
Lose influence	2	57	68	50
Stay the same	4	22	12	6
Gain influence	94	21	20	44
Kazakhstan				
Lose influence	4	15	53	72
Stay the same	18	68	41	25
Gain influence	78	17	6	4
Egypt				
Lose influence	12	15	3	11
Stay the same	29	27	11	32
Gain influence	59	58	86	57

proportion of respondents in these countries compared to Indonesia and Pakistan thought that the influence of Islam would remain the same. If we combine the response categories, 'stay the same' and 'gain influence' then the evidence clearly indicates that a majority of the respondents perceived the influence of Islam in future increasing or remaining the same. In Egypt, however, about one out of every ten respondents said that Islam will lose influence. A detailed analysis of the Egyptian data revealed that most of the respondents who saw a decline in the influence of Islam in future were men (only 4 per cent of Egyptian women compared with 17 per cent of the men saw a decline in the influence of Islam in the future). In this respect, the Egyptian respondents differed from the other three countries in which there were no significant differences between men and women.

There was significant variation in the responses about the future of Christianity. In Indonesia, 51 per cent of respondents said that the influence of Christianity will remain the same and 37 per cent said that it would lose influence. Twelve per cent were of the view that Christianity will gain influence. In Pakistan, 57 per cent of the respondents saw Christianity as losing influence and 22 per cent thought that it will remain the same and about the same proportion thought that its influence will increase in the future. Among the Kazakh respondents 68 per cent said that its influence will remain unchanged and 17 per cent thought that it will gain influence followed by about the same proportion who said that it will lose influence. The Egyptian pattern was very different from the general pattern of responses described above. Unlike the Indonesian, Pakistani and Kazakh respondents, 58 per cent of the Egyptian respondents said that Christianity will gain influence with another 27 per cent expressing the view that it will remain unchanged.

The perception of Judaism was similar to that of Christianity. In Indonesia and Pakistan 68 per cent of respondents expected Judaism to lose influence and a slightly lower proportion in Kazakhstan expressed the same view. Compared with Indonesia and Kazakhstan significantly more Pakistanis said that it would gain influence. The Egyptian responses were again strikingly different from the other three countries. Eighty-six per cent Egyptians were of the opinion that Judaism will gain influence in the future. Only 3 per cent said that it would lose influence.

The future of atheism was viewed differently. In Indonesia and Kazakhstan a large majority saw its influence declining and only a small proportion said that the influence of atheism would increase. In Pakistan while 50 per cent of respondents said the influence of atheism will decline, 44 per cent also saw atheism gaining influence. The Egyptian perception of atheism was similar to its perception of Christianity, with a majority of Egyptians seeing its influence to increase and a small percentage saying that it will decline. About one-third of Egyptians said its influence will remain unchanged.

Further analysis of the data showed no significant effect of gender, age, education and sample types on the attitudes of Indonesian respondents towards Islam, Christianity and Atheism. The only exception to this was that the more educated were less likely to say that Judaism will lose influence but the majority (64 per cent) with university education said that Judaism will lose influence in the future. In Pakistan the above mentioned independent variables did not influence opinions about the future of Islam but were found to have some effect on attitudes towards other religions. Pakistani women were significantly less likely to say that Christianity, Judaism and atheism will lose influence than Pakistani men and more likely to say that they will gain influence. In Pakistan additionally more educated respondents were more likely to say that atheism will lose influence and less likely to say that it will gain influence compared with the less educated.

In Kazakhstan significantly more educated respondents saw Islam gaining influence in the future compared with their compatriots with lower educational attainment. The majority of the Kazakhs saw the influence of Christianity remaining unchanged but women and younger respondents were more inclined to say that its influence would increase in the future. The Kazakh Muslims were equally divided about the future of Judaism. About half of them thought that its influence will decline but another half did not see much change in its future role. However, the majority of the Kazakhs saw the influence of atheism declining. This view was especially pronounced among older respondents and university graduates.

The majority of Egyptian Muslims, like those from Indonesia, Pakistan and Kazakhstan, also saw Islam gaining influence in the future but this view was much more widely held by Egyptian women (79 per cent) than men (53 per cent). Another feature of the Egyptian data was that compared with the Muslim professionals and the public, a significantly larger proportion of the religious activists saw the influence of Islam decline. Egypt was the only country displaying this pattern and this suggests that among Egyptian social groups there was considerable polarization of views about the future direction of the role of Islam in Egypt as well as in the world. Another unique feature of the Egyptian data was that 60 per cent of the respondents saw the influence of Christianity and Atheism increasing and 86 per cent saw Judaism gaining more influence. These views were generally much more widely expressed by the more educated respondents as well as by those who were religious activists.

These perceptions showed that compared with their fellow Muslims from the other three countries, the Egyptian Muslims held very different views about the future of Christianity, Judaism and Atheism. Furthermore, these views were more widely subscribed to by religious activists. If this represents a general pattern then it would suggest that, comparatively, the Egyptians take a much more pluralistic view of future religious and ideological developments, and that the internal evolution of the Egyptian society may follow a different pattern from the other three countries. One feature of this may be greater polarization among Egyptian Muslims leading to a different pattern of religious activism than other countries.

Perceptions of the 'Other' and Muslim Religious Piety

An investigation of the relationship between the perception of the 'Other' and Muslim religious piety showed that the Ideological dimension of Muslim piety and the response that Islam will gain influence in the future were statistically positively and significantly correlated in Indonesia, Kazakhstan and Egypt and positively although not significantly correlated in Pakistan. The ritualistic dimension of piety was statistically positively correlated in Indonesia, Pakistan and Kazakhstan but negatively and not statistically significantly correlated in Egypt (see Table 8.2). This negative relationship, as mentioned above, though not significant was unexpected but it does confirm the observation made earlier that in Egypt the perception of the

Table 8.2 Correlation between the ideological and ritualistic dimensions of piety and the future role of Islam, Christianity, Judaism, and Atheism

	Indonesia	Pakistan	Kazakhstan	Egypt
Islam				
Ideological dimension of piety	.084*	.047	.128**	.075*
Ritualistic dimension of piety	.062*	.133**	.114**	-.057
Christianity				
Ideological dimension of piety	-.036	-.063*	-.084*	.205**
Ritualistic dimension of piety	-.039	.042	-.113**	.278**
Judaism				
Ideological dimension of piety	.017	-.069*	-.007	.162**
Ritualistic dimension of piety	.031	.069*	-.105*	.182**
Atheism				
Ideological dimension of piety	-.101**	-.095**	-.122**	.067
Ritualistic dimension of piety	.00	.009	-.149**	.064

* Correlation is significant at the 0.05 level
** Correlation is significant at the 0.01 level

future roles of different religions was markedly different compared with the other three countries.

The relationship between the ideological dimension of piety and the response that Christianity will gain influence in future was negatively correlated in all countries except Egypt where the relationship was positive and statistically significant. The same pattern of relationship was observed between ritualistic piety and Christianity gaining greater influence except that in Pakistan the relationship was also positive but not statistically significant. The correlation between Judaism gaining more influence and the two dimensions was more complex. In Egypt, it was positive and statistically significant. In Pakistan and Kazakhstan, it was negative but only statistically significant in Pakistan. In Indonesia, the correlation between the ideological dimension and Judaism gaining greater influence was positive but not significant. The correlation between such a perception of Judaism and ritualistic piety was positive and statistically significant in Pakistan and Egypt but not in Indonesia. It was negatively correlated in Kazakhstan. The correlation between the two dimensions of piety and atheism gaining more influence in the future was in general negative in Indonesia, Pakistan, and Kazakhstan and positive but not statistically significant in Egypt.

The above evidence lends itself to the following broad conclusion: Muslim perception of the 'self' is very positive. They see Islam gaining greater influence nationally and internationally in the future. Their perception of the 'Other' on the other hand is markedly different. In Indonesia, Pakistan and Kazakhstan the respondents generally saw the influence of Christianity, Judaism and atheism declining or at best remaining the same. The exception to this pattern was Egypt where the respondents thought that Christianity, Judaism and atheism would also gain influence in the future.

These national differences in the perceptions of the 'Other' would suggest that the dynamics of relationship between Islam and Christianity, Judaism and atheism are going to follow a complex pattern, which would be shaped in part by nationally grounded social factors. The interesting question which unfortunately cannot be answered by the available data but needs further investigation is what social factors are instrumental in producing the observed different patterns in the perceptions of the 'Other'? This evidence, however, would suggest that future relationships between Islam and the West are likely to experience periodic political and social tensions and conflicts. This should provide a challenging opportunity for those individuals and organizations interested in promoting harmonious relationships between the two major world civilizations.

Muslim Perceptions of the Major Countries

Muslim perceptions of the 'Other' were further explored through a question that inquired about the respondent's opinion about the attitudes of some of the major non-Muslim countries towards Islam. The respondents were asked, 'What kind of attitudes do you think the governments of the following countries have towards Islam?' They were asked to indicate which one of the following responses came closest to their opinion: 'Pro-Islamic', 'Anti-Islamic', or 'Do Not Know' (if they had no opinion).

The categories 'Pro-Islamic' and 'Anti-Islamic' are broad and open to wide interpretations. The pre-test of the question before the fieldwork showed that most respondents were able to make a choice and if they did not have an opinion and were not sure they chose the 'Do not know' response. The decision to include the countries mentioned above was guided by the intention to include all those which were generally regarded as belonging to the West and whose influence in international and/or regional affairs made them prominent. The findings are reported in Table 8.3.

About half of the Indonesians said that the attitudes of the governments of the United States and Russia were anti-Islamic and 44 per cent expressed a similar view about the Chinese government. As for the other countries, the majority of the Indonesians were not sure or did not know what their governments' attitudes towards Islam were. On the whole only a small minority of Indonesians thought that the governments of

Table 8.3 Respondents' perceptions of the attitudes of governments of selected countries towards Islam (%)

	Indonesia		Pakistan		Kazakhstan		Egypt	
	Pro-Islamic	Anti-Islamic	Pro-Islamic	Anti-Islamic	Pro-Islamic	Anti-Islamic	Pro-Islamic	Anti-Islamic
US	4	52	4	84	12	15	3	80
UK	6	34	5	79	10	16	11	65
Germany	6	26	4	63	11	16	12	56
France	6	26	5	65	10	15	18	52
Russia	2	56	3	80	12	16	2	75
China	4	44	27	38	3	14	7	56
Australia	9	18	7	46	2	11	9	44
Singapore	23	10	8	42	5	10	10	40
Japan	9	13	10	44	4	12	13	41
India	17	19	3	86	9	12	2	21

Note: The figures are percentages of respondents. The percentage for 'Do Not Know' responses are not indicated above but can be calculated by adding the percentages of the two responses given above and subtracting it from 100.

major western countries were pro-Islamic. The major exceptions were Singapore and India which were seen by 23 and 17 per cent of respondents respectively as pro-Islamic.

About one out of every ten Indonesian respondents thought that the Japanese and Australian governments were pro-Islamic and about the same proportion saw them as anti-Islamic. The governments of Singapore and Japan were seen as least anti-Islamic followed by the Indian and Australian governments. These data were collected before the 1999 East Timor conflict in which Australia was seen by many Indonesians as taking an anti-Indonesia position and it would be interesting to assess whether events surrounding this conflict have resulted in a shift in the attitudes of Indonesians towards Australia.

About one-third of the Indonesian respondents regarded the attitudes of the other major Western powers, the United Kingdom, France and Germany as anti-Islamic but interestingly a majority of them expressed no opinion about their attitudes. The anti-Islamic perceptions of the United States were attributed to the American policies towards the Palestinians and Bosnian Muslims. The anti-Russian attitudes were largely attributed to the Russian treatment of the Muslims of Chechnya and to its past atheistic policies. The attitudes towards China were largely shaped by China's past support of Indonesian communists as well as to China's atheistic communist ideology that was seen as against Islamic teachings.

The Pakistani responses clearly demonstrate how the national political dynamics and concerns shape individual perceptions of the 'other'. Expectedly, given Pakistan's obsession with India and the history of military and political conflicts between them, an overwhelming majority of Pakistanis saw the Indian government as anti-Islamic. It was closely followed by similar perceptions of the American, Russian and British governments. This perception again appears to be influenced by the conflicts involving Muslim populations in former Yugoslavia, Palestine and Chechnya. At the time of the data collection for this study the Bosnian conflict was raging and many respondents blamed the above mentioned countries for not doing enough to stop the massive human tragedy being inflicted on the Bosnian Muslims. In addition Pakistanis also viewed these countries as supporting India in its conflict with Pakistan. The United States was often seen as blatantly pro-Israel in Israel's conflict with the Palestinians and Muslim Arabs, and in general hostile to Islamic countries such as Iran, Iraq and Libya.

The anti-Islamic perception of the German and French governments was also due to the same type of causes but about one third of the respondents had no opinion about these two countries. China has been for long seen as a close ally of Pakistan in its conflict with India. Consequently, notwithstanding that China is a communist country, about one-third of Pakistanis saw China's government as being pro-Islamic and only 38 per cent as anti-Islamic. While about half of the respondents were neutral about the governments of Australia, Singapore and Japan, slightly less than half of the respondents felt they were also anti-Islamic.

The majority of the Kazakh were surprisingly uncertain or neutral about what their perceptions were of various countries. About one in ten Kazakhs felt that the major Western countries were pro-Islamic and a slightly larger proportion felt that most of the countries were anti-Islamic. The governments of major Western countries and Russia were seen as slightly more anti-Islamic than Japan, Australia, Singapore and India.

Egyptian perceptions were somewhat similar to the perceptions of Pakistanis and Indonesians. A large majority of Egyptians regarded the United States government as anti-Islamic and this view was largely shaped by their perceptions of the American pro-Israel policies. A large majority also saw the Russian government as anti-Islamic primarily due to its policies towards Muslim minorities in Chechnya and former Yugoslavia. While the French government was seen as being the most pro-Islamic a majority of Egyptians saw the British, French, German and Chinese governments as anti-Islamic in their policies. Unlike the Pakistanis the Egyptians did not see India as anti-Islamic. In fact, most of them said that they did not know its policies. Slightly less than half of the respondents thought that the

Singapore, Australian and Japanese governments were anti-Islamic largely because they were perceived as allies of the Western countries assumed to be hostile towards Islam.

Concluding Remarks

Muslims in general were very optimistic and positive about the influence of Islam in the future. A large majority of them saw Islam gaining influence in world affairs. This view was almost universally held by Indonesians and Pakistanis. The Kazakhs and Egyptians were comparatively somewhat restrained in expressing such a view but still a large majority opined that Islam would gain influence. One main difference between the Indonesians and the Pakistanis, and the Kazakhs and the Egyptians was that a greater proportion of the latter held the view that Islam's influence in future will remain unchanged.

The opinions about the 'others' were more complex and appeared to be influenced by national factors such as demographic composition of the populations and the perception of the influence held by the 'others' in the national affairs. For example, in Pakistan the population is largely religiously homogeneous with Muslims constituting over 95 per cent of the population. This fact obviously had an impact on the Pakistani perception of the 'Other', with a majority of the respondents expressing the opinion that Christianity, Judaism and Atheism will lose influence. The demographic homogeneity in Pakistan precludes other religions influencing national affairs.

The populations of the other three countries are less homogeneous. Sizeable proportions of Indonesian, Kazakh and Egyptian populations are Christians. Consequently, their opinions about the future role of Christianity are less distorted. In Egypt, where Coptic Christians historically have been not only a sizeable proportion of the population but have also occupied a very prominent role in national affairs, especially in politics and the economy, a majority of the Egyptian respondents held the view that the role of Christianity will increase.

Surprisingly, an overwhelming proportion also expressed a similar view about Judaism. This can be possibly attributed to the impact of Egyptian and Israeli political and military conflicts on the national perceptions of Egyptians. Israel is not only militarily and economically more powerful than Egypt but it also enjoys the support of much of the West as well as of much of Western Jewish populations. All these factors obviously influence Egyptian Muslim respondents' perception of Judaism thus producing the pattern revealed by the data.

Atheism stills appeared to be viewed by many Pakistani and Egyptian respondents to be gaining influence in the future but not by the Indonesians and Kazakhs. Once again, this perception is influenced by specific national factors. For example, the Kazakhs having been part of the former communist Soviet Union probably did not see the restoration of communism to power. The Indonesians probably made their assessment based on the decline of communism in Indonesian society over the past thirty years under the New Order governments of former President Mohammad Suharto. They may have also been influenced by the fall of communism in the former Soviet Union and Indo-China where only Vietnam remains a communist country and is now part of the ASEAN (Association of South East Asian Countries).

But none of these factors appeared to forge the same type of change in the perceptions of Pakistanis and Egyptians. What factors influenced their attitudes is difficult to say. One possible reason may be that both of these countries have very robust and influential Islamic organizations seeking to establish an Islamic state. Their influence may be a factor in shaping their attitudes about atheism. The respondents in these countries may also be influenced by the increasing economic, military and political influence of the West in their countries, which is largely viewed as secular and non-religious.

The evidence also showed that religious piety was generally positively associated with the view that Islam will gain influence in future. This perception, together with the widespread view that the governments of the major western countries were anti-Islamic raises important questions about the nature of Muslim political consciousness and public opinion in Muslim countries. These perceptions tend to support the observation about how Muslims see an increasing moral polarization between themselves and the 'Other' globally. For many Muslims this belief is based on the evidence they see around them. In Muslim societies there is a visible increase in religious piety as discussed in Chapter 1. Additionally they also see in the popular cultures of the Western countries evidence of declining religious piety and increasing secularization. What the popular culture, however, fails to show is that in Western countries the decline in religious piety has been accompanied by an increase in social morality which emphasizes public responsibility for collective social well being and good citizenship.

However, irrespective of the fact whether Muslim perceptions of their own and that of the Western countries' moral and religious life are valid or not, their perception of the increasing moral polarization, in my opinion, does not auger well for promoting a better political relationship between the Western countries and the Muslim World. Just as Muslim perceptions of the future role of Islam in the world may be exaggerated, their perceptions about the western countries as anti-Islamic may also be exaggerated. At any rate the findings provide a glimpse of the social reality which requires the attention of both Muslims and the 'Others' who are interested in promoting a better understanding between the Muslim world and the rest.

9

CONCLUSIONS
Islamic Futures

The results of this study show that the Muslim world is undergoing a religious renaissance. In various chapters an attempt has been made to explore some of the main features of Muslim religious commitment and consciousness. As expected, the contours of this consciousness indicate its complexity. While fundamental Muslim religious beliefs and practices are an important constituent of Muslim religious consciousness, the empirical evidence discussed in the preceding chapters strongly suggests that its structure and expression are influenced by social factors. The complexity, therefore, inheres not in the sacred religious texts but in the social conditions in which they are read, interpreted, reflected upon and practised. In other words, there is nothing inherently Islamic in the ways different Muslim countries and the social groups within them conceptualize and express piety or invest their trust in religious institutions and functionaries. To elaborate on this point, I will first provide an overview of some of the main findings and then discuss their implications for future developments in the Muslim world.

This study provides robust evidence of strong religious commitment among a majority of Muslims from all walks of life. This commitment is grounded in the traditions of scriptural Islam and occupies a prominent place in the daily lives of the majority of Muslims, influencing their everyday activities. The evidence also shows that religious piety is socially constructed. This social construction is influenced by global and societal conditions. At the global level, the hegemonic cultural patterns of the West appear to provoke strong resistance in Muslim populations which expresses itself in the reassertion of Islamic identity, which in turn reinforces cultural pride and self-esteem as well as consciousness of an Islamic history which once bore the signature of superior cultural traditions.

At the local level, factors influencing social construction include dissatisfaction with the slow and often negligible progress made by national governments in their attempt to address gross economic, social and political inequalities. Consequently, many Muslims turn to Islam to rectify these problems. The evidence of social construction is also reflected in the marked characteristics of Muslim identity in the four countries under study. In Indonesia, Pakistan and Egypt, Muslim identity is linked to piety embedded in the knowledge of sacred texts, religious rituals, religious devotion and socio-cultural conditions. In Kazakhstan, Muslim identity is linked primarily to 'secular' factors such as ethnic and national histories and consciousness.

These two types of Muslim identities also correspond to the self-image of Islam. The dominant self-image of Islam among the majority of the respondents in Indonesia, Pakistan and Egypt has been referred to as 'traditional' and the dominant self-image of Islam among the Kazakh Muslims is 'liberal'. A minority of respondents in Indonesia, Pakistan and Egypt also subscribed to the liberal self-image; similarly a minority of respondents in Kazakhstan subscribed to the traditional self-image. The traditional self-image is positively related to religious piety and the liberal self-image is negatively correlated to religious piety. This further reinforces the observation about the two types of Muslim identities, namely, the traditional and the 'liberal' or secular.

These self-images and Muslim identities also appear to correlate with the two strands of Islam: 'High Islam' and 'folk Islam'. 'High Islam' is characterized by 'scripturalist puritanism', whereas 'folk Islam' is 'pluralistic and flexible', deeply influenced by the needs and proclivities of the believers. The majority of the respondents in Indonesia, Pakistan and Egypt subscribed to 'High Islam' and a minority to 'folk Islam'. In Kazakhstan the distribution was opposite; the majority of Kazakhs appeared to subscribe to 'folk Islam' and a minority to 'High Islam'. In other words strong religious commitment (piety), traditional self-image of Islam (religiously rigorous) and high Islam are different expressions of one type of Muslimness. The other type of Muslimness is expressed by weak religious commitment, liberal self-image (religiously lax) and folk Islam.

Muslim societies are dominated by two types of elites which, following Gellner, have been labelled as 'radical' and 'conservative'. The Radical elite prevail in Muslim countries where either colonialism has destroyed the old elite or where a new one has risen from below through popular and radical social change, claiming that it represents a purer type of Islam. The conservative or traditional elite are those who have their origins in one of the historical Khaldunian swings of the pendulum which brought them to power; once in power they maintained their position by claiming to represent the pristine puritanical Islamic tradition.[1]

The two types of Muslimness or religious commitment and the typology of elite lend themselves to the development of a typology of Muslim societies. This typology provides a useful framework to chart the religious and political futures of contemporary Muslim societies. It makes an important but often ignored distinction between the two types of rigorist/ fundamentalist societies. It also shows that a majority of Muslim countries can by and large be characterized as moderate social formations. Interestingly, those countries which are classified as fundamentalist-radical appear to evoke the most stringent political disapproval of the major western governments which are closely allied with the other type of fundamentalist societies.

The attitude of Western governments towards the fundamentalist-radical Muslim societies is a reaction to the ardent opposition of the latter to Western military and cultural hegemony. In this respect, this typology does provide some support to the Islamicist intellectuals' criticism of the West that it is intolerant of any ideologically grounded opposition to its hegemonic position in world affairs. As indicated by the evidence reported in Chapter 8, a large majority of respondents in the non-fundamentalist liberal Muslim countries like Indonesia, Pakistan and Egypt viewed the governments of the leading western countries as anti-Islam. This means that the fundamentalist-radical Muslim societies' perception of the West is not confined to them alone but is widely shared by Muslims from other countries with whom the western countries have friendly relations. These findings reinforce the perception of the 'moral-polarization' of the world which is widespread in Muslim countries. This perception holds Islam up as the embodiment of morality as compared with the 'other', especially the West.

Islamic Fundamentalism, the State and Civil Society

The findings provide some interesting insights into the sociological implications of different institutional configurations of religion and politics in Muslim societies. They show that in societies where religion and politics are integrated, religious institutions lose public influence and trust, and in societies where they are not integrated and function independent of state structures, they tend to gain influence and public trust. The reason for this appears to be the effect of different institutional configurations on the 'performance' role of religious institutions. Religious institutions gain public influence and trust when they efficiently carry out their 'performance' role. They are able to do this when they are autonomous relative to the state and other institutional sub-systems. If they are not, then they cannot carry out their 'performance' role effectively.

This has several important implications for the institutional configuration of the state in Muslim societies. When an Islamic state—that is, a state in which religion and politics are integrated—lacks trust, and consequently political legitimacy, in the public mind, it may in fact cause an erosion of trust in Islamic institutions. Among other things, this can severely weaken the fabric of civil society. The message of this finding for the Muslim religious elite seeking the establishment of an Islamic state is that such a state may not be in the best interests of Islamic institutions and religious elites. The broad conclusion that follows from this needs to be restated: In order to promote a constructive social-cultural, political, moral and religious role for religion, which the political and /or fundamentalist movements seek for Islam within Muslim societies, it may be prudent to keep faithlines separate from the state and thereby prevent them from becoming the faultlines of the political terrain. The case of Iran provides an appropriate illustration of this.

Contrary to the claims of many Islamicist intellectuals and other scholars of Muslim societies[2] who claim that the institutions of the state and religion are unified in Islam and that Islam is a total way of life which defines social and political matters, most Muslim societies did not and still do not conform to this model. In fact, most Muslim societies were built around separate institutions of the state and religion.[3] In other words, an Islamic state has not been the historical norm for Muslim social formations. The norm was and still remains the differentiated state-society formation in which religion and politics occupy different space. The findings of this study also have important implications for the ruling elite of the majority of contemporary Muslim societies, which are differentiated social formations.

These implications arise from the findings that the level of trust in religious institutions is directly related to the level of trust in the institutions of the state; that is what I have called 'the feedback effect' (see Table 5.4, Chapter 5). In other words, the attempts of the ruling elites of differentiated Muslim societies to promote radical secularist public policies which seek to diminish and disestablish Islam may have adverse consequences for the level of trust in and political legitimacy of the state itself. Some of the most dramatic illustrations of this 'feedback effect' have been the demise of the Pahlavi regime in Iran and the communist regime in Afghanistan, as well as the political and social tensions in a number of other Muslim societies, including Turkey, Egypt and Indonesia.

These findings also have implications for the international community. The most important being that a better understanding of the consequences of future political and social trajectories of Muslim society where religion and politics are integrated, i.e., of a Muslim state is warranted. If an Islamic state were to come into existence as a result of democratic, constitutional or even revolutionary means international support for such a state could in the long run pave the way for the development of a kind of differentiated Muslim social formation. The logic of this development is that, when in power, the Islamic ruling elite would likely have to make compromises with the state over time to ensure political stability, and more importantly, to gain political legitimacy. This development is a type of 'secularization of religion' that manifests itself in calls to limit the political role of religion in society.

Recent political developments in Iran provide an instructive example of the 'secularization of religion' hypothesis. The results of the 1997 presidential election showed that Iranian voters rejected the official candidate of the ruling clerical elite and instead elected a moderate cleric, Mohammed Khatami, as president. This was a big victory for the reformers seeking to change the theocratic nature of the Iranian State and replace it with a more liberal and democratic political system. The indications are that the reformers are winning, notwithstanding stringent opposition from the ruling conservative clerical establishment, which has labelled the reformers as 'revisionists'. The results of the parliamentary elections of February 2000 indicate that the reformers have won a major electoral victory, thereby consolidating support for a new Islamic democratic movement similar to the Christian democratic movements of several West European countries.

What is surprising is that this political movement is being supported by a number of theologians and philosophers, such as Mohsen Kavidar, Abdolkarim Soroush and Sheikh Mohammad Shabistari. These philosophers are all Islamic intellectuals with broad support among the masses and are also supported by President Khatami. Their ideas have gained great popularity among the Iranian public, including young clerics, and their works are now widely read in Iran. The central planks of the Islamic reform movement include: a state based on the rule of law, public freedom and human rights.

The Iranian press including widely read periodicals like *Sobhe Emrus, Khordad, Salaam, Nashat, Kian, Zanan* and *Hamshari*, now regularly publish writings and statements by the 'revisionist' theologians and philosophers. Although the authorities have attempted to stifle such writings, they have not been very successful in suppressing them. While there remain considerable religious, political and structural obstacles to these reforms the results of the May 1997 presidential elections, the March 1999 local elections and the February 2000 parliamentary elections clearly show that, short of complete subversion of the constitution, the momentum gained by the Islamic reformers is unstoppable.

There is general consensus that any subversion of the constitution by the conservative ruling clerical class would face strong resistance from the Iranian public. According to a noted Iranian intellectual Mohammed Sadeqol-Hoseyni Iranian reformers are seeking to restore three aspects of their ancestral heritage, namely, the western, the national and the Islamic. The last has smothered the other two; thus their restoration is on top of the agenda. Paradoxically, the policies of the Islamic Republic have bolstered support for the reform movements as well.

The state policy of not encouraging birth control has allowed the birth rate to soar over several years, so that the demographic balance has now shifted in favour of the young, especially those below twenty-five years old. With sixteen years being the voting age, the reformers have been successful in appealing to them for support. The vigorous literacy campaign and general provision of free education have reduced the rate of illiteracy by three-quarters and it is estimated to be now below 15 per cent. At the same time, there has been a tenfold increase in the number of university graduates to over four million (not counting the two million university students). These graduates are now swelling the ranks of the unemployed and demanding economic reforms.

The greatest irony of post-Islamic-revolutionary Iran has been the change in the educational and economic status of ordinary women. By making the *chadar* compulsory, the Islamic Revolution has unexpectedly given a powerful boost to the emancipation of women. It has made possible the mass enrolments in schools and universities of girls whose traditional families had refused to send them to school in the days of the monarchy when wearing the *chadar* was forbidden. Women now make up 50 per cent of students, compared with 25 per cent during the time of the Shah.

Modestly dressed women have also entered the labour market in large numbers since they are now under pressure to contribute to the family income. Women have gradually started demanding equality under the law in areas such as inheritance and divorce, rights that would have been seen to be a sacrilege for the conservative Muslim clerics who are now in power. In an unprecedented way feminist groups from all walks of life have decided to make the betterment of women's status in Iran a key plank of their reform agenda. Women's political activism is reflected in their willingness to run for elections. In the municipal election of 1999, a large number of women were successful in winning seats in the local councils. Some of them obtained more votes than their male counterparts. Even in the holy city of Qom a 'modern' female nurse defeated several of her turbaned male rivals. Two of the fifteen seats in the Tehran city council are held by women.[4]

Perhaps the most important evidence of the Islamic Iranian state's pragmatic accommodation of the 'secular' domain of society was the 1989 amendment to the Iranian constitution, which was personally sanctioned by Ayatollah Khomeini. It empowered the government to set aside Shariah principles, including the fundamental pillars of the faith such as prayers and fasting, if it is in the general interest of the Muslim nation. The amendment also gave the government far reaching powers to decide when the provisions of Muslim law are, or are not, binding.

Given that 'the tenets of Islam' are the ultimate constitutional limit on legislation and government power, their effective suspension affords the government and parliament unlimited powers. This kind of development could only have occurred in an Islamic state.[5] In conclusion, the general lesson of the Iranian situation is that over time the undifferentiated Muslim social formation (Islamic State) tends to evolve towards a kind of differentiated Muslim social formation. An Islamic state, therefore, may also be a route to the social and political development of Muslim societies in which religion and state co-exist in an autonomous but mutually cooperative relationship.

The Mainstreaming of Religious Fundamentalism in Muslim Countries

The developments in post-revolutionary Iran outlined above, as well as developments in countries like Egypt, Pakistan, Jordan, Malaysia, Tunisia and Indonesia over the past twenty years, suggest an important shift in the perception of religious fundamentalism and its place in the national politics of Muslim societies. In the case of Iran, it is obvious that Islam is very much the mainstream of the political process. The orthodox clerics who have ruled Iran since the Islamic Revolution have done so by institutionalizing some of the fundamental features of the democratic political system.

They have framed a constitution, which while recognizing that the ultimate sovereignty belongs to Allah also recognizes the principle of the sovereignty of the people in conducting state affairs. This is obvious from the fact that the constitution grants and guarantees universal franchise, elected representation and accountability of the elected representatives through periodic elections. These features of the Iranian Republic have been functioning effectively. The reform movement is now seeking to expand the limits of the political and constitutional rights to freedom of expression, the rule of law, the role of civil society and the right to personal privacy.

The evidence suggests that the reform movement has now obtained the political power to institutionalize these changes. Similar developments have been taking place in Pakistan, Indonesia and Egypt and over the past two decades Islamic parties have been gradually incorporated into the mainstream political processes. Recent developments in Indonesia such as the election of Abdurrahman Wahid, a prominent Muslim cleric and the leader of an Islamic party, as President of Indonesia indicates how much Islam has become a part of national politics. In other countries mainstreaming is taking place gradually and through the democratic process.

Even in the media and in academic circles in Muslim and western countries alike, the discussion of religious fundamentalism is no longer seen as a pathological expression of religious fanaticism but as a modern social movement which is seeking to establish a just and egalitarian social order. The most striking example of this shift in the perception of Islamic fundamentalism in Western academia is the establishment the Fundamentalism Project at the University of Chicago, funded by the American Academy of Science and the Humanities. The several volumes so far published by this Project clearly indicate the shift in the perceptions of religious fundamentalism in general and Islamic fundamentalism in particular.[6]

This is not to say that all variants of religious fundamentalism in Muslim societies have the same value. Judging from the reactions of Islamic movements in most Muslim countries to Afghanistan's Taliban variant of Islamic fundamentalism, it is obvious that they do not regard the Taliban with much sympathy or affection. But the general point is that, starting with Iran's Islamic Revolution, Islamic fundamentalism is gradually finding its way into mainstream national politics in Muslim countries and in the process it is giving powerful expression to the development of the Islamic democratic movement.

The mainstreaming or integration of religion into the national political process would go a long way towards redressing the imbalance between the two traditions of Islam. What is meant by this is that, in the colonial as well as in the postcolonial state in Muslim countries, the folk or popular tradition of Islam has been the main ally of the state's ruling elite. The orthodox or what Gellner has called the 'High Islam' has been largely excluded from state power. This situation had contributed to persistent tensions between the two traditions of Islam in most Muslim countries. One consequence of this tension has been the rise of the Islamization movements which in many cases was the struggle mounted by the partisans of 'High Islam' to displace the less 'pure' tradition of 'folk Islam' from its position in national politics.

This tension between the two traditions and the resulting social struggles have been a major source of political instability and sectarian violence. One Muslim country where these two traditions of Islam have been relatively equally developed is Indonesia. In Indonesia, Nahdatul Ulama and Muhammadiyah as representing respectively the folk or traditional Islam and the high or puritanical Islam are well organized with very large active memberships. The result has been that a kind of 'social contract' has evolved between them to allow each other to concentrate on the 'performance' role of promoting the well being of their followers.

Although Indonesia has been going through some difficult economic and political times over the past three years, it appears to me that due to the cooperative coexistence between the two Islamic traditions, Indonesian society has been spared from protracted violent instability. The remarkable success of Indonesia's social and economic development programme and social stability for the past two to three decades was predicated on this 'social contract' for cooperative coexistence between the two Islamic traditions. The recent political developments in that country also reflect the mainstreaming of Islam in the national political process. The point here is that the evidence of mainstreaming of Islam in Iran, Pakistan, Jordan, and Egypt augers well for social stability and political and economic development in the future, something which all Muslim countries need desperately.

Islamic Militancy: A New Paradigm?

What does the evidence of religious renaissance in the Muslim world mean? What are the implications of this for Islamic militancy? Does this mean greater support for the militant Islamic movements that are seeking to establish their versions of the Islamic State? Would this increase their militancy against those groups and countries they regard as anti-Islamic?

The overall weight of evidence suggests that religious piety appears to be associated with a decline in support for militant Islamic movements. A large majority of Muslims do not belong to any radical militant Islamic group. In fact, most of the respondents approved of moderate political leaders who are leading political and social movements for democratic and tolerant societies and political cultures. The declining support for radical and militant movements is paradoxically further radicalizing these movements and transforming them into more violent and secretive organizations. The ruthlessness of their violence reflects a desire to gain public attention and is symptomatic of their desperation.

The new form of violence is different from the earlier form that was carried out by such organizations, often with some degree of tacit support from the political structure. The new militancy appears to be fuelled by a sense of desperation and humiliation caused by globalization and the increasing economic, cultural, technological and military hegemony of the West. This pattern represents a kind of paradigm shift in the nature of terrorism carried out by the new militant groups. The old form of militancy aimed at establishing the legitimacy of political goals; the new form is guided by religious fanaticism, destruction and revenge. The old type of militancy had identified enemies. The new enemies are ephemeral global conspiracies.

A majority of Muslims regard major western countries as anti-Islam. The primary reason for this attitude is not religion, but the perceived indifference and inaction of the western countries to protect the Muslim populations of Bosnia-Herzegovina, Kosovo, Palestine and Chechnya from the random destruction being perpetrated upon them. Such views are widely held among the Muslim elite. This study provides new insights into the dynamics of the new Islamic militancy. It shows that, contrary to the general belief, increasing religiosity in Muslim countries is associated with political liberalization and diminishing support for militant Islamic groups. The impact of these developments is making the militant movements highly secretive and increasingly unpredictable and violent.

The globalization process in particular is creating a social and cultural hiatus that is affecting the nature and organization of militancy in Muslim countries. The new militancy is not motivated by attitudes towards colonialism and struggles to win the hearts and minds of Muslim populations. It is fuelled by a sense of powerlessness, revenge and religious fanaticism. How Muslim countries and the rest of the international community respond to these new developments will have a profound impact on the nature and activities of the new militancy. The solution would require more open and stronger political structures in Muslim countries to legally and politically pursue the solutions to the problems of the new militancy. It will also need a change in the mind-set that increasing religiosity does not increase support for militancy but in fact does the opposite: it diminishes support for it.

Piety, Economy and Society

As mentioned in the introduction, a majority of the estimated 1.2 billion Muslims in the world live in countries which are euphemistically called the 'Third World', meaning that they are economically, educationally, technologically and scientifically backward. Almost all Muslim-majority countries have relatively high inflation, low economic growth, low life expectancy and high illiteracy. The quality of human capital is adversely affected by low educational attainment, poor nutrition and gender bias. These conditions in the context of the so-called third industrial revolution, with its 'knowledge economy' in which the creation

of wealth will depend on scientific and technological skills, cast
a very unfavourable shadow on the future of the Muslim world.
In the words of one of the most prominent Muslim scientists,
the late Pakistani Nobel laureate, Dr Abdus Salam, 'of all
civilizations on this planet, science is weakest in the lands of
Islam'. He and other observers of this situation have pointed out
that this poses a major threat to the honourable survival of
Muslim countries in the future.

The evidence gathered by Anwar and Abu Bakar[7] from the
International Islamic University in Malaysia about scientific
productivity (cited in Chapter 4) provides a stark confirmation
of the relative scientific and technological backwardness of
Muslim countries. According to them between 1990 and 1994
the scientific output of all forty-six Muslim-majority countries,
as measured by publications in the scholarly scientific journals,
was a meagre 1.17 per cent of the total world output. It was less
than of Spain and India. The output of all Arab countries was
only 0.55 per cent of the total world output. In the same period,
Israel's contribution was 0.89 per cent.

These conditions are largely the result of the meagre resources
allocated by Muslim countries to science and development.
Muslim countries on average spend 0.45 per cent of their GNP
on research and development as compared with 2.30 per cent
for the OECD countries. Additionally, the historical experience
of colonial rule which most Muslim countries endured for
extended periods in the nineteenth and twentieth centuries had
the effect of severely limiting opportunities for research and
development. During the period of colonial rule Muslim
countries like other former colonies endured some of the worst
excesses of racial and economic exploitation and these were
instrumental in arresting their economic and social development.
Nevertheless, most of the causes of the present predicament in
which Muslim countries find themselves must be attributed to
the cultural features and practices which now prevail in them. I
say this because many other non-Muslim countries like Korea,
Taiwan, Singapore and even India have taken notable strides in

the fields of science and technology and are now among the major emerging modern industrial societies.

Islamic ulama such as Maududi and Qutb have their own explanation of the present predicament of Muslim countries. According to them, the real cause of the backwardness is weak and superficial religious commitment arising from the exposure of the Muslim masses and elites to godless secular education which has prevented them from thinking Islamically. They also argue that another result of this exposure is the pervasive sense of self-doubt among Muslims which is threatening their religious identity and character which is in turn affecting their intellectual creativity through the resulting moral disintegration and confusion.

Interestingly, such criticisms are internalized by Muslims themselves. The evidence reviewed in Chapter 2, however, strongly contradicts such assertions and explanations and emphatically shows a high and strong level of religious piety among a large majority of Muslims of all classes. The evidence also shows that this strong religious piety is accompanied by prevalence of the traditionalistic self-image of Islam. Is it plausible that these conditions may be a contributing factor to the scientific and technological backwardness of Muslim countries? I believe that this may well be the case.

In the course, of this research I got the opportunity to visit many universities in Muslim countries. The weight of the empirical evidence and my field observations have led me to the conclusion that strong religious piety is reinforcing the traditionalistic self-image of Islam in Muslim countries. This is producing a kind of cultural conditioning which is not conducive to the pursuit of rational and objective scholarship because of the ideological control imposed by the traditionalistic self-image of Islam. Let me illustrate this point by referring back to the three categories of thought proposed by Mohammad Arkoun. He labels these categories as thinkable, unthinkable and unthought. The cultural conditions emanating from the traditionalistic self-image encourage the Muslim masses and intellectuals to think only in terms of the thinkable and the unthinkable and discourage cognitive processes leading to the unthought.

The evidence of this can be gleaned from the responses to questions included in Chapter 4. To questions which can be classified as examples of the thinkable, such as 'Muslim society must be based on the Qur'an and Shariah law' and ' the Qur'an and Sunnah contain all the essential religious and moral truths required by the whole human race from now until the end of time', there was almost universal agreement among the respondents. But the responses to questions like 'A human element is present in the messages from Allah contained in the sacred texts' and 'Knowledge comes from human reason based on empirical evidence rather than from truths revealed to a select few by Allah', what was surprising was not that the agreement rates were lower but that a very large proportion of respondents simply did not want to answer these questions. I would argue that this type of response pattern is indicative of the validity of Arkoun's category of the unthought.

The conditions which prevent the realm of the unthought from flourishing and which prevail in Muslim countries will constitute perhaps the most significant barriers to the development of science and technology in those countries. Muslims, like non-Muslims, will be called upon to address and solve modern problems not only related to the development of science and technology but also other problems like equality of citizenship for women and children, the management of human sexuality, environmental degradation, the rule of law, and political and cultural freedoms. A proper understanding and resolution of these problems would require a common understanding based on rational and scientific knowledge.

One of the obvious ways to approach the problem of relative absence of the unthought would be the relative autonomy of various institutions from all stifling hegemonic political, cultural or religious influences. This is not an easy objective to achieve but human history bears testimony to its achievability. The evidence reviewed in Chapter 5 shows that the inevitable trend of the history of Muslim societies is towards the development of differentiated social formations, which would allow such institutional autonomies to evolve and develop.

The Self-image of Islam and Gender Issues

Islam was instrumental in introducing wide-ranging legal and religious enactments to improve the status and position of women, first in the Arabian society and later on among other populations which converted to Islam. As Rahman and other commentators have pointed out, the Qur'anic injunctions expressly demanded reforms of customs and beliefs which adversely affected the status of women and sought to confer a full-fledged personality on women. There is a general consensus among scholars of Islam that the protection and improvement of the status of women and children was an important plank in Prophet Muhammad's (PBUH) social project.

However, selective and sometimes deliberately manipulative interpretations of the sacred texts appear to have thwarted these aspects of Muhammad's (PBUH) social project. In most Muslim societies, there are widely-held views that women's autonomy and independence pose a problem for the general functioning of society and the family. In several Muslim countries, nationalist leaders have been trying to overcome centuries of male resistance and introduce modest changes to the laws and customs that subordinate women to men in the public and private domains. On the whole, progress in this area has been very slow and women in many Muslim countries continue to be deprived of full citizenship rights. The findings reported in Chapters 6 and 7 explored some of the cultural and social attitudes towards women's role and status in the surveyed countries.

The attitudes towards gender roles displayed two dimensions which appear to influence the attitudinal variations across countries. They have been labelled as the societal and gender dimensions. The societal dimension refers to the variations in attitudes across countries which are caused by material, social and political conditions. This finding counters the arguments about 'Islamic determinism' which regard Islamic values and norms as the sole determinant of Muslim attitudes towards gender issues. The evidence also shows that women in all countries displayed more modern attitudes than men. These differences tend to be greatest in countries where men's attitudes were generally traditionalistic. The degree of modernity of women's attitudes was positively related to the traditionalistic attitudes of men. The traditionalistic attitudes maintained an elective affinity with the 'traditional self-image' of Islam.

There also appears to be a close elective affinity between attitudes towards patriarchy and veiling and the social segregation of women, and the traditional self-image of Islam. Men in countries with a greater presence of the traditional self-image of Islam are also likely to hold attitudes supporting patriarchy and veiling and the segregation of women. This, once again, is evidence of the social construction of such attitudes. Furthermore, the intensity of positive attitudes towards patriarchy and veiling tends to be stronger in countries which have achieved comparatively greater progress in improving the quality of women's citizenship. The two countries in which this is the case are Indonesia and Egypt. What is interesting is that men and women in these countries share remarkably similar attitudes on these matters.

One plausible explanation of such attitudes among men is that under social conditions which promote and achieve equality of citizenship between men and women, men are likely to experience a sense of status loss. This is so because gender equality diminishes men's domination over women in the public and private spheres. One likely response to the relative loss of male status is that men consciously or unconsciously compensate for this by developing an affinity with more conservative movements like those which seek to implement the traditional Islamic norms in relation to the position and status of women in society.

This means that the fundamentalist Islamic movements which favour traditional gender relations and norms are at least in some part a male response to men's loss of social status. One implication of this may be that in countries which succeed in improving the status and position of women as a result of public policies, Muslim women can expect to encounter new forms of social resistance through the emergence of fundamentalist Islamic movements. It is a paradox that progressive trends in relation to gender equality coincide with the politicization and ideologization of Islam.

I believe the explanation of the absence of gender differences in attitudes towards patriarchy and veiling may lie in the socialization effect of the traditional values about gender relations. But the more plausible explanation, paradoxically, may have to do with the fact that since loyalty to social groups varies according to the perceived ability of the group to meet and satisfy the individual's needs and aspirations, a society which is more successful in promoting gender equality would also generate greater identification with the society. In other words, Muslim societies that are more successful in providing institutional equality for women may also be successful in generating more positive attitudes towards the acceptance of traditional Islamic norms regarding patriarchy, veiling and the segregation of women as well as the management of human sexuality.

Hybridity and Future of the Ummah

The concept of ummah is an important part of historical as well as contemporary discourse. Historical analysis credits the concept of ummah as an important contributing factor in the rise and development of Islam and Islamic civilization. In contemporary discourse, ummah has been used as an analytical concept to explain the current social, economic and political conditions in the lands of Islam. This study focuses on ummah as a sociological community. Using appropriate empirical indicators, the presence of ummah consciousness has been examined in the four Muslim populations surveyed in this study. Analysis of the empirical evidence indicates the presence of ummah consciousness in varying degrees among Indonesian, Pakistani, Egyptian, and Kazakh Muslims.

The variation in the degree of ummah consciousness can be attributed to the broader reality of the Muslim world which is now characterized by structural and cultural pluralism as well as by high level of fragmentation. It has been suggested that this is an outcome of the two processes of structural and cultural change in the world, namely globalization and modernization. The major consequences of modernization are institutional differentiation and functional specialization. Muslim societies have experienced these consequences just as other societies have. One major consequence of institutional differentiation has been the emergence of specialized 'performance roles' of the various institutions, which are becoming the basis of their public influence in society.

In order to carry out their performance roles effectively, these institutions must be autonomous of the state. In Muslim societies, these consequences of modernization are producing political struggles over the role and functions of the religious institutions. While these struggles are still going on in many Muslim countries, the general trend appears to be that religious institutions are adjusting to the institutional configurations of differentiated Muslim social formations. Even in Iran, which is perhaps the best example of the undifferentiated Muslim society, the trend appears to be a gradual but definite movement towards the separation of religion from politics. This is clearly indicated by Iran's 1989 constitutional amendment, which empowers the government to suspend or even abrogate the Shariah principles if it is in the general interest of the Muslim nation.[8]

The modernization process has also been contributing to the spread of globalization, another source of social and structural change in the modern world. Modern information technology has now made rapid communication a reality. As a result, the world is becoming a global village and a 'single space'. One major implication of this for the Muslim world is the impact information technology is having on ummah consciousness. In the pre-globalized world, 'knowing' of all Islamized people was seriously constrained or even rendered impossible by the limitations of technology. These limitations have now been removed. In the pre-globalized world ummah consciousness was largely determined by the practice of the 'five pillars' of Islam and certain key beliefs. The existence of these Islamic beliefs and practices was seen as evidence that the entire culture was Islamized, that is, had come to resemble the foundational Arabian Islamic culture. This transformation of all Islamized people was considered to be an integral part of the 'Islamic Project'. It was rather naively assumed by Islamic intellectuals that such a cultural trajectory was the common destiny of all Islamized people. Difficulties of communication and contact with people of far-off regions fed this myth.

A common Muslim belief is that Islam is not only a religion but also a complete way of life, which in Islamic discourse is known as the 'one religion, one culture' paradigm. Globalization is prompting reformation of this belief. The instantaneous and world-wide communication links are now allowing Muslims and non-Muslims to experience the reality of different Islamic cultures. Such experiences reveal not only what is common among Muslims but also what is different. One overwhelming consequence of this has been the realization that the Muslim world is in fact socially and culturally and even religiously a 'hybrid' world. This realization has provoked an unfavourable reaction among some groups of Islamic intellectuals towards this 'hybridity', which has given rise to some Islamic movements seeking to replace 'hybridity' with the 'authentic' Islamic way of life.

The struggle between 'hybridity' and 'authenticity' represents perhaps the most important challenge of globalization for the Muslim ummah. It has been argued that this is one of the underlying causes of the emergence of Islamic fundamentalist movements. Fundamentalism—as the term has been used in this study—refers to the strategy used by Islamic 'purists' to assert their construction of religious identity and Islamic social order as the exclusive basis for a re-created political and social order. Such purists feel that Islamic religious identity is at risk and is being eroded by cultural and religious hybridity. They try to fortify their interpretations of religious ways of being through a selective retrieval of Islamic doctrines and practices from a sacred past.

Religious fundamentalism is in other words, a problem produced by the encounter between modernity and the ummah in all its diversity and cultural hybridity and the strength of fundamentalism varies according to the intensity of attitudes towards these features. In a globalizing world, cultural diversity and cultural crossovers will become a matter of routine and, instead of eliminating hybridity this may in fact transform it into an autonomous symbolic universe, thus posing a challenge to the conventional categorical oppositions of existing symbolic systems. Such a challenge will create the conditions for cultural reflexivity and may confer on hybridity its own symbolism with a unique character and powers which will claim co-existence and recognition along with the existing symbolic universes.

These types of development would have far-reaching implications for the Muslim ummah. The Islamic regions may be transformed as unique religious and cultural systems claiming acceptance and recognition as authentic traditions of Islam. This transformation may lead to the 'de-centring' of the Muslim world from a supposedly uni-centred cultural and religious world to a multi-centred world. In Chapter 3, five such centres of the de-centred Islamic world have been identified. These are Arabic Middle Eastern Islam, African Islam, non-Arabic Middle Eastern Islam, South-East Asian Islam and the Islam of the Muslim minorities in the West. Demographic pressures in the Muslim countries will further accentuate the movement towards a regional ummah.

The de-centred Muslim ummah will confer a kind of legitimacy on the regional ummah, and thus may lead them to chart their own social, political, economic, religious and cultural developments along distinctive lines suitable to the history and temperament of their people. This will engender new opportunities for the Muslim ummah to again strive for the intellectual, cultural and material superiority that was achieved by the ummah in its formative centuries. In such a scenario, the Islamic ummah will gain strength not as a unified and unitary community but as a differentiated community consisting of the regional ummah all striving to gain material and ideological influences in a global system. These developments may also produce their own opposing and supporting movements requiring each ummah to find appropriate responses to them.

In a culturally and religiously differentiated ummah setting, it is possible that the political and cultural leanings of one or some of the regional ummah may not find approval with the governors of the holy centres of Mecca and Medina. This may pose difficulties for the members of these regional ummah regarding free access to these centres to perform their religious duties. This in turn may necessitate the formulation of new and appropriate governing structures for Islam's holy centres of Mecca and Medina.

In the course of this research, many comments were noted concerning an interest in reforms to the management and governance of the holy cities, including their placement under internationally constituted political structures representing the entire ummah, and independent of the political authority of the government of Saudi Arabia. Such comments were often prefaced with expressions of great dissatisfaction with the current management of these centres and the idiosyncratic policies of the Saudi ruling class. Policies and practices such as barring adult single women unaccompanied by a male member of the immediate family and banning non-Muslims from visiting the centres were seen as inappropriate, anarchistic and unsuitable to the conditions of modern times. While these and similar issues which are likely to arise may initially pose difficulties they may also be the harbingers of the new futures which await a differentiated Muslim ummah in the modernized and globalized world of the twenty-first century.

NOTES

1. Gellner 1983, pp. 62-69.
2. Maududi 1960; Qutb 1953; Lewis 1993; Weber 1978; Crone 1980; Huntington 1993.
3. Lapidus 1964; Keddie 1994.
4. Rouleau 1999; Kian 1996.
5. Zubaida 1997.
6. Marty and Applebly 1991, 1993, 1994.
7. Anwar and Abu Bakar 1996.
8. Zubaida 1995; Malat 1993.

APPENDIX A

METHODOLOGY: How the Study was Done

The empirical data reported in this volume were generated by an international study of Muslim religiosity. This study was funded by a three-year (1996-1998) grant from the Australian Research Council. The data were collected through a structured survey questionnaire which was administered to a sample of respondents in each of the four countries included in the study. The countries surveyed were Indonesia, Pakistan, Egypt and Kazakhstan. The following sections will describe in some detail various methodological steps and procedures which were followed in the study.

Focus of the Study

The main focus of the research was a comparative study of Muslim religiosity and Muslim conceptions of religion and society. More specifically, the following issues were investigated: Muslim piety, relationship between politics and religion, attitudes towards gender issues, ummah consciousness, the self-image of Islam, sociological correlates of religious fundamentalism and attitudes towards the 'other'.

Construction of the Survey Questionnaire

As mentioned above, the data were collected through a survey questionnaire. The development of the questionnaire took the first eight months of the study. A comprehensive search of the previous survey instruments used in studies of religiosity was conducted. The relevant instruments were reviewed for possible items. The key questionnaire that was used as the basis of the questions on religious piety was the questionnaire developed by Charles Y. Glock and Rodney Stark for their study of *Religion and Society in Tension*, published in

1965, which was also used in their study of *American Piety: The Nature of Religious Commitment,* published in 1968. The other questionnaires reviewed were: World Value Survey (R. Inglehart 1990); Social Stratification in Eastern Europe after 1989 Questionnaire (I. Szelenyi and D. Treiman); Survey of Religion (Indonesia) 1976 (Joseph B Tamney); Religion and Social Change in Pakistan Questionnaire, 1980 (R. Hassan); and the religious attitude questionnaires included in John P. Robinson and Phillip R. Shaver (eds.) *Measures of Social Psychological Attitudes* (1973).

The self-image of Islam questions were generated from the following texts: W. Montgomery Watt, *Islamic Fundmentalism and Modernity* (1988), Ernest Gellner, *Muslim Society* (1983); Fazlur Rahman, *Major Themes of the Quran* (1989) and *Islam and Modernity* (1982). There were other sources which also contributed to the development of the final questionnaire which are too numerous to mention. In addition, over twenty 'key' scholars and Muslim thinkers from Indonesia and Pakistan were interviewed in 1996 about their views on Muslim religiosity, religious fundamentalism, religious activism, role of religion in modern society and related issues.

The final questionnaire consisted of the following sections: respondent's sociodemographic, educational and occupational background, social and political attitudes, confidence in institutions, religious socialization, religious beliefs and practice, images of Islam, social class, housing and lifestyle, personality, media exposure, attitudes towards the 'other' and household composition. (A copy of the questionnaire is available with the author). The questionnaire was translated into Indonesian, Urdu, Arabic, Kazakh and Russian languages, the main languages of the countries surveyed. In each case the questionnaire was also translated back into English in order to minimize the translation bias.

Countries Surveyed and Local Collaborators

The countries included in the study were Indonesia, Pakistan, Egypt and Kazakhstan. The rationale behind the selection was guided by pragmatic and theoretical considerations. Indonesia was chosen because it is the largest Muslim country, and also, because of its vital political and security importance to Australia. Pakistan was selected as a non-Arabic Middle Eastern and South Asian country. Egypt was selected because of its position in the Arab world, and also, as representing the Arabic Middle East. Kazakhstan, which had been under communism until 1990, was chosen to represent West and Central Asian Islam. The main theoretical consideration was to include countries with different institutional configurations.

In Indonesia, the Population Studies Institute of Gadjah Mada University in Yogyakarta conducted the fieldwork. The Population Studies Centre is one of the leading research centres in the social sciences in Indonesia. It has a body of professionally trained and skilled staff specialized in conducting survey research. The staff was responsible for making all the necessary logistical arrangements to carry out the fieldwork. The interviewers were trained, and they conducted the fieldwork under the overall supervision of Dr Agus Dwiyanto and Drs Sukamdi, director and deputy director respectively of the centre. The fieldwork commenced in October 1996 and was completed in June 1997.

In Pakistan, the fieldwork was carried out by the Social Science Research Centre of the University of the Punjab at Lahore. This centre is reputed for social research and its professional staff is skilled in conducting survey research in Pakistan. The centre was responsible for all logistical and technical arrangements for the fieldwork, which was conducted under the supervision of its director, Professor Muhammad Anwar, who was assisted by Dr Muneer Ahmad, Ms Razia Rafiq, Mr Shaukat Abbas, and Mr Safdar A. Sohail. The survey interviews were conducted between November 1996 and July 1997.

In Egypt, the fieldwork was conducted by the Ibn Khaldoun Centre for Social Development in Cairo. The university centres as well as the government's centre for Population Mobilization and Statistics were approached, but for political reasons they were unable to carry out the survey. The Director of the Ibn Khaldoun Centre, Professor Saad Eddin Ibrahim, is a well-known and respected sociologist in Egypt. He is professor of sociology at the American University in Cairo. He was interested in the study for its sociological significance and undertook to carry out the survey fieldwork which was conducted from March to October 1997. The director for the survey in Egypt was Professor Saad Eddin Ibrahim, and Dr Hassan Eissa coordinated the fieldwork. They both were responsible for translating the questionnaire into Egyptian Arabic.

In Kazakhstan, the fieldwork was contracted out to the Kazakhstan Centre for Strategic Studies under the President of the Republic of

Kazakhstan in Almaty. The centre is a key social science research centre in Kazakhstan. The centre was responsible for all facets of the survey fieldwork which was coordinated by one of Kazakhstan's leading sociologists Dr Sabit E. Jousupov under the overall direction of the centre's director, the late Dr Oumirseric Kasenov. The translation into Kazakh and Russian languages was done under the supervision of Dr Oumirseric Kasenov and Dr Jousupov, and the survey fieldwork was carried out between March and September 1997.

I was able to observe survey work in each location. My teaching commitments at the Flinders University could only permit me to be away for limited periods of time to participate in the research activities at various sites. When I was not at the fieldwork sites personally, I maintained a close contact by phone, fax and e-mail with the country survey coordinators. It was a complex research exercise, but, fortunately, highly skilled, able and professional assistance and supervision of the country collaborators and their staff enabled us to complete the survey fieldwork satisfactorily.

Sampling and Sample Composition: General Comments

The original study design envisaged that in each country the sample would consist of three groups: religious elite, Muslim professionals constituting the elite from other sections of society, and the general public. It was also intended to select each of these samples randomly. The research funds granted for the study, however, were at a much lower level than required to administer the questionnaire to a randomly selected sample in each country. The sampling strategy was therefore revised after consulting colleagues in Indonesia and Pakistan. The concept of elite was reconceptualized to mean individuals with university education or individuals holding management positions in an organization. The sample composition was retained.

For religious elite, the targeted respondents were those who were active in legally established and functioning religious organizations. In addition to this, the preferred respondents were those who had university degrees or had religious qualifications to act as leaders in mosques or religious organizations. This group was called religious activists in the study. The Muslim professionals were expected to have university education and also to be active participants in formal organizations related to their professions. In all cases, the country research teams, under the direction of the local study coordinators, identified the organizations, individuals and the local areas.

Between fifty and fifty-five individuals were personally identified by the members of the research teams and invited to participate in the survey. If they agreed to participate, then a copy of the questionnaire was given to them for completion, and the interviewer was available to answer any questions or queries. They were requested to give names of five people who could be approached by the research team to participate in the study. This snowballing approach of sample selection proved most useful and aided considerably in meeting the targeted sample types and sizes in each country. All respondents were given the protocols approved by the Ethics Committee of the Faculty of Social Sciences, Flinders University of South Australia, for their information.

The selection of the general public respondents was made from the well-established working-class areas. The protocols for contacting and interviewing were the same as for the religious activists and Muslim professionals. One main difference was that most of them completed the questionnaire in face-to-face interviews. The details of sample selection and fieldwork in each country are provided in the following section. In each country the samples were also stratified by gender, details of which will be provided in the country sample profiles.

Egypt

The Ibn Khaldoun Centre for Social Development, Cairo recruited a team of five female and fifteen male interviewers. They all had post-graduate degrees in social sciences and most of them were staff members of universities in Cairo.

The interviewers received training in two four-hour sessions, which were followed by two hours of debriefing sessions. The interviewers were trained about the administration of the questionnaire and the selection of the samples. The samples were drawn from the Cairo metropolitan area. The religious sample was selected by Dr Hassan Eissa through the extensive contacts of the centre and its staff. Interviewers were assigned to interview specific respondents who resided in the vicinity of their place of residence. One consequence of this was that interviewers may have chosen respondents who lived near their home. However, every attempt was made to ensure a degree of randomness in the sample selection. The respondents were also asked to recommend other potential interviewees, who were then followed up and, whereever possible, interviewed.

The Muslim professionals were respondents who were university graduates with professional degrees and who were not actively involved in religious organizations. The general public respondents were selected from amongst the people living in the working-class areas of Cairo. The average time for administering a questionnaire in Cairo was approximately two hours. The survey fieldwork in Cairo took six months. One major problem which arose in Cairo was the unfavourable coverage in the section of the local press. This led to an investigation by the military intelligence, which frightened some of the interviewers. Two of them destroyed forty completed questionnaires just to be sure that if the military intelligence approached them, they did not possess any evidence of completed questionnaires. As a result of this, it was decided to stop the survey before the targeted number of 1000 respondents could be interviewed. In Egypt, only 766 respondents were interviewed. The survey samples were drawn from the following areas of metropolitan Cairo: Ains Sams and Matariyh (North Cairo), East Cairo—Shourbra area, Shara Biah (working-class area) and Mahidi.

Indonesia

In Indonesia, the survey fieldwork was conducted by the Population Studies Center of Gadjah Mada University in Yogyakarta. The fieldwork was directed and supervised Dr Agus Dwiyanto and Drs Sukamdi, director and deputy director respectively of the centre. The questionnaire was translated into Indonesian by the experienced staff under the supervision of Drs Sukamdi. It was also translated back into English to minimize translation bias. The centre was responsible for obtaining the formal approval of the authorities for the study and for sample selection.

The interviewers were trained staff of the Population Studies Centre. Altogether a total of fourteen interviewers, seven male and seven female, were responsible for conducting interviews. They were all trained by the country directors for the fieldwork. A total of 1472 respondents were interviewed. These respondents were drawn from the activists of two of the largest Islamic organizations, namely Muhammadiyah and Nahdatul Ulama, as well as activists from other religious organizations, Muslim professionals from other spheres of civil society, and the general public.

These samples were selected, using a purposive framework, from the province of Yogyakarta in Central Java. The Muhammadiyah sample was selected from the predominantly Muhammadiyah areas of Kauman in the sub-district of Gondomanan and from Preggan and Purbayan in the sub-district of Kotagede. A smaller number of respondents were selected from Karangkajen in the sub-district of Mergangsan. These areas were located in the Yogyakarta municipality. The Nahdatul Ulama sample was selected from Mlangi in Gamping sub-district (Seleman Regency), Krapyak Kulon and Wetan (West and East Krapyak), and Glugo in the sub-district of Sewon (Bantul Regency).

For each area, lists of all Muhammadiyah and Nahdatul Ulama activists were made, then a sample was selected from these lists after consultation with the local leader as to whether the respondents would be able to answer the questionnaire, and whether he/she was also available for the interview. From each area, except Kuaman and Karangkajen, 125 respondents were randomly selected from among those found to qualify for the interviews. From Kauman and Karangkajen a total of 125 respondents were interviewed. The sample for Muslim activists from other Muslim organizations was drawn from Yogyakarta, and the names of the respondents were randomly selected from the lists provided by the organizations.

Each sub-sample was expected to consist of 250 respondents, but owing to the difficulties in finding suitable respondents, the actual number of respondents in Nahdatul Ulama, and of activists from other religious organizations, were slightly smaller. General public respondents were also selected from the province of Yogyakata, as was the sample for Muslim professionals who included academics, government officials, doctors, engineers, lawyers, businessmen, and other professionals. A concerted attempt was made to ensure that there was no imbalance of occupations within the sample.

Pakistan
In Pakistan, the survey fieldwork was carried out by the Social Science Research Centre of the University of Punjab, Lahore. This centre is one of Pakistan's major academic centres for social research. The fieldwork was coordinated by the centre's director, Professor Mohammad Anwar, and supervised by four experienced researchers and educationists, Dr Muneer Ahmad, Mr Safdar Sohail, Mrs Razia Rafiq and Mr Shaukat Abbas. This team was responsible for the Urdu

translation of the questionnaire. However, as English is widely used in Pakistan, about 15 per cent of the interviews were administered in English. The survey team was responsible for sample selection and supervision of the fieldwork. The fieldwork was carried out by three female and twelve male interviewers, all of whom were social science graduates. All interviewers received training for the fieldwork before it commenced.

A total of 1162 respondents were interviewed. The Islamic activists were mostly drawn from Jamaat-i-Islami and Tablighi Jamaat and other regional religious organizations. The Muslim professional sample was drawn from various professional, business and occupational groups. The sample of general public was drawn from the working-class areas of Lahore. The main site of the fieldwork was the Lahore metropolitan area, although a small proportion of respondents came from Faisalabad, Multan, Rawalpindi, Karachi and Peshawar.

Kazakhstan

The Kazakhstan Institute for Strategic Studies in Almaty carried out the survey work, under the direction of the institute's director and deputy director. The institute was responsible for translating the survey questionnaire into Russian and Kazakh languages and for sampling design and selection.

Sampling design and selection in Kazakhstan presented a unique problem. As only Muslim respondents were being interviewed in this study, the first problem was how best to select them since about 40 per cent of Kazakhstan's population was non-Muslim, mostly of Russian origin and belonged to the Russian Orthodox Church. The situation was further complicated by the fact that during the years that Kazakhstan was part of the former USSR, the practice of religion was prohibited. Under the influence of the state's communist ideology, most Kazakhs were educated in a strictly secular educational system, and very few were considered to be interested in Islam. One historical consequence of this policy is that unlike Indonesia, Pakistan and Egypt there is no identifiable and recognized group of Islamic activists in Kazakhstan. In view of this, in Kazakhstan the study population was classified into only two sample groups, namely the Muslim professionals and the general public.

These problems were resolved in the following way by the local research coordinators. They divided the country by the level of prevalence of Islam. Southern, South Western and Western regions were classified as Islamic regions. These included South Kazakhstan, Zhambyl, Kzyl-Orda, Taldy-Korgan, Atyrau and Aktubinsk Oblasts (regions). Other regions of the country were classified as moderately Muslim areas. These regions included Almaty, Zhezkazgan, Semipalatinsk, Aktubinsk, Northern and Eastern Oblasts (regions). This classification was made on the basis of the coordinators' knowledge based on the state documents and personal experience.

Almaty and South Kazakhstan regions were selected for the study. Both regions had populations of about two million each. A sample of 500 was selected from each of the two regions. A sample of 250 was drawn from the city of Almaty and 250 were selected from the two large surrounding villages, one with a mosque and one without a mosque. Similarly, from the South Kazakhstan region, 150 respondents were selected from the city of Shymkent, 100 from the town of Turkestan, and 250 from two villages, one with a mosque and one without.

The method of selection of respondents was the same in the two regions. Unlike the other three countries, it was possible in Kazakhstan to draw the sample randomly because the institute had access to the lists of the municipal registers which are part of the old communist state apparatus. Since only Muslims were interviewed in the study, a random sample of 1000 was drawn from each region. This meant that from each of the two regions the interviewers first ascertained the religious affiliation of the respondents, and if it was Islam, then they were interviewed.

The interviewing process went very smoothly in Kazakhstan. The interviews were carried out by five institute staff members (one female and four male) and ten interviewers, all of whom were social science graduates. They were all trained by the survey coordinators. Most of the interviews were conducted in the Russian language. One feature of the fieldwork in Kazakhstan was that because of the distance involved between the two interview sites, it took much longer to complete the interviews in Kazakhstan than in the other three countries.

Fieldwork Protocols
A set of protocols was followed in conducting fieldwork in all countries. The main features of the protocols were as follows:

- All interviewers were trained and briefed about the study by the country coordinators, who were all well-trained and experienced social scientists.
- The sampling design and selection was made by the country coordinators.
- Respondents were first contacted by members of the research team and invited to participate in the study. If they agreed, a questionnaire was given to them and an appointment was made to collect the completed questionnaire.
- The interviewers were available to answer any questions either by phone or in person.
- The questionnaire to respondents from the general public was administered in face-to-face interviews by members of the research team.
- All completed survey questionnaires were checked twice, first by the interviewer and then by his or her supervisor. Only properly completed questionnaires were used in the study.
- Questions which the interviewers were unable to answer were referred to the supervisor or the country coordinators.
- All respondents, interviewers and members of the research team were Muslims.

Fieldwork Problems

It is imperative that in a study of this type fieldwork bias be minimized in order to ensure the comparability of the data. This was done by reducing the translation bias through the process of back translation and through the training and close supervision of the interviewers. But problems were encountered which may have influenced the answers of some of the respondents.

Some of the main problems encountered were the complaints about the length of the questionnaire, inquiry about the funding and purposes of the study, difficulty in understanding some of the questions in Section D, suspicion that the study was being conducted by a Western (American) intelligence organization to undermine Islam and Islamic resurgence. There were also concerns in each country that the questionnaire should have been constructed with the help of local Islamic scholars.

These questions were handled and answered frankly and openly by the research team. In Pakistan and Egypt the media attempted to raise public concerns about the study. In Pakistan the country coordinators were able to answer the media queries by the editors and consequently avoided the adverse publicity. In Egypt, however, a section of the media did carry very sensational stories which initiated an investigation of the study by the military intelligence. These stories were appropriately and promptly responded to by the country coordinators as a result of which public interest in them declined quickly. The investigation also did not lead to any adverse findings.

The study teams in all countries also received significant amounts of positive and complimentary feedback from respondents who fully approved of the study and were glad to be part of it. The survey teams also felt very positive about the study. Perhaps the following comment by one of the country coordinators in Kazakhstan captured the spirit of their feelings: 'I have conducted many surveys but there have been no surveys which have enabled me to have a vision of the future'. As for the respondents the most common positive feedback was that 'by completing the questionnaire I have learned something about myself'. It needs to be reiterated that the sampling frame on which this study is based was not random but purposive and, therefore, no claims are made that the findings of the study are generalizeable to the whole country.

Data Entry
After the completion of the interviews the initial data entries were done by the contracting centre in each county. The completed questionnaires were shipped to Flinders University. The main data analyses were carried out at the Flinders University in 1998 and 1999.

The Sample Profile
Table A.1 describes the composition of the country samples and their demographic and social characteristics. Tables A.2 a, b, c, d and A.3 a, b, c, d, report educational attainment and the number of people normally supervised by the respondents representing three types of sample groups included in the study, namely, religious activists, Muslim professionals and general public. These table show that Muslim professionals and religious activists were significantly more educated and also a significant proportion of them occupied supervisory positions in their respective place of work compared with the respondents from the general public.

Table A.1 Social, economic and demographic characteristics of the sample

		Indonesia	Pakistan	Kazakhstan	Egypt
Social and Demographic characteristics					
Gender	Male	74.3	79.1	53.8	75.8
	Female	25.7	20.9	46.2	24.2
Age	<25 years	20.3	11.5	17.0	16.0
(Lifecycle)	26-40	34.6	50.5	40.2	54.6
	41-55	31.7	23.7	26.1	19.1
	>56	13.3	14.6	16.7	10.3
Marital status	Married	63.2	63.6	56.9	65.5
	Divorced	0.5	0.6	9.1	1.3
	Separated	–	0.1	2.4	0.4
	Widowed	2.7	2.9	6.1	2.4
	Never married	33.6	32.8	25.5	29.4
Level of education	Less than high school	10.7	4.4	12.9	7.6
(Human Capital)	High school/Some College	48.7	25.8	85.4	15.4
	College/professional	40.6	69.8	2.4	77.0
Socio-economic characteristics					
Currently Employed	Yes	68.1	77.8	75.8	83.5
	No, but usually employed	7.0	0.5	10.0	14.6
	No	24.9	21.5	14.2	0.4
Self reported social class	Upper class	–	2.2	2.3	3.3
	Upper middle	10.5	38.8	20.8	35.8
	Lower middle	44.4	32.3	11.1	21.8
	Working class	24.6	13.3	22.6	31.6
	Lower class	–	1.2	7.4	2.3
	Do not know	20.6	11.4	35.8	4.8
Quality of housing	Above average	20.9	24.8	18.0	46.4
	Average	71.5	50.8	47.4	40.2
	Below average	6.7	17.4	19.2	12.5
Other Attributes					
Self-reported Religiosity	Very religious person	3.3	14.1	3.9	12.1
	Somewhat religious person.	65.0	60.1	19.0	70.7
	Not very religious	23.7	15.6	36.2	9.5
	Not religious at all	0.3	2.7	17.1	1.4
	Not sure–do not know	7.7	7.5	23.8	5.9
Self reported	Very conservative person	2.3	8.4	11.5	14.8
conservative vs. modern	Somewhat conservative	36.0	54.2	39.7	62.2
	Somewhat modern	59.4	33.8	38.4	19.3
	Very modern	2.0	0.9	10.4	1.5
	Not sure-do not know	0.3	2.8	–	1.0
Sample type	Religious Activists	49.9	41.9	–	36.4
(Social Location)	Muslim professionals	15.9	26.1	49.3	50.2
	Public	34.2	32.0	49.3	13.4
		1472	1185	1000	788

Table A.2 Educational Attainment

a. Indonesia

Education	Religious activists	– Sample Type – Muslim professionals	Public	Total
Less than high school	43 5.9%	10 4.3%	105 20.8%	158 10.7%
High school – some college	409 55.7%	47 20.1%	261 51.8%	717 48.7%
Completed college/university	282 38.4%	177 75.6%	138 27.4%	597 40.6%
Total	734 100%	234 100%	504 100%	1472 100%

b. Pakistan

Education	Religious activists	– Sample Type – Muslim professionals	Public	Total
Less than high school	33 6.7%	7 2.3%	12 3.2%	52 4.4%
High school – some college	162 32.9%	18 5.9%	123 32.6%	303 25.8%
Completed college/university	297 60.4%	282 91.9%	242 64.2%	821 69.8%
Total	492 100%	307 100%	377 100%	1176 100%

c. Kazakhstan

Education	Muslim professionals	– Sample Type – Public	Total
Less than high school	12 4.9%	49 19.9%	61 12.4%
High school – some college	226 91.9%	190 77.2%	416 84.6%
Completed college/university	8 3.3%	7 2.8%	15 3.0%
Total	246 100%	246 100%	492 100%

d. Egypt

Education	Religious Activists	– Sample Type – Muslim professionals	Public	Total
Less than high school	12 4.4%	7 1.8%	33 32.0%	52 6.9%
High school – some college	71 26.2%	48 12.6%	65 63.1%	184 24.4%
Completed college/university	188 69.4%	325 85.5%	5 4.9%	518 68.7%
Total	271 100%	380 100%	103 100%	754 100%

Table A.3 Number of people supervised by respondents who were employed by sample type

a. Indonesia

| People supervised | – Sample Type – | | | |
	Religious activists	Muslim professionals	Public	Total
None	345	94	275	714
	68.0%	40.5%	75.1%	64.6%
1 to 9	93	63	58	214
	18.3%	27.2%	15.8%	19.4%
10 or more	69	75	33	177
	13.6%	32.3%	9.0%	16.0%
Total	507	232	366	1105
	100%	100%	100%	100%

b. Pakistan

| People supervised | – Sample Type – | | | |
	Religious activists	Muslim professionals	Public	Total
None	186	75	103	364
	51.0%	27.3%	44.4%	41.7%
1 to 9	119	95	88	302
	32.6%	34.5%	37.9%	34.6%
10 or more	60	105	41	206
	16.4%	38.2%	17.7%	23.6%
Total	365	275	232	872
	100%	100%	100%	100%

c. Kazakhstan

| People supervised | – Sample Type – | | |
	Muslim professionals	Public	Total
None	111	66	177
	51.6%	80.5%	59.6%
1 to 9	55	10	65
	25.6%	12.2%	21.9%
10 or more	49	6	55
	22.8%	7.3%	18.5%
Total	215	82	297
	100%	100%	100%

b. Egypt

| People supervised | – Sample Type – | | | |
	Religious activists	Muslim professionals	Public	Total
None	105	154	51	310
	41.8%	46.7%	62.2%	46.8%
1 to 9	106	106	26	238
	42.2%	32.1%	31.7%	35.9%
10 or more	40	70	5	115
	15.9%	21.2%	6.1%	17.3%
Total	251	330	82	663
	100%	100%	100%	100%

BIBLIOGRAPHY

Abduh, M. 1965, *The Theology of Unity*, translated by Musa, I. and Cragg, K. London: Ayer Company Publishers

Abdullah, T. 1988, The Pesantran in Historical Perspective, in Abdullah, T. and Siddique, S. eds., *Islam and Society in Southeast Asia*, Singapore: Institute of Southeast Asian Studies.

Abu Sulayman, A.H. 1997, *Crisis in the Muslim Mind*. Hendon: International Institute of Islamic Thought.

Adnan, Z. 1990, Islamic Religion: Yes, Islamic (Political) Ideology: No! Islam and the State in Indonesia, in Budiman, A. ed., *State and Civil Society in Indonesia*, Monash Papers on Southeast Asia, 22. Melbourne: Monash University Press.

Ahmad, K. 1997, *Muslim Ummah at the Threshold of the 21st Century*, Lahore: Islamic Publishing.

Ahmad, L. 1992, *Women and Gender in Islam: Historical Roots of a Modern Debate*, New Haven: Yale University Press.

Ahmad, M. 1991, Islamic Fundamentalism in South Asia: The Jamaat-i-Islami and Tablighi Jamaat, in Marty, M. Appleby and R.S. eds., 1991, Fundamentalism Observed, Chicago: University of Chicago Press.

Ahmad, M. 1995, Pakistan, in Esposito, J.L. et al. eds., *The Oxford Encyclopedia of Modern Islamic World*, New York: Oxford University Press.

Ahmad, R. 1994, Redefining Muslim Identity in South Asia: The Transformation of the Jamaat-i-Islami, in Marty, M. and Appleby, R.S. eds., 1994, *Accounting for Fundamentalism*, Chicago: University of Chicago Press.

Akhavi, S. 1992, The Clergy's Concepts of Rule in Egypt and Iran, *The Annals*, 524: 92-102

Akiner, S. 1990, *Islamic Peoples of the Soviet Union*, London: Kegan Paul.

Al-Attas, S.M.N. ed. 1979, *Aims and Objectives of Islamic Education*, London: Hodder & Stoughton.

Ali, C. 1970, The Position of Women, in Ahmad, A. and Von Grunebaum, G. eds., *Muslim Self Statement in India and Pakistan 1857-1968*, Weisbaden: Otto Harrassowitz.

Ali, M.M. 1950, *The Religion of Islam*, Lahore: The Ahmadiyyah Anjuman Ishaat Islam.

Altoma, R. 1994, The Influence of Islam in Post-Soviet Kazakhstan, in Manz, B.F. ed. 1994, *Central Asia in Historical Perspective*, Boulder: Westview Press.

Anderson, J.N.D. 1976, *Law Reform in Muslim World*, London: Athlone Press.

Anwar, M. and Bakar, A. 1996, Current State of Science and Technology in the Muslim World. Paper presented at the International Conference on Values and Attitudes in Science and Technology, International Islamic University Malaysia, Kuala Lumpur, 3-6 September 1996.

Arkoun, M. 1994, *Rethinking Islam*, trans. Lee, R. Boulder: Westview Press.

Armstrong, K. 1993, *A History of God*, London: Mandarin.

Auda, G. 1994, The 'Normalization' of the Islamic Movement in Egypt from the 1970s to the Early 1990s, in Marty, M. and Appleby, R.S. eds. 1994, *Accounting for Fundamentalisms*, Chicago: University of Chicago Press.

Ayubi, N.H. 1991, *Political Islam: Religion and Politics in the Arab World*, London: Routledge.

Bari, F. 1998, 'Women and the 15th Amendment,' *Dawn-Opinion*, 17 November.

Bayat, A. 1998, Revolution without Movement, Movement without Revolution: Comparing Islamic Activism in Iran and Egypt, *Comparative Studies in Society and History*, 40/1: 136-169.

Beinin, J. and Stork, J. eds. 1997, *Political Islam*, Berkeley: University of California Press.

Bell, C. 1997, *Ritual: Perspectives and Dimensions*. New York: Oxford University Press.

Beyer, P. 1994, *Religion and Globalization,* London: Sage publications.

Binder, L. 1963, *Religion and Politics in Pakistan,* Berkeley: University of California Press.

Bodman, H. and Tohidi, N. eds. 1998, *Women in Muslim Societies: Diversity within Unity.* London: Lynne Rienner Publishers.

Boudibha, A. 1985, *Sexuality in Islam*, trans. Alan Sheridan, Boston: Routledge and Kegan Paul

Budiman, A. ed. 1990, *State and Civil Society in Indonesia*, Monash Papers on Southeast Asia, 22. Melbourne: Monash University Press.

Bullough, V.L. 1973, *The Subordinate Sex: A History of Attitudes Toward Women*. Urbana: University of Illinois Press.

Butterworth, C.E. and Zartman, I.W. 1992, Preface, *The Annals*, 524: 8-12.

Cardwell, J.D. 1969, The Relationship Between Religious Commitment and Premarital Sexual Permissiveness: A Five Dimensional Analysis. *Sociological Analysis*, 30: 70-81.

Chaudhri, M.A. 1994, *The Muslim Ummah and Israel*, Islamabad: National Institute of Historical and Cultural Research.

Clayton, R.R. 1971, 5-D or 1? *Journal of Scientific Study of Religion*, 10: 37-40.

Clayton, R.R. and Gladden, J.W. 1974, The Five Dimensions of Religiosity: Towards Demythologizing a Sacred Artifact, *Journal for the Scientific Study of Religion*, 13: 135-143.

Cornwall, M. 1988, The Influence of Three Aspects of Religious Socialization: Family, Church and Peers, in Thomas, D.L. ed., *The Religion and the Family Connection: Social Science Perspective*, Salt Lake City Brigham Young University Press.

Crone, P. 1980, *Slaves on Horses: The Evolution of the Islamic Polity*, Cambridge: Cambridge University Press.

Dallal, A.S. 1995, Ummah, in Esposito, J. et al. eds. *The Oxford Encylopedia of the Modern Islamic World (vol. II)*, New York: Oxford University Press.

Darrow, W.R. 1987, Ummah. In Eliade Mircea et al. eds., *The Encyclopedia of Religion (vol. 3)*, New York: MacMillan.

Deeb, M. 1992, Militant Islam and the Politics of Redemption, *The Annals*, 524: 52-65.

DeJong, G.F., Faulkner, J.E. and Warland, R.H. 1976, Dimension of Religiosity Reconsidered: Evidence from a Cross-Cultural Study, *Social Forces*, 54: 866-889.

Denny, F.M. 1975, The Meaning of Ummah in the Quran, *History of Religions*, 15:1, 35-70.

Denny, F.M. 1977, Ummah in the Constitution of Medina, *Journal of Near Eastern Studies, 36* (1), 39-47.

Dhofier, Z. 1980, The Pesantren Tradition: A Study of the Role of the Kiyai in the Maintenance of the Traditional Ideology of Islam in Java, Ph.D. dissertation, Australian National University, Canberra, Australia.

Egypt. 1990, *The Constitution of the Arab Republic of Egypt*. http://www.parliament.gov.eg/en_aconst41.htm.

Eisenstadt, S.N. and Giessen, B. 1995, The Construction of Collective Identity, *European Journal of Sociology, XXXVI*, 72-102.

El Guindi, F. 1999, *Veil: Modesty, Privacy and Resistance*, New York: Berg

Erickson, J.A. 1992, Adolescent Religious Development and Commitment: A Structural Equation Model of the Role of the Family, Peer Group and Educational Influences, *Journal for the Scientific Study of Religion, 31*:131-152.

Esposito, J.L. 1982, *Women in Muslim Family Law*, Syracuse: Syracuse University Press.

Esposito, J.L. ed. 1983, *Voices of Resurgent Islam,* New York: Oxford University Press.

Esposito, J.L. 1991, *Islam: The Straight Path*, New York: Oxford University Press.

Esposito, J.L. 1995, *The Islamic Threat: Myth or Reality*, New York: Oxford University Press.

Faulkner, J.E. and De Jong, G.F. 1966, Religiosity in 5-D: An Empirical Analysis. *Social Forces*, 45: 246-254.

Folliet, J. 1955, The Effects of City Life Upon Spiritual Life, in Fisher R. ed. *The Metropolis in Modern Life*, New York: Doubleday.

Gallup Pakistan. 1996, *Pakistan Public Opinion on Important Social Issues*. Islamabad: Pakistan Institute of Public Opinion.

Geertz, C. 1960, *The Religion of Java*, Chicago: University of Chicago Press.

Geertz, C. 1968, *Islam Observed: Religious Development in Morocco and Indonesia*, Chicago: University of Chicago Press.

Gellner, E. 1969, 'A Pendulum Swing Theory of Islam' in Robertson, R. ed. *Sociology of Religion*, Harmondsworth: Penguin.

Gellner, E. 1969, *Saints of the Atlas*, London: Weidenfeld and Nicolson.

Gellner, E. 1981, *Muslim Society*, Cambridge: Cambridge University Press.

Gellner, E. 1992, *Postmodernism, Reason and Religion*, London: Routledge.

Gellner, E. 1994, *Conditions of Liberty*, Harmondsworth: Penguin Books.

Giannakis, E. 1983, The Concept of Ummah, *Graeco-Arabica*, 2, 99-111.

Gibbs, J.O. and Crader, K.W. 1970, A Criticism of Two Recent Attempts to Scale Glock and Stark's Dimensions of Religiosity: A Research Note, *Sociological Analysis*, 31, 107-114.

Glock, C.Y. and Stark, R. 1965, *Religion and Society in Tension*, Chicago: Rand McNally.

Glock, C.Y. 1962, On the Study of Religious Commitment, *Religious Education, Research Supplement*, 57:4, S98-S110.

Gul, H. 1997, The Encounter between Islam and the West, *2*, 3: 3-40

Haddad, Y.Y. and Esposito, J.L. eds. 1998, *Islam, Gender and Social Change*, New York: Oxford University Press.

Haeri, S. 1989, *Law of Desire: Temporary Marriage in Shi'i Iran*. Syracuse: Syracuse University Press.

Haeri, S. 1993, Obedience versus Autonomy: Women and Fundamentalism in Iran and Pakistan, in Marty, M. and Appleby, R.S. eds. *Fundamentalisms and Society*, Chicago: University of Chicago Press.

Hardacre, H. 1993, The Impact of Fundamentalism, on Women, the Family and Interpersonal Relations, in Marty, M. and Appleby, R.S. eds. *Fundamentalism and Society*, Chicago: University of Chicago Press.

Hassan, R. 1980. Social and Religious Attitudes in Pakistan (Unpublished Questionnaire).

Hassan R. 1984, Iran's Islamic Revolutionaries: Before and After the Revolution, *Third World Quarterly*, 6: 3.

Hassan, R. 1985, Islamization: An Analysis of Religious, Political and Social Change in Pakistan, *Middle Eastern Studies*, 21:3.

Hassan, R. 1987, Pirs and Politics: Religion Society and State in Pakistan, *Asian Survey*, 26:5.

Hassan, R. 1992, The Muslim World in the International Economic System— An Overview, *Journal of Muslim Minority Affairs*, 13:2.

Hassan, R. and Effendi, S. 1995, *Social Structure and Access to Education in Indonesia: Some Observations on the Trends Between 1978 and 1986*. A paper presented at the Asian Sociological Conference, Beijing, China, November 1995.

Hathout, M. 1998, The Nature of Islamic Discourse in America, *Minaret* 20/1 (January): 21-23.

Higgins, P.J. 1985, Women in the Islamic Republic of Iran: Legal, Social, and Ideological Changes, *Signs* 10/3 (Spring): 477-494.

Hilty, D.M. and Stockman, S.J. 1986, A Covariance Structure Analysis of DeJong, Faulkner, and Warland Religious Involvement Model, *Journal for the Scientific Study of Religion*, 25, 483-493.

Himmelfarb, H.S. 1975, Measuring Religious Involvement, *Social Forces*, 53, 606-618.

Hitti, P.K. 1943, *History of the Arabs*, London: Macmillan.

Hodgson, M.G. 1975, *The Venture of Islam*, Chicago: University of Chicago Press.

Hoodbhoy, P., *Islam and Science: Religious Orthodoxy and the Battle for Rationality*, London: Zed Books.

Hooglund, E. 1995, Managing Metropolis, *Middle East Insight*, 11/5 (July-August): 72-73.

Hooker, B. 1984, *Islamic Law in South-East Asia*, Kuala Lumpur: Oxford University Press.

Hume, D. 1976, *The Natural History of Religion*, Oxford: Oxford University Press.

Huntington, S. 1993, *The Clash of Civilizations and the remaking of World Order*, New York: Simon & Schuster.

Ibrahim, S.E. 1996, *Egypt, Islam and Democracy*, Cairo: American University of Cairo Press.

Inglehart, R. 1990, World Value Survey Questionnaire, http://wvs.isr.umich.edu.

Irfani, S. 1983, *Revolutionary Islam in Iran*, London: Zed Books.

James, W. 1902, *The Varieties of Religious Experience: A Study of Human Nature*, Cambridge: Harvard University Press.

Karawan, I.A. 1992, Monarchs, Mullahs, and Marshals: Islamic Regimes, *The Annals*, 524: 103-119.

Kazakhstan. 1993, *Constitution of the Republic of Kazakhstan*, http://www.kz/eng/kzinfo/kz6.html.

Keddie, N. 1972, *Scholars, Saints and Sufis: Muslim Religious Institutions in the Middle East since 1500*, Berkeley: University of California Press.

Keddie, N. 1994, The Revolt of Islam, 1700 to 1993: Comparative Considerations and Relations to Imperialism, *Comparative Studies in Society and History*, 36:3.

Keddie, N. 1999, 'Fundamentalism' New Religious Politics and Women Worldwide: A Comparative Study, *Journal of Women's History*, 10:4.

Khaldun, I. 1958, *The Muqaddamah*, trans. Rosenthal, F., London: Routledge.

Kian, A. 1996, *Iranian Women take on the Mullahs*, Paris: Le Monde.

King, M.B. and Hunt, R.A. 1969, Measuring the Religious Variable: Amended Findings, *Journal for the Scientific Study of Religion*, 8, 321-323.

King, M.B. and Hunt, R.A. 1972, Measuring the Religious Variable: Replication, *Journal for the Scientific Study of Religion*, 11, 240-251.

King, M.B. and Hunt, R.A. 1975, Measuring the Religious Variable: National Replication. *Journal for the Scientific Study of Religion*, 14, 13-22.

King, M.B. and Hunt, R.A. 1990, Measuring the Religious Variable: Final Comment, *Journal for the Scientific Study of Religion*, 29, 531-535.

Kotb (Qutb), S. 1953, *Social Justice in Islam*, trans. John B. Hardie, Washington: American Council of Learned Societies.

Lapidus, I.M. 1996, State and Religion in Islamic Society, *Past and Present*, 151, 3-27.

Lapidus, I.M. 1992, The Golden Age: The Political Concepts of Islam, *The Annals*, 524: 13-25.

Lapidus, I.M. 1988, *A History of Islamic Societies,* Cambridge: Cambridge University Press

Levy, R. 1971, *The Social Structure of Islam*, Cambridge: Cambridge University Press.

Lewis, B. 1993, *Islam and the West*, New York: Oxford University Press.

Liddle, R. 1996, The Islamic Turn in Indonesia: A Political Explanation, *The Journal of Asian Studies*, 55:3 (August): 613-634.

Luhmann, N. 1977, *Funktion der Religion*. Frankfurt: Suhrkamp.

Luhmann, N. 1982, *The Differentiation of Society*, trans. Stephen Holmas and Charles Lamore, New York: Columbia University.

Madjid, Nurcholish. 1980, Islam in Indonesia: Challenges and Opportunities, in Pullapilly, C. ed. *Islam in the Contemporary World*, Notre Dame, Indiana: Cross Roads Books.

Mallat, C. 1993, *The Renewal of Islamic Law,* Cambridge: Cambridge University Press.

Maranell, G.M. 1968, A Factor Analytic Study of some Selected Dimensions of Religious Attitude, *Sociology and Social Research*, 52, 430-437.

Marsot, A. 1992, Political Islam in Asia: A Case Study, *The Annals*, 524: 156-169.

Marty, M. and Appleby, R.S. eds. 1991, *Fundamentalism Observed*, Chicago: University of Chicago Press.

Marty, M. and Appleby, R.S. eds. 1994 *Accounting for Fundamentalisms: The Dynamic Character of Movements*, Chicago: University of Chicago Press.

Marty, M. and Appleby, R.S. eds. 1993, *Fundamentalism and Society*, Chicago: University of Chicago Press

Marty, M. and Appleby, R.S. eds. 1992, *The Glory and the Power: The Fundamentalist Challenge to the Modern World*, Boston: Beacon Press.

Maududi, A. 1960, *The Islamic Law and Constitution,* Lahore: Islamic Publications.

Maududi, A. 1973, *Risala-e-Diniyat*, Lahore (1966). English translation, *Towards Understanding Islam*, trans. Khurshid Ahmad, Indiana: American Trust Publication 1977.

Maududi, A. 1987, *Purdah and the Status of Women in Islam*, Lahore: Islamic Publications Limited.

Maududi. A. 1966, *The Economic Problem of Man and its Islamic Solution*, Lahore: Islamic Publications.

Mayer, A. 1967, Pir and Murshid: An Aspect of Religious Leadership in West Pakistan, *Middle Eastern Studies*, 3:2, 160-169.

Mernissi, F. 1987, *Beyond the Veil: Male-Female Dynamics in Modern Muslim Society*, Indiana: Indiana University Press.

Mernissi, F. 1989, *Women and Islam*, trans. Mary Jo Lakeland, Oxford: Basil Blackwell.

Mernissi, F. 1991, *The Veil and Male Elite: A Feminist Interpretation of Women's Rights in Islam*, Reading: Addison-Wesley.

Mernissi, F. 1996, *Women's Rebellion and Islamic Memory*, Atlantic Highlands: Zed Books.

Minces, Juliette 1994, *Veiled: Women in Islam*, trans. S.M. Berrett, Masachusetts: Blue Crane Books.

Mol, J.J. 1972, *Western Religion*, The Hague: Mouton.

Muhammad, Mahathir. 1989, Islamization of Knowledge and the Future of Islamic Ummah, in *Towards Islamization of Disciplines*, Hendon: International Institute of Islamic Thought.

Muslim Women's National Network of Australia Newsletter. 1998, Vol. 16 (March).

Muslim, I. 1980, *Sahih Muslim Vol. 1*, trans. Abdul Hamid Siddiqi, Lahore: Sh. Muhammad Ashraf.

Muzaffar, C. 1988, Islamic Resurgence: A Global View, in Abdullah, T. and Siddique, S., eds., *Islam and Society in Southeast Asia*, Singapore: Institute of Southeast Asian Studies.

Myers, S. 1996, An Interactive Model of Religiosity Inheritance, *American Sociological Review*, 61:5.

Nash, Manning. 1991, 'Islamic Resurgence in Malaysia and Indonesia', in *Fundamentalisms Observed*, ed. Martin E. Marty and R. Scott Appleby, Chicago: University of Chicago Press.

Nasr, S.V.R. 1994, *The Vanguard of the Islamic Revolution; The Jamaat-i-Islami of Pakistan*, London: I.B. Tauris Publishers.

Nieuwenhuijze, C.A.O. Van. 1959, The Ummah: An Analytical Approach, *Studia Islamica 10*, 5-22.

Olcott, M.B. 1995, Kazakhstan in Esposito J.L. ed. *The Oxford Encylopedia of Modern Muslim World*, New York: Oxford University Press.

Pakistan. 1973, *The Constitution of the Islamic Republic of Pakistan*. http://www.stanford.edu/group/pakistan/pakistan/constitution.

Peacock, J. 1978, *The Muhammadiyah Movement in Indonesian Islam*, Menlo Park: Benjamin Cumming Publishing.

Pipes, D. 1981, *Slaves, Soldiers and Islam: The Genesis of a Military System*, New Haven: Yale University Press.

Pratt, J.B. 1907, *The Psychology of Religious Belief*, New York: Macmillan.

Rahman, F. 1966, *Islam*, Chicago: University of Chicago Press.

Rahman, F. 1982, *Islam and Modernity*, Chicago: University of Chicago Press.

Rahman, F. 1984, The Principles of Shura and the Role of the Umma in Islam, *American Journal of Islamic Studies, 1* (1), 1-9.

Rahman, F. 1989, *Major Themes of the Quran*, Minneapolis: Bibliotheca Islamica.

Rashid, A. 1998, Pakistan and the Taliban, in Maley, W. ed. *Fundamentalism Reborn? Afghanistan and the Taliban*, Lahore: Vanguard Press.

Robertson, R. 1987, 'Church- State Relations and the World Order' in Robbins, T. and Robertson, R. eds., *Church-State Relations: Tensions and Transitions*, New Bunswick: Transactions Press.

Robinson, J. and Shaver, P. eds. 1973, *Measures of Social Psychological Attitudes*, Ann Arbor: Institute of Social Research.

Rohrbaugh, J. and Jessor, R. 1975, Religiosity in Youth: A Personal Control Against Deviant Behaviour. *Journal of Personality*, 43, 136-155.

Rouleau, E. 1999, *Much at Stake for the Muslim World: In Iran Islam Confronts Islam*, Paris: Le Monde.

Rugh, A. 1984, *Reveal and Conceal: Dress in Contemporary Egypt*, Syracuse: Syracuse University Press.

Sadowski, Y. 1997, The New Orientalism and the Democracy Debate in Beinin J. and Stork, J., eds. *Political Islam*, Berkeley: University of California Press.

Sivan, E. 1985, *Radical Islam: Medieval Theology and Modern Politics*, New Haven: Yale University Press.

Stark, R. and Glock, C.Y. 1968, *American Piety and the Nature of Religious Commitment*, Berkeley: University of California Press.

Syed, A.H. 1982, *Pakistan: Islam, Politics and national Solidarity*, New York: Praeger.

Szelenyi, I. and Treiman, D. 1992, Social Stratification in Eastern Europe (Unpublished Questionnaire).

Tamney, J.B. 1976, Religious Attitudes in Indonesia (Unpublished Questionnaire).

Tamney, J.B. 1980, Modernization and Religious Purification: Islam in Indonesia, *Review of Religious Research*, 22:2.

Tapp, R.B. 1971, Dimensions of Religiosity in a Post-Traditional Group, *Journal for the Scientific Study of Religion*, 10, 41-47.

The Holy Qur-an: English Translation of the Meanings and Commentary (ca. 1994 [A.H. 1410]). Medina: King Fahd Holy Qur-an Printing Complex.

The World Bank, 1998, *World Development Report, 1997*, New York: Oxford University Press.

Thurow, L.C. 1996, *The Future of Capitalism*, New York: W. Morrow.

Thurow, L.C. Building Wealth, in *The Atlantic Monthly*, June 1999.

Tibi, B. 1988, *The Crisis of Modern Islam*, Salt Lake City: University of Utah Press.

Tonnies, F. 1953, *Community and Society (Gemeinschaft and Gesellschaft)*, New York: Harper and Row.

Turner, B.S. 1974, *Weber and Islam*, London: Routledge.

United Nations Development Programme. 1996, *Human Development Report*. New York: Oxford University Press.

United Nations Development Programme. 1996, *Kazakstan:* Human Development Report, Almaty: UNDP.

Vakhabov, A. 1980, *Muslims in the USSR*, Moscow: Novosti Press Agency.

Voll, J.O. 1994, Central Asia as Part of the Modern Islamic World, in Manz, B. F. ed., *Central Asia in Historical Perspective*, Boulder: Westview Press.

Von Grunebaum, G.E. 1962, *Modern Islam: The Search for Cultural Identity*, Berkeley: University of California Press

Von Grunebaum, G.E. 1961, Nationalism and Cultural Trends in the Arab Near East, *Studica Islamica*, 14, 121-153.

Von Hugel, F. 1908, *The Mystical Element of Religion, as studied in Saint Catherine of Genoa and Her Friends*, Vol. 1. London: J.M. Dent and Sons.

Wahid, A. 1988, The Nahdatul Ulama and Islam in Present Day Indonesia in Abdullah, T. and Siddique, S. eds., *Islam and Society in Southeast Asia*, Singapore: Institute of Southeast Asian Studies.

Watt, W.M. 1953, *Muhammad at Medina*, Oxford.

Watt, W.M. 1954, Economic and Social Aspects of the Origins of Islam, *Islamic Quarterly*, 1, 90-103.

Watt, W.M. 1955, Ideal Factors in the Origin of Islam, *Islamic Quarterly*, 2, 160-174.

Watt, W.M. 1979, *What is Islam?* London: Longman.

Watt, W.M. 1983, 'Self Image of Islam in the Quran and Later' in Hovannisian, R.G. and Vryonis, S. Jr. eds., *Islam's Understanding of Itself*, Malibu: Undena Publications.

Watt, W.M. 1988, *Islamic Fundamentalism and Modernity*, London: Routledge.

Weber, M. 1964, *The Sociology of Religion*, trans. E. Fiscoff, Boston: Beacon Press.

Weber, M. 1978, *Economy and Society*, eds., Ross, G. and Wittich, C. Berkeley: University of California Press.

Weiss, A. ed. 1986. *Islamic Reassertion in Pakistan*, Syracuse, NY: Syracuse University Press.

Werbner, P. and Madood, T. eds. 1997, *Debating Cultural Hybridity*. London: Zed books.

Wolf, E.R. 1951, The Social Organization of Mecca and the Origins of Islam, *Southwestern Journal of Anthropology,* 7 (4), 329-356.

Woodward, M.R. 1989, *Islam in Java*, Tucson: University of Arizona Press.

Wulff, D.M. 1997, *Psychology of Religion Classic and Contemporary*, New York: John Wiley & Sons.

Yap, M.E. 1980, Contemporary Islamic Revival, *Asian Affairs Journal of the Royal Society for Asian Affairs*, 11:2.

Zubaida, Sami. 1989, *Islam, the People and the State*, London: Routledge.

Zubaida, Sami. 1995, Is There a Muslim Society? Ernest Gellner's Sociology of Islam, *Economy and Society*, 24 (2), 151-188.

Zubaida, Sami. 1997, Is Iran an Islamic State, in *Political Islam*, ed. Beinin, J. and Stork, J. Berkeley: University of California Press.

INDEX